Contents

Communicate!

Reading

1 Skim the following text to find out answers to these questions.

1 What is it about?
2 Who are the main characters?
3 Where do you think the text is taken from? Give reasons for your answer.
   A a research paper
   B a newspaper article
   C a book about wildlife

⏱ about 350 words

N'Kisi knows what he's talking about

2 Scan the text again and answer the following questions.

1 Where does N'Kisi live?
2 What can he do that other parrots can't?
3 What else, besides speaking, have African greys been known to do?
4 How many words does Aimee Morgana think N'Kisi knows?
5 How old is N'Kisi?
6 What has the parrot had difficulty doing?

3 In the IELTS Reading Module, you won't be allowed to use a dictionary. It's important that you try to guess the meaning of words you aren't sure of. The following words are taken from the article. Look at the words in context and try to think of another word or phrase which means the same. When you have finished, check your answers in an English-English dictionary.

EXAMPLE: mastered (line 4) ....*learnt*........

1 a running commentary (line 7) ....
2 to mimic (line 9) ....
3 making up (line 12) ....
4 cognitive powers (line 17) ....
5 to carry out (line 20) ....
6 complex (line 20) ....
7 chipped in (line 30) ....
8 linguistic conventions (line 39) ....

Squawking 'Pretty Polly' just isn't enough for some parrots. N'Kisi is able to hold a conversation. The African grey parrot, living in New York, has a vocabulary of almost 1,000 words and has mastered
5 basic grammar and sentence construction. He is able to ask for food and attention, but is far happier keeping up a running commentary on what is going on around him and talking to anyone who comes close.

African greys are well known for being able to mimic
10 human speech, but N'Kisi is believed to be the first to develop this ability into creating his own language. Owner Aimee Morgana has recorded him making up sentences 15 words long. The bird, according to her, takes into account past, present and future tenses.

15 Professor Donald Broom of the School of Veterinary Medicine at the University of Cambridge, who is an expert on the cognitive powers of animals, said that the parrot's conversational abilities should not cause too much surprise. African greys are intelligent birds
20 and can be taught to carry out complex tasks, like completing jigsaws when the pieces fit into shaped holes. They can also respond to circumstances, such as by saying 'good night' when you turn the lights off at night or 'goodbye' when you put a coat on.

Ms Morgana, an artist with an interest in animal 25 behaviour, believes N'Kisi's vocabulary is in the region of 972 words. But she is more impressed by the comments he comes out with, such as when she was picking up the beads of a necklace from the floor and N'Kisi chipped in 'Oh no, you broke your 30 new necklace.'

The six-year-old bird is also able to recognise different objects, shapes and colours and describe what he sees. When he first met Dr Jane Goodall after seeing a picture of her with one of the 35 chimpanzees she studies, the parrot asked 'Got a chimp?' Seeing another parrot hanging upside down, N'Kisi called out 'You got to put this bird on the camera.' However, some linguistic conventions have proved difficult for the parrot. While trying to put 'fly' 40 into the past tense, he said 'flied' instead of 'flew', just as young children often do.

Grammar

The passive

G ⋯⋮ STUDENT'S BOOK page 138

4 Scan the article again and find two examples of the passive.

5 Complete this chart of past forms. It contains both regular and irregular verbs from Unit 1 of the Student's Book.

Infinitive	Past tense	Past participle
send	*sent*	*sent*
take		
teach		
make		
form		
be		
spend		
find		
say		
use		
speak		
give		

6 Complete the sentences below using one of the verbs from exercise 5. Some verbs may be used more than once. Think carefully about which tense to use – you may need to use a modal passive with *can*.

EXAMPLE: The information about the Internet survey _was sent_ to households last week.

1 Progress .... (recently) on plans for the new IT building.
2 Last year, more money .... on new computer terminals than on anything else in the department.
3 It .... that more research is needed into whether mobile-phone masts are dangerous to health.
4 Latin .... (very rarely) nowadays.
5 Grey parrots .... to speak.
6 When you enrol next Tuesday, you .... more details of the course.
7 Ice .... when the temperature of water is below freezing point.
8 Information on a range of subjects .... on the Internet.

Vocabulary

7 Complete this puzzle of words to do with communication by solving the clues below. The number of letters in each word is given in brackets. What word appears vertically?

1, 2 It is very common to send a .... to a friend these days. (4, 7)
3 N'Kisi has learnt to .... (4)
4 The Principal will give a .... at the end of term. (6)
5 In order to be heard, you need to .... clearly into the microphone. (5)
6 I often call my friends to have a .... about college. (4)
7 It's good to have someone you can .... a conversation with. (4)
8 Give me a .... sometime, and we'll arrange to go out somewhere. (4)
9 If you want to attract someone's attention from a distance, you can always .... (7)

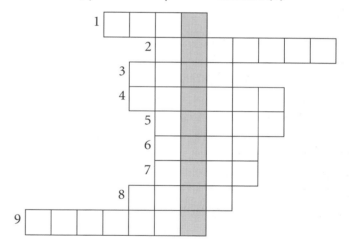

8 Match the verbs (1–8) with the correct nouns (a–h) to form collocations to do with communication.

1	tell	**a**	a question
2	whistle	**b**	a foreign language
3	ask	**c**	an answer
4	speak	**d**	advice
5	offer	**e**	surprise
6	make	**f**	a tune
7	have	**g**	a lie
8	express	**h**	a speech

A healthy diet

Reading

1 Quickly read this article about fast food.
Time yourself as you read.

⏱ about 580 words

FAST FOOD – behind the image

We all know what a fast-food outlet looks like and what it serves. This is because when a big modern business offers fast food, it knows that we, its customers, are likely to want No Surprises. We are hungry, tired and not in a
5 celebratory mood.

The building itself is easy to recognise and designed to be a 'home from home', on the motorway or in the city. However, the usual things you find in a restaurant are a little different – tables and chairs are bolted to the floor,
10 and cutlery is either non-existent or not worth stealing. Words and actions are officially laid down, learned by the staff from handbooks and teaching sessions, and then picked up by customers in the course of regular visits. Things have to be called by their correct names
15 (cheeseburger, large fries); the staff have a script they must learn – you know the sort of thing: 'Will that be with cheese, sir?', 'Have a nice day' – something I find particularly irritating. The staff wear a distinctive uniform, menus are always the same and even placed in the same
20 spot in every outlet in the chain; prices are low, and the theme of cleanliness is repeated endlessly.

The company attempts to play the role of kind and concerned parent. It knows people are suspicious of large corporations and so it tries to stress its love for children; it
25 often has cottagey-style buildings for warmth and cosiness or large glass walls and smooth surfaces to show cleanliness and modernity. It responds to social concerns, but only if beliefs are sufficiently widely held and

therefore 'correct'. Take, for example, the worry about fat in our diets. Fast-food chains only responded by putting
30 salad on the menu when there was pressure in various countries from doctors and health ministers. Some chains are busy at present showing how much they care about the environment, too.

Fast-food chains know that they are ordinary. They want
35 to be ordinary and to be thought of as almost inseparable from the idea of everyday food consumed outside the home. They are happy to allow their customers time off for holidays – Thanksgiving, Christmas and so on – for which they do not cater. Even those comparatively rare
40 holiday times are turned to a profit because the companies know that their favourite customers – families – are at home together then, watching television, where carefully placed commercials will spread the word concerning new fast-food products and re-imprint the
45 image of the various chains for later. Families are the customers the fast-food chains want; good, law-abiding citizens who love their children, teaching them how good hamburgers are for them. The chains even have very bright lighting to make sure that 'undesirable' people
50 don't want to come in.

Supplying a hamburger that is perfect in terms of shape, weight, temperature, together with selections from a pre-set list of extras, to a customer who knows what to expect, is a difficult thing to do. The technology involved
55 has meant spending huge sums on research, and there are also political and economic questions to consider – how to maintain supplies of cheap beef and cheap buns. However, the image that is maintained is of a 'casual' eating experience. Make up your own mind, but there's
60 more to a hamburger than just beef in a bread roll.

2 Do the following statements agree with the information given in the reading passage? ⤳ TF1

Write

TRUE	if the statement agrees with the information
FALSE	if the statement contradicts the information
NOT GIVEN	if there is no information on this

EXAMPLE: Customers often choose to eat in fast-food outlets because they know what to expect. *TRUE*

(See underlined text.)

1 Each employee is encouraged by the chain to have his/her own individual way of communicating with customers.
2 Fast-food companies started selling salads because of worries about health.
3 Salad is one of the more popular choices at certain fast-food outlets nowadays.
4 Fast-food companies want to attract people who are too busy to cook at home.
5 There are certain types of customers who are not welcome at fast-food outlets.
6 Supplying hamburgers to customers is very straightforward.
7 More money needs to be spent on research into new fast-food technology.

Grammar

Comparatives and superlatives

G ⋯⟶ STUDENT'S BOOK page 138

3 Make sentences, using a comparative adjective and other necessary words.

EXAMPLE: Mount Everest / Mount Kilimanjaro – a lot / high
Mount Everest is a lot higher than Mount Kilimanjaro.

1 the River Nile / the River Thames – considerably / long
2 London / Mexico City – far / small
3 fruit / sweets – much / good
4 Rolls Royce car / bicycle – a good deal / expensive
5 fast food / cooking yourself – more / convenient
6 Australia / New Zealand – far / big

4 What can you say about the following things?

EXAMPLE: the Pacific Ocean
It's the biggest ocean in the world.

1 the Sahara Desert
2 the Great Wall of China
3 Bill Gates
4 Pluto
5 redwood tree
6 the cheetah

5 These sentences contain errors made by IELTS students. Correct them.

1 Fast-food outlets are open longer that ordinary restaurants.
2 I would rather have a sandwich then a pizza.
3 The number of people who eat rice is considerably greater the number who eat potatoes.
4 The amount of meat eaten in the USA is far more that eaten in China.
5 Hamburgers are more popular as noodles in Europe.
6 Pizza is not so expensive than steak.
7 Producing meat is twice expensive in some countries than in others.
8 The number of customers we had today was much few as last night.

Vocabulary

6 Look at the clues and find the words in the wordsearch. The number of letters is in brackets. The words go vertically and horizontally. (↓→)

1 Indian food is often like this. (5)
2 If you leave milk for a long time, it will go like this. (4)
3 I prefer to eat bread which is like this. (5)
4 Too many of these aren't good for your teeth. (6)
5 Bananas are like this when they are yellow. (4)
6 What you do when you want to lose weight. (4)
7 The person who does the cooking. (4)
8 Food which has no taste is like this. (5)
9 Fish and chips and burgers are this. (4, 4)
10 You look at this when choosing your meal in a restaurant. (4)

A	L	K	R	E	M	E	N	U	P
S	P	I	C	Y	N	C	S	K	R
N	F	A	S	T	F	O	O	D	I
M	Q	F	W	A	Q	L	T	T	P
L	R	R	D	S	S	O	U	R	E
D	I	E	T	N	W	D	C	V	N
S	H	S	T	Y	E	I	C	D	E
V	H	H	E	Z	E	G	H	H	J
C	M	Q	G	N	T	A	E	F	R
B	L	A	N	D	S	X	F	C	M

7 Complete the table with the other forms of the words given. Take care with spelling. Use an English-English dictionary to help you.

Noun	Adjective	Adverb	Verb
1	hungry	2	3
4	celebratory		5
6	distinctive	7	8
cleanliness	9	10	11
12	suspicious	13	14
warmth	15	16	17
cosiness	18	19	
20	21	comparatively	22
23	political	24	25

3 City attractions

1 2
3 4

Reading

1 The four paragraphs below describe the cities shown in the photographs. Skim the text quickly. Can you match each photograph to the appropriate paragraph and identify the cities?

⏱ about 430 words

A Although there aren't many historic sites to attract tourists, this is a fascinating city. It's a major business centre, and its port is one of the busiest in the world. A construction boom that began in the early 1990s means there are now a large number of high-rise buildings. In January 2004, an exciting new transport link went into service – 'maglev' trains (using magnetic levitation technology) run between the city centre and the international airport, reaching a speed of 430km per hour. A traditional garden in the Old City contains a teahouse that may be the model for the well-known 'willow pattern' design, which is used on plates around the world.

B This city was probably founded in the 16th century and is laid out in a grid – that is, most of its streets are straight, like lines drawn on a sheet of paper from top to bottom and from side to side. One very impressive avenue is 140m across and is said to be the widest in the world. The main government building is called *la Casa Rosada*, which is Spanish for 'the Pink House'. One of the main attractions for tourists is watching – or even dancing – the tango. The hottest months of the year are January and February.

C This city was founded in the early 18th century to increase trade by sea with western Europe. A lot of canals were excavated, which made it resemble the city of Venice. As a result, this city is often called 'the Venice of the North'. Between 1712 and 1918, it was the country's capital. Although its name was changed to Petrograd and Leningrad in the past, it is again known by its original name. One of the famous attractions in this city is the Hermitage, an art gallery largely located in the Winter Palace. It contains an amazing collection of paintings.

D This ancient, historic city is over 2,600 years old. It was first called Byzantium and then Constantinople before adopting its present name. It's on both sides of a narrow stretch of water separating the two continents of Europe and Asia. There's plenty to interest and amuse tourists, so they need never get bored! Topkapi, the magnificent palace, used to have over 50,000 people living and working in its grounds, and even had its own zoo. Another impressive building is the Grand Bazaar, the largest indoor market in the country, with more than 3,000 shops and restaurants. It used to be the commercial centre of the city and is usually crowded with both tourists and local people.

2 Complete these notes. The notes come in the same order as the relevant part of the passage. Choose NO MORE THAN ONE WORD from the passage for each answer. ⋯⊱ TF3

City A
EXAMPLE: There is a great deal of activity in this city's ....*port*.......... .

1 A large amount of .... has taken place in recent years.
2 Very fast .... connect the city with its airport.

City B
3 Most streets in this city form a ....
4 'The Pink House' is used by the ....
5 A popular dance in this city is the ....

City C
6 Like Venice, this city contains a large number of ....
7 This city used to be the .... of the country.
8 Many people visit a palace here to see the impressive display of ....

City D
9 The two parts of this city are located in different ....
10 There used to be a zoo in the grounds of a ....
11 The Grand Bazaar is a covered ....

3 The passage contains four paragraphs labelled A–D. Which paragraph contains the following information? You may use any letter more than once. ⋯⋮ TF7

EXAMPLE: a similarity between this city and another one. ....*C*....

1 a description of how roads are arranged ....
2 the possibility that famous representations may be of a building in this city ....
3 a reference to activities that no longer take place in a certain building ....
4 the reason for establishing this city ....
5 a potential disadvantage for the tourist industry ....
6 a reference to a name that has come back into use ....

Vocabulary

4 Find the word in the reading passage that matches each definition. The definitions are in text order.

1 a large increase, particularly in economic activity ....
2 in a style that has continued for a long time without changing ....
3 an object or person that is represented by an artist ....
4 brought into existence, set up ....
5 a pattern of horizontal and vertical lines crossing each other to form squares ....
6 dug (a hole or channel in the ground) ....
7 look or be like something else ....
8 in a particular place ....
9 choosing as its own ....
10 dividing into parts ....

5 Complete each sentence with the word from the box that best suits the meaning. More than one answer is possible in some cases. Pay attention to any preposition after the space.

amazed	amused	astonished	bored	excited
fascinated	frightened	interested	surprised	
terrified	thrilled			

1 I saw a cat trying to catch fish in the canal, and I was so .... I started laughing.
2 I thought Helen was on the other side of the world, so I was .... to see her in Shanghai.
3 Takuya is very .... in the history of Topkapi Palace, so he has bought a book about it.
4 Juan has got the whole day free, but he can't think of anything to do, so he's ....
5 The side of the bridge had been damaged, and Brad was .... that a child might fall into the river.
6 Tania was .... with her prize of a round-the-world trip, because it was something she'd always dreamed of.
7 Hasan couldn't take his eyes off the people dancing in the street, he was so .... by them.
8 The band gave such a fantastic performance that the crowd became more and more .... , and started dancing and cheering.

Grammar

Cause, purpose and result

G ⋯⋮ STUDENT'S BOOK page 138

6 Complete each sentence with one of the words or phrases in the box.

because	because of
so that	so

1 Shanghai doesn't have many historic attractions, ... not many tourists realise what an interesting city it is.
2 There are now a great many high-rise buildings in Shanghai .... the recent construction boom.
3 An old teahouse in Shanghai is a popular place to visit .... it might have inspired the famous 'willow pattern' design.
4 The main government building in Buenos Aires has been painted pink, and .... it is now known as *la Casa Rosada* – the Pink House.
5 A lot of people visit Buenos Aires .... they can learn the tango.
6 The weather is warmest in Buenos Aires in January and February .... the city is in the southern hemisphere.
7 The site of St Petersburg was chosen .... ships could sail between the city and western Europe.
8 St Petersburg is known as 'the Venice of the North' .... its canals.
9 Istanbul is over 2,600 years old, ... it is much older than St Petersburg.
10 The Grand Bazaar in Istanbul attracts plenty of tourists .... the large number of shops and restaurants it contains.

4 Ways of learning

Grammar

Present tenses

G ⋯⟶ STUDENT'S BOOK page 139

1 Look at these sentences. Most of the verbs in **bold** contain errors which are typical of those made by IELTS candidates. Put a line through the wrong words and write the correct ones. One sentence is completely correct.

EXAMPLE: Those people who ~~are taking~~ part in sports like scuba diving usually ~~spends~~ a lot of money. *take, spend*

1 Service-oriented companies often **giving** mobile phones to their sales force. ....

2 I **am writing** to tell you that I **become** a full-time student. I started my course last week. ....

3 Since I was a child, I **want** to be a nurse. ....

4 The table **is showing** that the number of students **is rising** to over five million since 1980. ....

5 We **don't see** each other for a long time, so I **want** to meet soon. ....

6 I **want** to be an engineer. This is the reason I **have decided** to go to college. ....

7 In this way, I feel I **am being** able to repay the hours and effort that **have been spent** on me. ....

8 In the past decade, computers **are becoming** the most useful tool in offices and factories. ....

9 This letter is to tell you what I **doing** recently. ....

10 This development **is being happening** for many years. ....

2 Complete this passage by using the correct present tense in each space. One verb should be in the passive. There is an example to help you.

Ever since I was a child I **0** (love) *have loved* piano music, though until recently I never had the chance to play myself. But at last I **1** (start) .... having lessons at the adult education college in my town. It was hard at first, but Sarah, my teacher, says that now I **2** (make) .... good progress.

I'm a computer programmer, and usually **3** (work) .... long hours, so I **4** (not have) .... much spare time. I **5** (practise) .... several times a week, but unfortunately the piano **6** (belong) .... to my neighbours, so I only **7** (play) .... when it's convenient for them. Now I **8** (think) .... about buying my own piano, so that I can play whenever I **9** (like) ....

Every year, there's a concert at the college, and some of the music students **10** (ask) .... to perform. Recently I **11** (practise) .... a piece by Shostakovich, and I **12** (hope) .... I'll be good enough to play it in the next concert.

Sarah **13** (suggest) .... that I take a piano exam next year, but I **14** (not decide) .... yet. It **15** (depend) .... on whether I can afford to buy a piano for myself.

Prepositions

3 Prepositions are normally followed by a noun, pronoun, *-ing* form or *wh-* word. They can't be followed by any other verb forms. Look at these sentences, based on the recording in 4.1 of the Student's Book (page 26). Complete each sentence with a preposition from the box.

about	at	from	on	to	with

Preposition + noun or pronoun
1 We've been looking .... different forms of education.
2 I don't really look forward .... English lessons.
3 What about your future career – have you thought much .... it?

Preposition + -ing

4 My parents thought I could cope .... being taught at home.

5 Apart .... working on projects, what subjects do you study?

6 I'm thinking seriously .... becoming a doctor.

Preposition + wh- word

7 My mother and I talk .... what exactly the project should cover.

8 In my next project, I want to focus .... why some people choose one-to-one education for their children.

4 These sentences include errors that are often made by IELTS candidates. Put a line through the wrong words and write the correct ones. One sentence is correct.

EXAMPLE: I'm interested in ~~find~~ out about the people who live in my town.
........*finding*........

1 Writing a project takes a lot of read. ....

2 Let's talk to what you've done. ....

3 I'm interested from finding out about people's jobs.
....

4 I've been thinking about what you said. ....

5 How do you feel about use a computer? ....

6 I'm looking forward to start a new project. ....

7 I'm quite good to find information on the Internet.
....

8 I enjoy most lessons, apart of history. ....

9 Children are usually better at learn foreign languages than adults. ....

10 Next, we'll look to the best way to plan a report.
....

Reading

5 This passage is similar to Section 2 of General Training Reading. Read it quickly, timing yourself as you read.

⏰ about 300 words

Southmoor College – Policies and Procedures

The College has introduced a number of policies and procedures which are briefly summarised here. A leaflet containing full details is available on request.

- The College Charter is a series of statements which explain what is being done to promote high standards for people who use College services. It has been designed in accordance with a national framework aimed at maintaining and improving standards, while at the same time being tailored to meet the specific needs of the College.
- Formal complaints should be submitted in writing to the Principal, who will refer each complaint to the appropriate member of staff and then provide a response.
- The College has developed both informal and formal appeals procedures in connection with its own internal examinations. Appeals against external examination bodies must follow their own procedures, and details are available from the Examinations Officer.
- The College is a designated No Smoking Area. Smoking is not permitted inside any part of the building unless specifically authorised.
- All accidents must be reported to Reception as soon as possible and the appropriate form completed.
- Students are responsible for the apparatus, tools or machinery with which they are working. If items are damaged or broken as a result of careless use or failing to follow instructions, the person concerned will be required to cover the cost of repairing or replacing the items. All equipment must be left in a clean state and in good working order.
- Mobile phones are part of everyday life, but they must be used with consideration for other people. Please ensure that you have switched them off before entering classrooms or the library. They must not be taken into any examination room under any circumstances.

6 Do the following statements agree with the information given in the passage? ⋯⋗ TF1

Write

TRUE *if the statement agrees with the information*
FALSE *if the statement contradicts the information*
NOT GIVEN *if there is no information on this*

1 Anyone wishing to see the complete policies and procedures should ask for them.

2 The Charter was written after consultation with groups of people who use the College.

3 The Charter is identical to the charters of the other colleges in the country.

4 Replies to formal complaints will be given by the Principal.

5 The College's appeals procedure applies to all examinations taken in the College.

6 Smoking inside the College is allowed in certain circumstances.

7 The College can provide medical help if an accident occurs.

8 Students may have to pay for equipment that they break.

9 Mobile phones can be taken into examination rooms if they are switched off.

5 Discovering the past

Vocabulary

1 Match these people (1–10) to their field of study (a–j).

EXAMPLE: archaeologist *someone who studies the physical remains of the past*

1 biologist		**a**	someone who studies animal and plant life
2 botanist		**b**	someone who studies the basic characteristics of substances, including their reactions
3 economist		**c**	someone who studies the past
4 mathematician		**d**	someone who designs buildings
5 paediatrician		**e**	someone who helps clients who have legal problems
6 anthropologist		**f**	someone who is interested in the consumption and production of goods and services
7 architect		**g**	someone who studies number, shape and quantity, among other things
8 historian		**h**	someone who specialises in children's diseases
9 lawyer		**i**	someone who studies human beings, their customs and relationships
10 chemist		**j**	someone who specialises in plant life

2 What are these shapes?

EXAMPLE: *circle*

3 Look at these sets of words. Which is the odd one out and why? Use an English-English dictionary to help you.

1 circle   square   triangle   rectangle
2 cylinder   cube   sphere   circle
3 enormous   tiny   huge   vast
4 average   medium   minute   standard
5 sizeable   immense   minuscule   colossal

4 Complete each sentence below using a verb from the box in the appropriate form.

analyse	carry out	evaluate	make
perform	put forward	reach	support

1 Dr Jones .... the conclusion that the bones weren't 5th century.
2 After .... the analysis, they found that the people had come from Polynesia.
3 The test results .... at the laboratory.
4 The builders who .... the discovery were given a reward.
5 Our findings .... Professor Rice's theory.
6 After .... the statistics, Peter decided to publish them.
7 The person who .... the experiment on the bones was Stephen Doughty.
8 No one has yet officially .... the theory that the city inhabitants died of starvation.

Grammar

Past tenses and sequencing

G ···❯ STUDENT'S BOOK page 139

5 Put the verbs in brackets in the most suitable past tense.

EXAMPLE: Last year, I (join) ......*joined*...... a dig in Egypt.

1 When I arrived at the museum, everyone (go) .... home and the place was empty.

2 Zara and Ali (arrive) .... early at the hotel before the others and (eat) .... immediately without waiting for anyone else to arrive.

3 They (pass) .... the Chinese exhibit when something about it (catch) .... their eye.

4 I (not enjoy) .... studying Economic History when I was at college.

5 Anna was in the library all evening and so (miss) .... seeing the film.

6 I (work) .... on my coursework when I (see) .... that I (make) .... a huge mistake and would have to start again.

7 I (see) .... my tutor in the city centre yesterday, but he (not see) .... me – he .... (talk) to his wife.

8 The tourists (climb) .... the path to Machu Picchu when there was a sudden thunderstorm overhead.

9 Before entering the tomb, the archaeologist (make) .... a speech.

10 While I (dig) .... the trench, I (cut) .... my hand.

6 Read through these sentences about some new research. Put them in the right order and provide punctuation.

a ...*1*... it has been known for a long time that the ancient egyptians imported copper from cyprus

b .... the fortress was only needed for a brief period only 50 years or so and was abandoned in the 13th century bc

c .... the men grew their own food and baked bread but imported luxury items such as wine and olive oil

d .... the fortress was built around 1270 bc by rameses II to protect maritime trade

e .... the complex covered five acres and was home to at least 500 soldiers

f .... new research carried out by a team from liverpool university has shown how the egyptians built a huge fortress on this coast

g .... it was 20 metres long and ten metres wide with three central rooms

h .... as well as a bakery and a palace a temple was also discovered

i .... what historians had not realised until recently was the threat posed to these imports by aggressive tribesmen along the mediterranean coast

6 What is job satisfaction?

Reading

1 Read the text below about how people may choose their career and say where this text is taken from.

A a scientific conference journal
B a newspaper article about a new book
C a textbook on motivation at work

⏱ about 600 words

The Douglas family

Meet Bernard Shapiro. He is a friendly 64-year-old and the Principal of McGill University, in Canada. He's an extremely tidy person and listens to opera. Before he accepted his current job, he worked as a statistician.

5 Many of the same things could be said of Harold Shapiro, Bernard's identical twin. He's also a former statistics expert and an opera lover with a taste for order in the workplace. And he is President of Princeton University in the USA. Both seem a little taken aback

10 by the way their lives have followed a similar pattern. 'It never occurred to me – or, I believe, to my twin – to deliberately plan similar careers,' Bernard says.

Easily the strangest thing about Principal and President Shapiro, though, is how far from unusual they actually

15 are. For they are just one of many pairs of twins to feature in a major new work by Professor Nancy Segal that provides the most important evidence so far that career choice, working style and job satisfaction can be significantly influenced by our genes. The implications

20 reach far beyond identical twins. The headline finding in her study is that at least 30% of the factors that make an individual choose their career path could be genetic. 'I'm not saying that there is a single gene for being a carpenter or a gene for being an artist,' Segal says, 'but

25 our studies do suggest that the choice of any job reflects many characteristics that are genetically based, from physical size to personality.'

Her evidence is clear enough. It is based on studies of career parallels between identical twins – including,

30 importantly, many who have been brought up separately – and twins who are non-identical, or fraternal. Identicals, who usually share 100% of genes, showed a far greater degree of similarity in their working lives than fraternals, who typically share an average of 50%.

35 'We're not in the occupations we have by accident,' she says. 'I'm a teacher and researcher, and I could probably have been a clinical psychologist. But I couldn't have been an investment banker or plumber.'

Career dynasties are nothing new – there are the tycoon Murdochs, film star Douglases and political Churchills, 40 all well-known examples of a phenomenon that occurs in any walk of life. But the idea that there might be more to such coincidences than parental pressure and a ready-made set of contacts just waiting to be networked has some important implications. Not least among them 45 is the possibility that parents intent on forcing their child towards a specific career may have less influence than they believe.

However, Professor Val Dusek is sceptical. 'One of the problems with this research is that when identical twins 50 are raised together, because of their striking physical similarities, they can be treated by their parents in very particular ways. And as for all the stories of coincidences – well, one can often find some quality between any two people that appears strangely similar.' 55

A much less controversial but arguably more significant finding from Segal's research is the idea that job satisfaction may also be in the genes. Furthermore, Segal's results suggest that job satisfaction seems to play a much greater role than expected. Employers take 60 note: changing the lighting or the seating arrangements, providing free coffee or even increasing salaries may not contribute to their employees' happiness as much as giving them meaningful and personally satisfying goals. So, whatever it is that motivates an actor to endure the 65 poverty of lengthy 'resting' periods in return for the occasional bit of acting, or a lecturer to tolerate poor pay in order to pursue his or her academic passion, may be buried deep in their ancestry.

2 Complete each sentence with the correct ending A–G below. ⋯⟩ TF3

1 Professor Nancy Segal
2 An employer
3 A parent

A has clear evidence to show that there is a gene for particular jobs.
B needs to rethink his or her strategy for motivating the workforce.
C will try to bring up each twin as a separate individual.
D believes that a third of people choose a career because of their genes.
E is less likely to be the most important factor in their child's choice of job than previously thought.
F has shown that people don't choose a job by chance.
G concludes that some jobs are harder than others.

3 Do the following statements reflect the claims of the writer? ⋯⟩ TF1

Write

YES *if the statement reflects the claims of the writer*
NO *if the statement contradicts the claims of the writer*
NOT GIVEN *if it is impossible to say what the writer thinks about this*

1 The Shapiros were a bit surprised when they found that they had both chosen the same career.
2 It is unusual to find twins who have both reached high positions.
3 Families who follow the same career are usually limited to specific fields.
4 Parents can help their child find a job by talking to people they know.
5 Professor Val Dusek believes Segal's research is correct.
6 People sometimes find their career disappointing.

Grammar

Past simple or present perfect?

G ⋯⟩ STUDENT'S BOOK page 139

4 Complete each sentence with the verbs in brackets, using either the past simple or present perfect.

EXAMPLE: Over the years, many famous people (follow) *have followed* in the footsteps of their parents.

1 Unemployment (not rise) .... for the past two years.

2 I (be) .... a doctor for ten years now.
3 Lisa (study) .... chemistry at school and then (go) .... on to college.
4 My brother (ring) .... me one morning and (say) .... he (have) .... a job in Australia.
5 Tom (never be) .... a hard worker – he prefers to stay in bed in the morning.
6 I (see) .... a career adviser two years ago.
7 My cousin (enjoy) .... her job ever since she was promoted.
8 We (spend) .... many years building up our business before we retired.

5 Complete the sentences with the correct tense of the verbs in brackets and with *for, since* or *ago*.

EXAMPLE: I (not see) *haven't seen* him *since* 1999.

1 I (last see) .... Michael Douglas in a film five years ....
2 One actor I know (not work) .... many years and he still isn't working.
3 Peter (have) .... a holiday three months ....
4 Val Dusek (be) .... sceptical about the book ever .... it was published.
5 When Sue (teach) .... in Zambia eight years .... , she (not enjoy) .... it.
6 Paul (not had) .... a job .... the past year.
7 We (last go) .... on a marketing trip four weeks ....
8 I (learn) .... French at school, many years ....
9 'How long (you be) .... manager of the company?' '.................... 2003.'

Vocabulary

6 Find ten verbs that collocate with *money* in this wordsearch. (→↓)

C	H	A	N	G	E	Z	P
A	L	E	N	D	I	S	A
T	L	S	Q	U	N	P	Y
L	E	A	V	E	V	E	M
Y	S	V	Y	L	E	N	A
T	R	E	M	J	S	D	K
W	A	S	T	E	T	P	E
T	N	F	G	I	V	E	D

7 Selling dreams?

Reading

1 In the General Training and Academic Reading Modules, you may be asked to match questions to short texts or sections of a longer text. Read these web pages, A–D, which advertise various events and organisations. Then read the sentences below and decide which advertisement each one refers to. Write the correct letter A–D next to each question. ⋯⋰ TF2

⏱ about 430 words

A

Nathan's Famous
International Hot-Dog Eating Contest

The preliminary ceremonies of this famous annual competition will begin at 11.30 a.m., with bands, rappers and children's chorus. 12.25 p.m. sees the introduction of this year's eaters, who represent nations from all over the world, and at 12.40 p.m., the historic 12-minute all-you-can-eat contest will begin. Will anyone beat the world record, which stands at over 50 hot dogs and buns in 12 minutes?

Viewing is available on a first-come-first-served basis. Television crews are invited to use a two-tiered stage 3m from the main stage. The area in front of the main stage is reserved for still photographers and television cameras without tripods.

B

fröjel viking re-enactment society

Few periods in history stimulate the imagination as much as the era when the Vikings were known – and sometimes feared – throughout Scandinavia, the British Isles, Russia, all the Mediterranean, Africa and even America. Fröjel (pronounced Fro-yel) is a family-based Viking re-enactment society depicting the Vikings from a harbour that was one of the richest trading centres in the Viking world – Fröjel, on the Swedish island of Gotland.

The members' aims are to re-create the clothing, weapons, tools, jewellery, games, food and furniture of that long-gone period, and enjoy an escape to a simpler, more relaxed time, with like-minded people. We will also use the items we have made by reliving that age at various public entertainments.

C

Drive a steam engine!

Now anyone can be an engine driver! Join us for a day's introductory course, during which you will learn the basic techniques of driving a 60-year-old steam locomotive, under the eye of an experienced instructor. Then, why not try the advanced course, giving you first-hand experience of operating a locomotive? Lunch and refreshments are provided on both courses at no extra cost. You are also given one-year membership of the railway society, which gives you the opportunity to become a volunteer on our educational programme.

D

The Wedding Fair

One of the most popular events in the Barnwell Centre's annual programme, the Wedding Fair, takes place every March and September. As well as displays from leading suppliers of wedding dresses, caterers, photographers and many more, a wide range of specialists will be on hand to give expert advice on planning your wedding.

The full programme of events includes a fashion show, which features wedding outfits for brides, grooms, bridesmaids and page boys. The Great Hall is decorated to show how it could look for your wedding reception. Refreshments are available in our self-service restaurant.

1 The charge for attendance includes food. ....
2 You will be able to take part in displays for others to watch. ....
3 This event takes place once a year. ....
4 You will be taught certain skills. ....
5 Participants have the opportunity to see clothes being modelled. ....
6 Spectators will have the chance to listen to musical entertainment. ....
7 If you pay for an activity, you are automatically enrolled in this organisation. ....
8 Facilities are provided for the media. ....
9 Participants make copies of everyday objects from the past. ....
10 Information is available about organising an event. ....

Grammar

Relative clauses

G ···> STUDENT'S BOOK page 139

2   In the advertisements above there are six relative clauses introduced by *who, which* or *that*. Underline those words, and decide whether the clauses are defining or non-defining.

3   There are two other forms of *who*: *whose* (the possessive form, similar to *my* and *his*) and *whom* (which normally follows a preposition). The passage that follows is part of an article about advertising techniques. For each space, choose the right word from the box. In some cases, there is more than one possibility. There is an example to help you.

that	which	who	whom	whose

How advertisers make you buy

Are you one of those people **0** ....*whose*.... expenditure is greater than their income? If so, read on – you might find out why you spend so much on goods **1** .... you don't really need.

One of the most common techniques with **2** .... advertisers try to persuade you to buy their products is for a person **3** .... name and face you know well to tell you that they can't live without that particular product. These celebrities, most of **4** .... can hardly need the money **5** .... they receive for it, may endorse the most unexpected products – like the footballer **6** .... appeared in an advertising campaign for packets of snack food.

Another common style is the advert in **7** .... we're told that everybody else has already bought the product, so you'd better hurry if you don't want to be the one person **8** .... doesn't have it. This high-pressure approach generally works because it's difficult for you to find out whether or not the product is really selling well. You have to take the advertiser's word for it, **9** .... means you're at their mercy. Adverts using this technique often tell us to 'hurry while stocks last' or give the date when the 'special offer' ends.

4   Relative pronouns can be omitted when they are the object in a defining relative clause:

The advertising is about the benefits (which/that) we hope to gain.

In the passage in exercise 3, the relative pronoun can be omitted from two spaces. The first one is number 1. Which is the other one?

5   The relative pronoun and the verb *be* are often omitted in front of the -*ing* and past participle forms of verbs and in front of adjectives. Put a line through those that can be omitted.

EXAMPLE: The agency ~~which is~~ running the fruit juice campaign is a very small company.

1   The new commercial for fruit juice, which was first shown on TV last month, has led to a jump in sales.
2   The advertising agency that was responsible for the fruit juice campaign won an award.
3   Newspapers, which first appeared in England around 1622, transformed advertising.
4   Adverts that were missing from early newspapers were ones for household goods.

Vocabulary

6   Answer these questions with phrases from the advertisements on page 16. Each answer contains an adjective made up of two or more words joined with hyphens.

EXAMPLE: Which words describe the length of a competition? *the 12-minute contest*

Which words …
1   mean people who share similar interests?
    ....
2   describe the way in which places are allocated to spectators? ....
3   refer to a period of belonging to an organisation?
    ....
4   mean that you do something yourself?
    ....
5   refer to a place where you collect and eat food?
    ....
6   explain what happens in a competition?
    ....
7   suggest the different ages of people who belong to an organisation? ....
8   give something's age? ....
9   mean a time that has finished?
    ....

Apart from the hyphen, what other difference is there between *12 minutes* and *(the) 12-minute (contest)*? One of your answers should follow the same rule: which one?

8 Time to waste?

Grammar

Talking about the future

G ⋯▸ STUDENT'S BOOK page 140

1 Complete this letter, using the verbs in brackets with *will* (*'ll*), *going to*, present simple or present continuous. As this is an informal letter to a friend, use contractions, like *'ll* and *'m*.

The future can be seen in different ways, so there are usually several ways of talking about a future event. However, in this exercise, express the meanings given in the notes on the right. This will help you to remember the differences between the various ways of expressing the future.

Dear Sarah

How **1** (you celebrate) .... your birthday next month? If you haven't arranged anything, do come to a concert by the orchestra I've just joined. We **2** (play) .... music by your favourite composer, and I'm sure you **3** (not regret) .... it, as we're pretty good!

The concert **4** (be) .... on a public holiday, and the tickets are already selling very fast, so clearly it **5** (be) .... a sell-out.

My only problem is that the performance **6** (start) .... quite late — at 9 p.m. — and I **7** (fly) .... to the West Indies the following day. The plane **8** (leave) .... early in the morning, so it **9** (be) .... quite a rush! I **10** (not spend) .... the next few weeks worrying about it though.

Do come — it **11** (be) .... great to see you. I **12** (send) .... you a leaflet about the concert as soon as they're available.

Love
Jenny

1 already decided
2 already arranged
3 prediction
4 timetable
5 result of something in present
6 timetable
7 already arranged
8 timetable
9 prediction
10 already decided
11 prediction
12 making a decision

2 These three passages were written by IELTS candidates. Correct the errors in the phrases in bold. Four of them are already correct.

Dear Friend
This letter is to invite you to my grandmother's birthday party. It's a special occasion, because my grandmother **1 is going to be** 100 years old. I've decided to give her a big surprise, so **2 I'll make** dinner. The dinner **3 is** on 1st July at seven o'clock in the Hacienda Club, and the night **4 would begin** with a favourite song of my grandmother's.

Dear Helen
Do you remember that in my hurry to travel back home, I left a big suitcase in your basement? Would you please send it to me and tell me the cost of shipment? **5 I'm going to pay** you back as soon as possible.

There is much controversy nowadays about whether the radio **6 will continue** to exist or not. Some people claim that the radio **7 will use** for a very long time. Those who disagree argue that TV and the Internet create a lot of problems. Some people spend all their spare time watching TV or playing on the Internet, and by doing this they **8 will waste** a lot of time which they could spend with their family or friends. But I firmly believe that reasonable use of the TV and Internet and keeping the radio are very important and necessary. Decreasing the negative effects of all the media **9 will to make** our society more secure than before. Otherwise, they **10 will have** a bad impact on our way of life.

3 Rewrite the part of each sentence in italics, using the words in brackets and keeping as close as possible to the sentence given. Don't change the meaning.

1 *Maybe there will be another opportunity* to go to a rock concert next month. (may)

....

2 I'm looking forward to the outdoor concert, and luckily *the weather promises to be fine*. (likely)

....

3 Jill and Dave see every play at the local theatre, so *I'm convinced they'll be there tonight*. (bound)

....

4 So many people want to see this musical that *you're unlikely to get tickets*. (probably)

....

5 Our performance was so good that *we may win the drama competition*. (chance)

....

6 *I doubt whether* many people will go to see a play in a foreign language. (unlikely)

....

7 *We probably won't* have time to go to the show. (little chance)

....

8 *This is definitely* one of the best exhibitions we have seen locally. (no doubt)

....

Reading and grammar

4 Read the article below about the history of juggling. Ignore the spaces. Choose the best heading for each paragraph from the list below. ⋯⦂ TF4

1 Paragraph A ....
2 Paragraph B ....
3 Paragraph C ....
4 Paragraph D ....
5 Paragraph E ....

⏱ about 325 words

List of Headings

i Recent discoveries
ii The end of a form of entertainment
iii Join a juggling class!
iv Anyone can try it
v Jugglers as celebrities
vi The technical demands increase
vii Different functions in different regions
viii Jugglers get organised
ix Audiences expect more from jugglers

A short history of juggling

A The history of juggling can be traced back 4,000 years to paintings of female jugglers **1** .... the walls of Egyptian tombs. In ancient civilizations in India, China, Japan, Iran and Central America, some form of ball manipulation was associated **2** .... religious rituals. Through the Middle Ages in Europe, juggling was practised only by wandering entertainers and court musicians.

B After several centuries when juggling was not recorded, it surfaced again in England in 1819. **3** .... the late 19th century, jugglers had become well established in the variety theatre in Europe. The best of them were incredibly creative and skilful, fully deserving the star status they achieved. Paul Cinquevalli, for instance, juggled an umbrella, a top hat and a bottle of water tied at the top with paper. He ended the act **4** .... tossing the hat to his head, opening the umbrella above him and throwing the bottle so that its open end stuck on the point of the umbrella, cascading water over the umbrella and all around him!

C In the late 1920s and 1930s, radio and talking movies attracted audiences away **5** .... live performances. Hundreds of small-time jugglers had filled the variety theatres, but few of them survived the death **6** .... those venues.

D Times were tough **7** .... jugglers through the 1940s, 50s and 60s. In the USA, some of them formed the International Jugglers Association in 1947. Through a newsletter and annual conventions, they communicated, sharing juggling tricks and tips on good locations for performing.

E In the 1970s, juggling became a craze in California, with teenagers taking **8** .... the streets and beaches to perform. Some were politically motivated, but most were just youngsters looking **9** .... a way of earning a little money. The kids who started on the street began a process that has removed juggling from the exclusive domain of the circus and nightclub and turned it **10** .... an approachable endeavour for everyone.

5 Now read the article again, and choose one of these prepositions for each space. You will need to use some of them more than once.

by	for	from	into	of	on	to	with

Reading

1 Scan the text for the following information.

  1 When did drilling begin?
  2 How big are the pieces in which the ice cores are stored?
  3 How many ice ages do the ice cores show?
  4 Without global warming, how long would it be before we had another ice age?

⏱ about 500 words

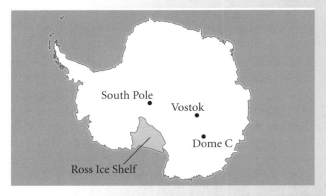

South Pole
Vostok
Dome C
Ross Ice Shelf

Drilling ice cores in Antarctica

Antarctica is both beautiful and very remote, being 2,700km from Australia and 3,500km from Africa. It is one-and-a-half times the size of Europe and is covered by a layer of ice up to 4,700m thick in places. Scientists
5 from ten European countries have been drilling into the ice since 1996, as part of the European Project for Ice Coring in Antarctica (EPICA).

An ice core is produced by a drill cutting through the ice and retrieving a cylinder of ice. These ice cores are
10 stored in slices 10cm in diameter and 3m long. When they first come out of the ground, they are at a temperature of –50˚C. They are then kept until they reach –20˚C when they are ready to be analysed in laboratories around the world.

15 Scientists find the ice cores invaluable because they contain tiny bubbles of air which were trapped when snow turned into ice. This air is being analysed to see how much carbon dioxide and other greenhouse gases, such as methane, have been present in the atmosphere
20 over many hundreds of thousands of years. Results show that the levels of methane and carbon dioxide are much higher today than in the past.

The deepest ice cores have been drilled at a site known as Dome C, where the East Antarctic ice sheet is about
25 3.4km thick. The ice sheet here is one of the most inhospitable places on Earth with average surface temperatures of –54˚C. At an altitude of 3,233m above sea level, Dome C is so cold and dark for much of the year that the scientists can only carry out drilling for
30 two out of every 12 months.

At Dome C, the deepest and oldest ice core yet drilled in the Antarctic suggests that the world's climate is heading for a period of abnormal weather conditions brought about by man-made greenhouse gases.
35 Chemical analysis of the ice within the core has revealed details of eight ice ages that have affected the Earth during the past 740,000 years. Scientists say that the present climate most closely resembles the warm 'interglacial' period about 470,000 years ago, but with
40 the difference that this time temperatures are set to go upwards as a result of global warming. Scientists from EPICA report that without the extra carbon dioxide being pumped into the atmosphere, it appears that our present climate would remain stable well into the future.

45 Some people have argued that human-induced global warming is beneficial because it averts the next ice age. However, according to Eric Wolff of British Antarctic Survey, this is misguided. 'If the climate is left to its own devices,' he says, 'we would have about another
50 15,000 years to go before the next ice age. If people say global warming is good because it stops us going into another ice age, they are wrong because we are not about to go into another ice age quite yet.'

2 Do the following statements agree with the information given in the article? ⋯⟶ TF1

Write

TRUE   *if the statement agrees with the information*
FALSE   *if the statement contradicts the information*
NOT GIVEN *if there is no information on this*

1 The ice cores need to warm up before they are sent to scientists.
2 Scientists have found similar levels of methane and carbon dioxide in the ice cores.
3 The previous ice ages were brought about by abnormal weather conditions.
4 Global warming is universally believed to be a bad thing for the Earth.
5 Eric Wolff believes there will be another ice age at some point in the future.

3 Which definition, a or b, best matches the following words or phrases as they are used in the text?

EXAMPLE: retrieving (line 9)
     a (bringing out)   **b** saving
1 inhospitable (line 26)
     a unwelcoming   **b** unsociable
2 heading for (line 33)
     a starting at   **b** going in the direction of
3 brought about (line 34)
     a happened   **b** created
4 are set to (line 40)
     a are likely/certain to   **b** are programmed to
5 stable (line 44)
     a unchanged   **b** firm
6 averts (line 46)
     a prevents   **b** moves
7 misguided (line 48)
     a misunderstood   **b** mistaken

Grammar

G ⋯⟶ STUDENT'S BOOK page 140

Noun/verb agreement

4 The *Cambridge Learner Corpus* tells us that IELTS candidates find the agreement of verbs, nouns and determiners (*the/any*, etc.) difficult. Correct the following errors from IELTS scripts. There may be more than one error.

1 One of the factories near me are causing a lot of problems.
2 Many things worries me about what are happening to the environment.
3 Every things in the town were hidden in thick smog.
4 There is many advantage to using solar power.
5 A number of problem has arisen recently in low-lying towns.
6 Another thing to mention are that we need to plant more trees.
7 Every countries has problem with a lack of fossil fuels.
8 These thing is now being used to make all kind of products.
9 A lot of thing to remember are that children needs a safe world to grow up in.
10 All kind problem will happen if the government don't do something soon.

Countable and uncountable nouns

5 Complete the following sentences with *much, many, few* or *little*.

1 The sea level is rising. We haven't got .... time.
2 Very .... research was done on climate change before 1950.
3 'How much work have you done?' 'Very .... , I'm afraid.'
4 There isn't .... news from the project manager this week.
5 .... scientists are finding it hard to get funding these days.
6 How .... research activities are you involved in?
7 There's very .... accommodation available at the research station.
8 We haven't had .... good weather recently – very .... sunshine.
9 .... people have heard of the ice-core drilling project.
10 There's very .... time left before our climate changes for good.

Vocabulary

6 Unjumble these words to do with the environment.

EXAMPLE: UPTLLNIOO   P *ollution*

1 GDEREANEND PEECISS   E............ S............
2 GCCYNLERI   R............
3 LLBAGO GRWAIMN   G............ W............
4 BOACNR XIODEID   C............ D............
5 EENHGUSROE SSGEA   G............ G............
6 CEI GAES   I............ A............
7 IMTAECL EGACNH   C............ C............
8 EAS EELVL   S............ L............

A place to work or live in

Reading

⏱ about 550 words

HOW SKYSCRAPERS WORK

A

Throughout the history of architecture, there has been a continual quest for height. Thousands of workers toiled on the pyramids of ancient Egypt, the cathedrals of Europe and countless other towers, all striving to create something awe-inspiring. Although today people build skyscrapers primarily because they are convenient, ego and grandeur still sometimes play a significant role in the scope of the construction, just as they did in earlier times.

B

Up until relatively recently, however, builders could only go so high – the main obstacle being the downward pull of gravity. In order to build upwards, there has to be more material at the bottom to support the combined weight of all the material above. For example, if you increase the base of a pyramid, you can build it up indefinitely, but this becomes unworkable as the base would take up too much land. As a result, people didn't construct many buildings over ten stories.

C

But in the late 1800s, a number of advances and circumstances converged, and engineers were able to break the upper limit. In the USA, the social circumstances that led to skyscrapers were the growing metropolitan American centers, most notably Chicago. Businesses all wanted their offices near the center of town, but there wasn't enough space. In these cities, architects needed a way to expand the metropolis upward, rather than outward. The main technological advancement that made skyscrapers possible was the development of mass iron and steel production. New manufacturing processes made it possible to produce long beams of solid iron. Narrow, relatively lightweight metal beams could support a lot of weight, while taking up very little space. Then, with the advent of the Bessemer process, the first efficient method for mass steel production, architects moved away from iron to steel.

D

The central support structure of a skyscraper is its steel skeleton. Metal beams are riveted end to end to form vertical columns. At each floor level, these vertical columns are connected to horizontal girder beams. Many buildings also have diagonal beams running between the girders, for extra structural support. In a typical skyscraper substructure, each vertical column sits on a spread footing. The column rests directly on a cast-iron plate, which sits on top of a grillage. This is basically a stack of horizontal steel beams, lined side by side in two or more layers. The grillage rests on a thick concrete pad which is on the soil. Once the steel is in place, the entire structure is covered with concrete.

E

Once you get more than five or six floors in the building, you need to have something to move people up through the building quickly and efficiently. Skyscrapers would never have worked without the development of elevator technology. Ever since the first passenger elevator was installed in New York's Haughwout Department Store in 1857, elevator shafts have been a major part of skyscraper design.

F

Experts are divided about how high we can really go in the near future. Some say we could build a mile-high (1,609m) building with existing technology, while others say we would need to develop lighter, stronger materials before these buildings were feasible.

1 Read the article on page 22 from an American magazine. It has six paragraphs labelled A–F. Which paragraph contains the following information? ⋯⟩ TF 7

EXAMPLE: a necessary addition to tall buildings *E*

1 the way a tall building is constructed today
2 the outlook for tall buildings
3 the emotional need for tall buildings
4 breakthroughs in building materials
5 the disadvantage of old building techniques

2 Label the diagram below. ⋯⟩ TF 10

A typical skyscraper substructure – (**1**) ....

(**2**) ....
(**3**) ....
(**4**) ....
(**5**) ....
soil

Vocabulary

3 The article on skyscrapers contains American English spelling and words, for example *center* for *centre* and *elevator* for *lift*. Match the American words in column A with the British words in column B.

A		B	
1	apartment	a	post
2	train station	b	cinema
3	drugstore	c	garden
4	check	d	note
5	mail	e	rubbish
6	fall	f	sweets
7	candy	g	maths
8	bill	h	autumn
9	garbage	i	flat
10	math	j	railway station
11	backyard	k	chemist's
12	movie theater	l	bill

Grammar

-*ing* forms and infinitives

G ⋯⟩ STUDENT'S BOOK page 141

4 Complete the sentences below, using the correct form of the word in brackets and adding a preposition, if needed.

1 There's no point (decorate) ...., as I'm only living here for a couple of months.
2 We've decided (share) .... a house in the city centre.
3 Stephen can't stand (live) .... with untidy people.
4 Toni suggested (move) .... to New York.
5 Tina succeeded (buy) .... her dream house in Italy.
6 Pablo's parents made him (study) .... medicine instead of letting him (do) .... art history.
7 Repairing the roof now will involve (do) .... a lot of work in cold weather.
8 We put off (get) .... a new shower put in until December.
9 After (interview) .... several people, we couldn't decide who (ask) .... to move in.
10 Would you mind (open) .... the window for me?
11 The builder carried on (work) .... all evening.
12 Dr Fisher apologised (keep) .... the architect waiting.
13 Marco can't afford (leave) .... home yet.
14 We hope (move) .... soon (get away) .... from the neighbours.
15 I agreed (give) .... him £50 a month towards the electricity bills.
16 She stopped (smoke) .... in her room after her mother shouted at her.
17 Could you recommend somewhere (stay) .... when I'm in Paris?
18 Lisa was advised (study) .... architecture at college.
19 I want (go) .... to see the new art gallery tonight.
20 My dad's not very good (fix) .... things.

Grammar

Articles

G ···▷ STUDENT'S BOOK page 141

1 Read the passage below quickly. As you read it, decide which of these sentences best sums up what it is about.

A Some animals are more intelligent than some human beings.
B Research into animal behaviour is making us reassess our ways of measuring human intelligence.
C Some animals are able to learn from human beings.
D We are increasing our understanding of animal intelligence.

2 Read the passage again, and write *a*, *an*, *the* or nothing in each space.

Intelligent animals

It used to be thought that only 1 .... human beings were able to use 2 .... tools. In recent years, however, 3 .... research has shown that some animals have developed 4 .... same ability.

5 .... chimpanzees appear to be among the most intelligent animals, and 6 .... study of some living in 7 .... certain region of West Africa found that they use 8 .... crude stone tools to crack open 9 .... nuts when they are hungry. Even more surprisingly, perhaps, they teach 10 .... skill to their young. The chimps that were studied show precise control over the force needed to break open 11 .... nuts. They use enough pressure to crack them open, but not so much that they break into 12 .... very small pieces that cannot be eaten.

13 .... chimps select 14 .... heavy stones and carry them to where the nut trees grow, which is 15 .... sophisticated behaviour for 16 .... animal of any species. They collect their nuts, put them on 17 .... flat, horizontal piece of 18 .... wood and hit 19 .... nuts with 20 .... stones. Mothers show their young how to crack 21 .... nuts, just as 22 .... human beings teach their children.

3 The *Cambridge Learner Corpus* shows that IELTS candidates make a large number of errors with articles. These sentences, written by IELTS candidates, contain errors with the article. Those in **bold** are the wrong article or are used when there shouldn't be one. The spaces show where an article is missing. Correct the errors.

1 I expect you to send **a** people to repair the power supply.
2 I hope you are in **a** good health.
3 Today you may buy the latest car in the market, but in .... few weeks' time it will be outdated.
4 Some people believe that traditional skills are disappearing due to .... development of technology.
5 There is a big demand for **a** fast food.
6 I do a lot of hobbies in my spare time. Generally I listen to **the** music.
7 The experience gained from working when they are young will help these children to find .... good job much faster.
8 I wouldn't say that everywhere is .... same.
9 These two charts show **the** information about the sale of cars last year.
10 Unfortunately, we had **a** bad service when we went to your restaurant for dinner.

Reading

4 Read the article on page 25 quickly. Which of these is the main topic?

A the different abilities of various types of animals
B how some animals interact with other species
C differences between human and animal behaviour

⏱ about 375 words.

The social life of **mammals**

5 The passage has four paragraphs labelled A–D. Which paragraph contains the following information? (You may use any letter more than once.) ···▸ TF7

1 a reference to possible harmful effects of not knowing about other individuals
2 examples of what individuals need to know about connections between group members
3 a reference to human beings sharing a social skill with other mammals
4 what makes it possible for mammals to spend time growing up
5 how individual members of a species identify themselves
6 where knowledge is located in the individual
7 a contrast between the social organisation of mammals and of other species
8 a suggestion concerning a connection between length of childhood and the amount of learning the individual requires

A When it comes to social behaviour, mammals are far more highly developed than other creatures. Some birds may form pairs or even co-operate to hunt, but the complexity of their relationships can hardly compare to those within a group of dolphins, elephants or humans. What makes mammalian 5 social groups different from, say, a flock of starlings or a shoal of fish is that in many cases the individuals recognise each other. Although we may think that all elephants look pretty much the same, we can easily tell individuals of our own species apart, and it has become clear through studies 10 that the same is true of other species of mammals. Dolphins have their own signature whistles that act like names, and elephants can recognise and greet other individuals they have known but not seen for many years. This is something that only a few species of birds appear to be able to do. 15

B Mammals in complex social groups not only recognise each other as individuals, they also remember a lot of information about that individual. Social groups often rely on this memory – such as knowing who is dominant to whom, who is related to whom, and who has done what to 20 whom in the past. They have to learn who to trust, who their friends are and who to watch out for.

C All this remembering goes on in a particular part of the brain called the neocortex. If you compare the size of a mammal's social group with the size of this part of the brain, you find 25 they are remarkably closely related. This area, though, seems to take a long time to develop fully, and animals in which it is very large take a very long time to grow up to adulthood. During this time, the youngster has to learn all the rules of social behaviour in their group and to piece 30 together all the relationships between the group members: knowledge that will be needed to avoid getting into trouble.

D Like all the advanced and specialised features that mammals have, social behaviour has developed because of the one defining characteristic that mammals possess: 35 the production of milk, allowing baby mammals to have a period of childhood in which they can develop their own distinctive and successful characteristics.

6 Complete the summary below. Choose no more than ONE WORD from the passage for each answer. ···▸ TF5

The social life of mammals

Mammals behave in a much more complex way than **1** .... or **2** ....
For example, **3** .... make individual sounds that distinguish them from each other.
4 .... are another non-human species that can remember individuals after a long absence.
Certain mammals retain **5** .... about individuals, partly because they need to know which ones they can **6** .... This memory is located in the **7** .... area of the brain. Animals in whom that part of the brain is large take a long time to reach **8** .... While they are growing up, they need to work out the social rules of their group and the **9** .... among its members. Mammals are only able to have a long period of growing up because they can be provided with **10** ....

Vocabulary

7 The adverbs in the box are used in the reading passage of 11.1 of the Student's Book or in this unit of the Workbook. Choose the best word to complete each sentence.

closely	eventually	hardly	highly
independently	respectively	relatively	
remarkably	simultaneously		

1 For a long time, very little was known about what animals do underground, but modern technology .... made it possible to film them.
2 .... , certain species of birds can make tools which they use to get access to food.
3 Dolphins and sharks are mammals and fish ....
4 When male frogs sing .... , they are more likely to attract females than if they sing alone.
5 Although elephants are .... harmless, it is unwise to go too close to them.
6 The development of social behaviour seems to be .... connected with having a long childhood.
7 Many nature programmes on TV are .... thought of.

Sport: just for fun?

Reading

1 You are going to read two short articles about using psychology to help athletes to improve their performance. Read the article below quickly, and as you read it, try to answer this question.

Which is the best summary of the writer's opinion?
A Sports psychology is of most use to athletes at the top of their field.
B The media give insufficient information about the value of sports psychology.
C Sports psychology is of great value to all athletes.
D Too much emphasis is placed on the usefulness of sports psychology.

⏱ about 125 words.

There's more to winning than just physical ability

Sports psychology involves preparing the mind of an athlete just as thoroughly as one prepares the body. For many top-level, professional, recreational and even youth athletes, successful performances cannot
5 simply be reduced to superior physical performance. Mental preparation includes setting clear, short-term goals, thinking positively, etc.

Thanks to the extensive media coverage of athletic events nowadays, the sports enthusiast can
10 understand the need for and benefits of sports psychology. Examples of mental training surround us; for instance, skiers, divers and gymnasts picturing their routines before they perform. Concepts such as motivation training and relaxation
15 are the basis for strong mental preparation, whether for a team or an individual sport, for an amateur or a professional, for a coach or an athlete.

2 Complete the sentences below with words taken from the passage above. Use NO MORE THAN ONE WORD for each space. ⸱⸱⸱⟩ TF3

1 Psychological preparation is just as important as
.... preparation.
2 Athletes should decide on their ....
for the near future.
3 Most people interested in sport are now aware of
the .... for sports psychology.
4 Many athletes imagine their .... in
order to improve their performance.
5 Basic mental preparation is useful for both
.... and .... sports.

⏱ about 450 words

A Critical View of Sports Psychology Consultants

A good sports psychology consultant can be of great value for a sportsman or woman. However, after many years' experience, I have reluctantly come to the conclusion that a large number of these consultants –
5 that is, people claiming expertise in working with athletes on psychological aspects of competition in sport – fail to reach the required standard. Many professionals claim to be the key to improving a sportsman or woman's concentration, team
10 performance and virtually every other skill they require. They are interviewed in local and national newspapers and heard on radio shows, and a surprising number of professional teams use one. However, the opinion that I have reached in my experience as a sports psychology
15 consultant seems to be shared by many players, and not a few consultants: too many professionals in this line of work are not worth the money they cost. Because of the incompetence of these people, the idea has gained ground that working with a sports
20 psychology consultant is a mistake. Yet this should not be the general view, as a skilled consultant can make a major contribution to success in sport.

Several reasons can be identified for poor performance by sports psychology consultants. One is a tendency to
25 overvalue qualifications. Most consultants believe that their qualifications are the most appropriate and effective way to impress potential clients. I beg to differ. Numerous examples can be given of consultants who have the necessary skills without a certificate from a
30 sports psychology organisation. Many, too, are far more effective than some consultants with a qualification.

3 Skim the passage above, on the same subject, and answer this question.

Which is the best summary of the writer's opinion?
A Sports psychology is useful, but too many consultants are bad at their job.
B The media give a false image of the value of sports psychology.
C Sports psychology can never be of value to athletes.
D Few sportspeople realise how sports psychology could help them.

4 Scan the article again and answer this question.

What is the writer's job?
A sports psychology consultant
B athlete
C journalist

Another cause for concern is the number of consultants who lack the necessary skills or experience. Some sports psychology professionals work only on performance issues, and are unable to engage in individual counselling for personal, or life, issues, which is an essential aspect of the work. Others have plenty of clinical skills, but no idea how to help sportspeople to become more successful at sport. Most have neither the skills nor the expertise needed to help their clients get results. 40

Even if they have all the other skills required, most sports psychology consultants are inadequate because they lack the interpersonal skills needed to work effectively with their clients. I have seen 45 consultants behaving very unprofessionally, for instance by guaranteeing results or becoming angry when faced with a client's decision to change to another consultant.

The bottom line is this: when choosing a sports 50 psychology consultant, it is important to get information about them, for instance from past or present clients. Then it is possible to make an informed decision regarding hiring them. Clients should not be afraid to demand both quality and character; if they 55 don't, plenty of money will be wasted.

5 Do the following statements agree with the views of the writer of the second article? ⋯⫶ TF1

Write

YES   *if the statement agrees with the views of the writer*

NO   *if the statement contradicts the views of the writer*

NOT GIVEN   *if it is impossible to say what the writer thinks about this*

EXAMPLE: The media pay too much attention to sports psychology consultants. *NOT GIVEN*

(In lines 11–12, the writer mentions the media attention given to sports psychology consultants, but does not say that this is too much.)

1 Newspapers are responsible for the increasing demand for sports psychology consultants.
2 A number of sports psychology consultants overcharge their clients.
3 Qualifications are essential for a good consultant.
4 Consultants should help clients with both personal and performance issues.
5 Consultants should promise clients that their help will be successful.
6 Clients should only change consultants if they have a good reason.
7 It is useful to speak to people who have used a particular consultant before hiring him or her.

Grammar

should, had better, ought to

G ⋯⫶ STUDENT'S BOOK page 141

6 Decide which of the following each sentence is being used to do.

A give advice
B express probability

1 You shouldn't wear glasses during your bungee jump because they might fall off.
2 Recent evidence should convince doubters that the Aztecs played far more challenging sports than those we have today.
3 You want to become a champion? Then you should do a lot of practice.
4 The number of events in the Winter Olympics has increased in recent years, so there should be around 80 next time.
5 You're in peak condition, so you shouldn't have any problem completing the marathon.

7 These sentences were written by IELTS candidates. In each one, decide if the phrase in **bold** is used correctly or not, both in meaning and grammar. If not, correct it.

1 It is very cold these days, so I hope you **should take** care of yourself.
2 In my opinion, governments **shouldn't subsidise** bodies such as orchestras and drama companies.
3 People **should not to be encouraged** to take part in dangerous sports like scuba-diving or mountain-climbing.
4 It will be cold when you visit Shanghai, so you **had better to take** warm clothes with you.
5 We **not ought to spend** our time cooking dinner after working all day.
6 The fire was caused by old electric wiring, so I think we **had better ask** the landlord to replace it.
7 It is a little cold, so I think **it's better you bring** warm clothes and your boots.

Grammar

Conditionals

(G) ⋯⟫ STUDENT'S BOOK page 141

1 Make conditional sentences from these situations.

  1 I can't decide. You have to help me.
    I can't decide unless ....

  2 Eating cheese makes me fat, so I don't eat it.
    If I don't eat cheese, ...

  3 I didn't go to Spain. I didn't learn Spanish.
    If I had gone to Spain, ...

  4 I'm unhappy. I have to make a lot of choices.
    I wouldn't be unhappy if ....

  5 I want to go to a good university. I will get a good job.
    As long as I go to a good university, ...
    ....

  6 I spend too much in restaurants. I need to learn to cook.
    If I learnt to cook, ...

  7 I went to a party last night. I woke up late this morning.
    If I hadn't been to a party last night, ...
    ....

  8 Nick can have the job, but he needs to learn to drive first.
    Nick can have the job as long as ....
    ....

  9 Susanna isn't here. She could help us.
    If Susanna were here, ...

  10 I was unhappy. I married the wrong man.
    I wouldn't have been unhappy if ....
    ....

Vocabulary

2 The following are important nouns which are often used in academic writing. Complete the sentences below using one of the words from the box.

analysis	evidence	factor	paper
process	research	source	theory

  1 Your .... of the situation is correct.

  2 His .... on 'Choice' was widely publicised.

  3 The .... of applying to college can be complicated.

  4 One .... in his promotion was his excellent research.

  5 Can you put a tick to indicate that you've read the research .... ?

  6 There is no .... of original ideas in this work.

  7 The .... of evolution was put forward by Darwin.

  8 In your bibliography, you must quote every .... that you use.

3 Form nouns from the words below. All the nouns occur in the passage in 13.1 of the Student's Book.

  1 satisfy   ....
  2 grow   ....
  3 able   ....
  4 politics   ....
  5 opt   ....
  6 tend   ....
  7 decide   ....
  8 expect   ....
  9 economise   ....
  10 differ   ....
  11 govern   ....
  12 recommend   ....

4 **Find the nouns from exercise 3 in this wordsearch. (They are all singular.) (→↓)**

D	T	H	E	O	P	T	I	O	N	R	E	I	S
I	O	N	L	G	O	V	E	R	N	M	E	N	T
F	Y	O	N	E	L	G	S	O	E	D	A	N	D
F	H	E	T	I	I	S	A	O	C	U	R	L	O
E	X	P	E	C	T	A	T	I	O	N	R	G	D
R	J	E	N	S	I	U	I	S	N	C	H	R	I
E	S	T	D	E	C	I	S	I	O	N	H	O	E
N	I	S	E	S	I	O	F	V	M	E	R	W	E
C	I	G	N	N	A	M	A	B	I	L	I	T	Y
E	A	Y	C	H	N	I	C	S	S	W	I	H	L
L	B	E	Y	D	O	N	T	E	T	I	N	H	E
A	V	E	N	A	N	D	I	O	N	E	A	R	T
H	A	M	E	N	C	W	O	B	M	M	V	P	B
R	E	C	O	M	M	E	N	D	A	T	I	O	N

5 **Complete each sentence with the best adverb. More than one answer may be possible.**

badly   hardly   highly   perfectly
totally   widely

1 'I'm afraid your work is so .... written that I refuse to mark it,' the teacher said.
2 The product was .... recommended by some friends of mine.
3 To be .... honest with you, no, I didn't enjoy the shopping trip.
4 Tom was .... amazed to find his cat asleep in the washing machine.
5 'It's .... necessary to take such a large bag when you go shopping,' she said.
6 The new restaurant was .... advertised in all the papers and on radio.
7 Professor Sims has always been a .... respected member of the faculty.
8 These types of machine are .... available in the shops.

6 **Which word/phrase in each set doesn't collocate with *decision* or *choice*?**

1 a *great / total / wise / unanimous* decision
2 a *popular / smooth / hard / snap* decision
3 to *make / have / offer / stop* a choice
4 a(n) *obvious / odd / soft / wide* choice
5 to be *spoilt for / given a/the / made a/the / left with no* choice

7 **Complete these sentences with one of the collocations from exercise 6.**

1 In the end, everyone agreed, making it a .... decision.
2 Dr Peters was given the Chair in Physics – he was the .... choice, as he had been acting Chair for the past two years.
3 When the rain came down, we had to make a .... decision – time wasn't on our side.
4 In the shop, we were .... the choice of either having a refund or a credit note.
5 Stella was .... choice in the shoe shop and didn't know which pair she liked most.

8 **Complete the text with the appropriate form of one of these phrases to do with shopping.**

a bargain   to cost a fortune   half price
to keep the receipt   a reasonable price
a refund   to try something on
to window shop

During the holidays, I decided to do a bit of
1 .... As I walked through the mall, I could
see that there were quite a few 2 .... to be
had. Some things were 3 .... or less. The last
pair of shoes I bought 4 .... , and so I really
wanted something at a more 5 .... Suddenly,
I saw a pair of trainers – they were just what I
needed, so I asked the assistant if I could
6 .... They fitted perfectly, and I made up
my mind immediately to get them. As the assistant was
putting them in a bag for me, she told me to
7 .... , just in case I changed my mind and
needed to get a 8 ....

The importance of colour

Reading

1 Look at the words in the box. Put them in pairs with similar meanings.

EXAMPLE: *a colour – a pigment*

2 Read the text below. Time yourself as you read.

⏱ about 700 words

clear ~~a colour~~ a consideration to create
to extract genuine an issue to make real
~~a pigment~~ to take out transparent

Colour in Art

A

There are no 'real' colours in nature – only the various wavelengths that make up light, which are absorbed and reflected by all the objects around us. The reflected wavelengths enter the eye, which, in turn, sends signals to
5 the brain: only then do we 'see' the impact of all these wavelengths on the eye. This white light contains the colours of the rainbow, which can be seen when the rays are separated by a glass prism. Each colour has its own wavelength: violet has the shortest, and red the longest.
10 When these colours are combined with nature's pigments – the chlorophyll in grass, for instance – millions of shades can be created. Painters have reproduced these using the powdered colours of natural or artificial pigments which are themselves only the colour of the light they reflect.

B
15 However, before we can adequately explore what colour means to the artist, we must ask what we mean by the word 'colour'. This may seem straightforward enough, but is my 'red' the same as your 'red'? Linguistic considerations are often central to an interpretation of
20 the historical use of colour in art. The Japanese *awo* can mean 'green', 'blue' or 'dark', depending on the context; Vietnamese also declines to distinguish green from blue. The indigenous Australians, the Aborigines, only have two colour terms – white and black – even though they
25 use other colours in their paintings. English uses 11 colour words – black, white, red, orange, yellow, green, blue, purple, pink, grey and brown – and thousands of other 'borrowed' names – apricot, avocado, gold, peach and so on.

C
30 Before the 19th century, when artists were deciding which colour paint to use, they generally had to use 'natural products', which is to say organic substances derived from animals and plants. The earliest cave paintings were made using red from iron oxides, black
35 from charcoal and white from chalk and ground bones. Later, Tyrian purple, the imperial colour of ancient Rome,

was extracted from a particular shellfish – just under half a kilo of royal purple dye required the crushing of four million molluscs. Cochineal red, discovered by the Aztecs, was made using the female cochineal beetle. 40

D
Interestingly, however, the blue pigment known as Egyptian frit or Egyptian blue, which has been identified in artefacts dating from around 2500 BC, is not a naturally occurring product. It was made by the ancient Egyptians who needed to first of all mix different compounds 45 together and then heat them. This resulted in the oldest synthetic pigment, a Bronze Age blue. This use of nature's materials reveals ancient Egypt as a civilisation with a genuine command of chemistry.

E
The cost and quality of the colours used were factors to be 50 born in mind by both artist and patron when a painting was commissioned. The dramatic red, made from a substance called cinnabar, used to paint wall panels in Pompeii, Italy, around 60 BC, was mined in Spain and was so expensive that a law was passed setting a ceiling 55 price. Another colour, ultramarine blue, was extracted from the lapis lazuli stone, which had to be quarried and shipped from Afghanistan. The expense of this meant that, in western art, ultramarine blue was reserved for paintings of very special or important people. 60

F
A new technique in the early 15th century expanded the range of colours that could be portrayed with oil paint. In this technique, the powdered pigment is mixed with a slow-drying oil – such as linseed or walnut – which absorbs oxygen from the air, forming a transparent skin 65 that locks the colour in. This meant that oil paint could be built up in layers and so only three or four pigments could be used to create over 20 different shades of, say, red. In the 19th century, the invention of collapsible tin paint-tubes to replace pigs' bladders made paint much 70 more portable.

G
So, where will artists get their colour inspiration from next? Perhaps more metallic or fluorescent colours will be used, or perhaps artists will use liquid crystals that change colour with temperature or that offer an 75 iridescent rainbow all at once. One thing is certain: technology will always open new doors for artists.

3 Which paragraph contains the following information? You may use any letter more than once.
···⟩ TF7

1 why there was a need for state intervention
2 an account of how humans perceive colour
3 the reason why the use of a colour was limited
4 details of the first known production of an artificial colour
5 a reference to different living organisms used in the production of colours
6 the part played by two important technical developments
7 different ways of putting the idea of colour into words
8 the way in which a colour could be made lighter or darker
9 an example of languages using the same word for more than one colour
10 where raw materials had to be dug out of the ground

Grammar

-*ing* forms and infinitives

G ···⟩ STUDENT'S BOOK pages 141 and 142

4 Correct these errors which IELTS candidates have made.

1 I have experience to design colour schemes for offices.
2 Can I suggest to go to see the science museum?
3 The interior of the car is designed for improving driving.
4 Leila learned using watercolour paints at college.
5 Let Pablo going into the room first.
6 He will be under pressure to meet deadlines and completing tasks and coursework.
7 You must to go and see the new colours at the fashion show.
8 In conclusion, to study abroad has fewer advantages than in this country.
9 To let everyone to know where the talk will be held, there'll be a map.
10 She intends to going away after term ends.
11 Pete can't remember to get into the car and to drive to the station.
12 We prevented to him draw on the walls.
13 A lot of time was spent to teach them to write.
14 Try to walk rather than to drive everywhere if you want to lose weight.
15 It was years ago, but I'll never forget to see Venice for the first time.
16 You'd better ringing up your tutor to tell him you'll be late.
17 Elisa's interested to do fashion design next term.
18 Remember posting that letter on your way to work.
19 Children often dream to be football stars.
20 You need giving up staying up late watching TV.

Vocabulary

5 Complete the definitions with the words in the box.

appreciative   cautious   competent
honest   impatient   impulsive
independent   sensitive

1 A(n) .... person is one who quickly gets annoyed if they have to wait for someone.
2 A(n) .... person is helpful and kind and knows what other people need.
3 A(n) .... person always writes a note to thank someone who gives them a present.
4 A(n) .... person always does things well.
5 A(n) .... person is not easily influenced by other people.
6 A(n) .... person avoids taking risks.
7 A(n) .... person can always be trusted.
8 A(n) .... person does things without planning or considering what might happen.

Vocabulary

1 These words come from the reading passage and exercise 3 in 15.1 of the Student's Book. Using the clues, write the words in the grid and find the secret word.

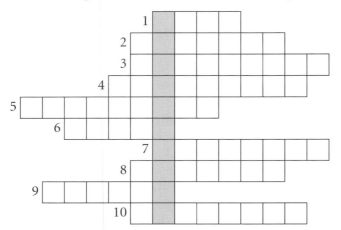

1 someone who invites another person to their home
2 complicated
3 crucial
4 dear, costing a great deal
5 food bought from shops and markets
6 someone invited to another person's home
7 sufficient, enough for a particular purpose
8 to watch carefully, to notice
9 informal
10 someone who lives in a particular place

Secret word: friendly and welcoming to people invited to one's home ....

Grammar

Must and *can't*

G ···⟶ STUDENT'S BOOK page 142

2 The *Cambridge Learner Corpus* shows that many IELTS candidates find modal verbs difficult. Read these sentences and correct any mistakes in the phrases in **bold**. Some of them are correct.

1 Young people like to use the telephone and watch TV at night. If their parents want to sleep, the noise **must make** them unhappy.
2 My brother felt shy when my aunt and uncle visited us. We concluded that he **must be spent** too much time watching television.
3 The leak is low, near to the floor, so it **should be related** to the pipes of the shower behind it.
4 I invited Abdul to come tomorrow, so that **mustn't be** him now.
5 Many people take part in dangerous sports, so there **must be** some who have accidents.
6 You **must haven't attend** a Chinese wedding before, as you are surprised by this one.
7 I believe that retirement at 60 or 65 is a good idea. One reason is that people **should be** tired at that age.
8 This food contains so much sugar that it **not can be** healthy.
9 I keep seeing Deirdre in town, so she **mustn't be working** in France any more.

Reading

3 Read the passage on the next page. Which paragraph mentions the following information? You may use any letter more than once. ···⟶ TF7

1 a list of motives for developing social relationships
2 an example of people wishing to learn about a future experience from others
3 various forms that social activities can take
4 how social relationships can be used to evaluate one's own feelings
5 a classification of occasions when people prefer to be alone or with other people
6 a comparison between the behaviour of adults and children
7 an outline of stages in the development of social relationships
8 how an investigation was carried out
9 why children behave as they do
10 a reason for a claim concerning the role of social relationships in daily life

Social relationships

A Imagine for a minute what life would be like without social relationships: not swapping news with your family at the end of the day, not gossiping with your friends about the party you went to last night, not chatting with colleagues at the coffee machine, not having any close relationship involving mutual support and caring. Imagining this kind of life is so difficult as to be almost impossible, which neatly illustrates the importance of social relationships in our lives. [10]

B From the earliest age, humans want to belong to their world and to feel a sense of connectedness with it. This need for belonging can be observed as the motivation for infants in their earliest interactions with others. From the moment of birth, babies seek [15] to establish an enduring social relationship with their main carer, extending their circle of relationships outwards as skills and circumstances allow. Later, as their social skills improve, children modify their behaviour to others in order to fit in with other [20] people and gain a sense of belonging.

C Wanting to belong is thought to be a basic need, which makes us set up, keep and – when necessary – repair good social relations with others. It has been suggested that we create social relations for [25] four main reasons: to enable us to compare ourselves with others, thereby reducing uncertainty; to obtain the reward of stimulating company; to be valued; and to gain emotional support.

D Social comparison allows participants to measure [30] their own uncertainty against that of other people and decide, for instance, whether their fear is justified. It can thus be a strategy for reducing anxiety.

E Relationships can also be used for information seeking. Just as young children refer to their parents [35] for information in new or ambiguous situations, adults will also seek out someone with more information when in difficulty. Hospital patients facing an operation the next day generally prefer to spend the night with others who have already had [40] the operation and can provide information about the potential danger, rather than with someone who is about to undergo the same operation.

F In one piece of research, people were asked to specify the conditions under which they would like [45] to be with others. The researcher found that people preferred the company of others in pleasant conditions, such as enjoying a concert, when feeling happy or in the work environment. Company was also preferred in threatening conditions, such as [50] when in danger or feeling afraid. In unpleasant conditions, such as when feeling tense or having just failed a test, people preferred to be alone, as they did in conditions requiring them to concentrate, such as solving a complicated problem [55] or making a decision.

4 After each adjective there are five nouns. Four of them often collocate with the adjective. Cross through the one that does NOT normally collocate. It will help if you find the adjectives in the passage.

EXAMPLE: mutual *advantage / benefit / respect / ~~situation~~ / support*

1 (a) complicated *history / problem / relationship / rules / value*
2 (an) emotional *appeal / motivation / relationship / response / support*
3 (a) social *conditions / group / interaction / operation / skills*
4 (a) stimulating *approach / belonging / company / discussion / effect*
5 (a) potential *consequences / customer / difficulty / danger / hospital*
6 (a) threatening *behaviour / conditions / environment / need / situation*

Check your answers before you go on to exercise 5.

5 Choose one of the four nouns from the appropriate set in exercise 4 to complete these sentences. Check both the meaning and the grammar.

EXAMPLE: Almost everyone participates in social ....*interaction*...... at home and at work.

1 As babies develop, they manage to work out and learn the complicated .... of the language they hear around them.
2 Any relationship between two people can be damaged by the threatening .... of one participant.
3 If the two participants in a relationship lack mutual .... , the relationship is unlikely to be long-lasting.
4 As children become more skilful, they learn to identify, and to some extent avoid, the potential .... of their actions.
5 The presentation was followed by a stimulating .... of the role of emotions in social relationships.
6 The speaker made an emotional .... for conflict to be resolved by peaceful means.
7 Social .... is important for children, as it helps them to learn how to behave.

16 Books, writing and signs

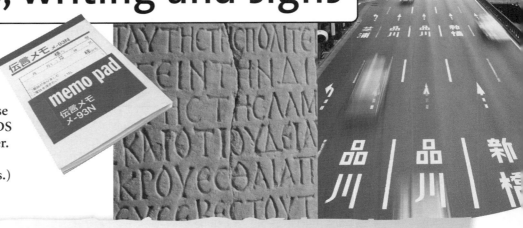

Reading

1 Read this book review, and complete the table below. Choose NO MORE THAN TWO WORDS from the passage for each answer.
···▸ TF3 (Completing a table is very similar to completing notes.)

⏱ about 340 words

Insights into the alphabet

In his book *Letter Perfect* (originally published under the title *Language Visible*), David Sacks proves that an area of language that we generally overlook is much more interesting than we might imagine: as the 26 building
5 blocks of our written language, the letters of our alphabet have an enormous impact on our lives. Serious linguists might find this book frustrating, but Sacks's target audience seems to be casual linguists, and they will love it. He sets out to educate and entertain us by exploring
10 both the history and the modern significance of each letter of the alphabet in turn.

Sacks is the author of *Encyclopaedia of the Ancient Greek World* and numerous articles on cultural topics, including 26 on the alphabet that he wrote for a
15 Canadian newspaper. These were so popular that he was encouraged to develop them into this book, which is full of fascinating information. He writes about how the Roman, Cyrillic, Arabic, Greek and Hebrew alphabets have descended from a common ancestor which was

created around 4,000 years ago. We learn why in English 20 the letter C is sometimes pronounced like S and sometimes like K, why Americans say *zee* for Z while the British prefer *zed*, and why Q is always followed by U. His comments on the letters in the present day cover everything from B-movies, through the character M of 25 James Bond films, to the Thomas Pynchon novel *V*.

The downside of the one-chapter-per-letter structure, however, is that it leads to considerable repetition: for instance, several chapters tell us about the origins of the Roman alphabet. Another drawback of the book is that 30 the dual focus on history and modern culture doesn't quite work. When he writes about the past, it is scholarly but can appear uninteresting, while what he says about the present sometimes seems unscholarly.

Many people will find plenty to interest them in this 35 book, though it's probably better to dip into it at random, rather than read it from cover to cover. It's a book that's sure to give plenty of pleasure.

Outline of book review	
Introduction	
Title	1 ....
Author	2 ....
Category	3 ....
Subject area	*alphabet*
Intended readers	4 ....
Overview	
Author's purpose	*to educate and entertain*
Main topics	*the 5 .... and current 6 .... of every letter*
Analysis and evaluation • Qualifications to write about subject • Strengths • Weaknesses	• *has written an encyclopaedia and many 7 ....* • *contains plenty of interesting 8 ....* • *too much 9 .... between chapters* • *sections about the past can seem 10 ....* • *sections about the present can seem 11 ....*
Conclusion Overall response	*Enjoyable, especially if you don't read it from 12 .... to ....*

Vocabulary

2 The words in the box are related to ones in the reading passage in 16.1 of the Student's Book. Use them in the correct form to complete the sentences below. A brief definition is given in italics.

> abstract   alphabetical   combine
> communicative   evolve   indicate
> modify   predecessor   regular
> representational   significant   unrelated

1 English spelling has .... over a period of about 1,300 years. (*develop*)
2 One category of Egyptian hieroglyphs .... what type of meaning a word has. (*show*)
3 The vast majority of Chinese characters are very .... , and so it is impossible to guess their meanings. (*non-realistic*)
4 When the Latin alphabet was adopted for Turkish in 1928, it was partially .... so that all the sounds of the language could be represented. (*adapt*)
5 Letters are used for the sounds of a language that are .... for distinguishing between words, for example, *fed* and *red*. (*important*)
6 Finnish spelling is much more .... than English. (*consistent*)
7 The sign 'No dogs allowed' consists of a fairly .... image of a dog, with a diagonal red line that symbolises prohibition. (*pictorial*)
8 The Egyptian hieroglyphic system was a far more effective means of communication than its .... (*the one that it replaced*)

3 Write these words under the verb that they are more likely to follow.

> ~~a book~~   a (book) review   a dissertation
> an email   an essay   an experiment
> an investigation   a letter   a report
> research   a survey   a threat   a thesis

to write	to carry out
a book	

4 Complete these sentences with words from exercise 3. In some cases, more than one answer is possible.

1 The museum asked the police to carry out a detailed .... into the disappearance of some valuable books.
2 A telephone .... of 1,000 people showed considerable support for the idea of simplifying spelling.
3 When Jane wrote up the results of her .... , she realised that some of her claims were contradictory.
4 I found that another student had chosen the same research topic for her .... , so I had to change my focus.
5 The college has just issued its annual .... , which shows a major investment in equipment for the library.
6 Dr Barton was delighted to read a favourable .... of his new book in a leading journal.

Grammar

Non-finite clauses

G ⋯⋮ STUDENT'S BOOK page 142

5 Rewrite each pair of sentences as one sentence, using one of the words in the box and a non-finite verb. This will help you to write in an academic style.

> after   before   by   despite   for   while

EXAMPLE: Sacks sets out to educate and entertain us. His method is to explore both the history and the modern significance of each letter.

Sacks sets out to educate and entertain us, by exploring both the history and the modern significance of each letter.

1 I recommend that you read this book. Then you should write your assignment about the Roman alphabet.
2 I only managed to finish the book before the deadline. I read it without stopping.
3 Writing a book review is a useful tool. It helps you to think carefully about what you have read.
4 I enjoyed reading *Letter Perfect*. This was even though I found it repetitive in places.
5 I read *Letter Perfect*. I then understood much more about the alphabet.
6 Many readers will be irritated by some parts of the book. At the same time, they will enjoy other parts.
7 They are related. However the Latin and Arabic alphabets are very different from each other.

Vocabulary

1 Match the sentences in column A with the *time* collocations in column B.

A
1 That film I saw was terrible.
2 I'd better go or I'll be late.
3 I won't rush.
4 I have nothing to do until the shift ends.
5 It's a great place to relax.
6 I'm not going to do an evening class.
7 I waste most of my evenings.

B
a I wasted my time going to see it.
b I spend too much time watching TV.
c I pass the time walking and reading.
d I don't have the time.
e I'll take my time.
f I'll kill time reading a magazine.
g I've run out of time – lunch is over.

2 Complete the health-related sentences below using the verbs in the box in the appropriate form.

| catch   come down with   come out in   feel (×2)   get over   have (×2) |
| lose (×2)   make (×2) |

1 I .... sick, so I'm not going into work today.
2 I really can't eat anything – I .... (completely) my appetite.
3 Luisa .... a bad cold last week and had to have a couple of days off.
4 Come back to work when you .... a bit better.
5 When Anna had measles, she .... spots all over her body.
6 Marco carried on with the job, even though he .... a terrible headache.
7 Our manager .... a full recovery from his operation last month.
8 The doctor asked Rory if he .... a temperature.
9 It only takes a few days .... a cold and return to normal.
10 When Paula .... her voice, she had to suck lozenges all day.
11 The factory was closed, as half the workers .... flu.
12 Don't eat too many biscuits – you'll .... yourself ill.

3 Complete the sentence with an appropriate form of *make* or *do*.

EXAMPLE: 'What do you ...*do*... for a living?' 'I ...*do*... shift work at the local factory.'

1 Pete .... a course at the local college at the moment.
2 I think you .... a mistake working nights.
3 We should .... a complaint about the number of hours we work.
4 My boss .... a fortune from his tyre factory.
5 My brother's so lazy – he .... (never) a day's work in his life.
6 You need to have a hot drink – it .... you good and .... you feel better.
7 We'll all have to .... without our tea breaks in future.
8 The manager .... his best to be fair about the night shift this month.
9 We're not allowed to .... phone calls from work.
10 .... me a favour, will you? Don't .... a noise when you go to bed.
11 Marcia .... a huge fuss when she found her hours had been changed.
12 'What time .... (you) it?' 'Ten past three.'

4 These words are all taken from 17.1 of the Student's Book. Complete the table, where possible, with the other forms of the words given. Use an English-English dictionary to help you.

Noun (abstract)	Adjective	Verb	Noun (person)
1	2	regulate	3
4	psychological		5
6	7	8	consultant
evolution	9	10	11
12	13	vary	
14	communicative	15	16
17	18	manage	19
20	21	destroy	22
23	natural		24
information	25	26	27
length	28	29	
30	31	32	humans

Grammar

Modals: obligation, lack of obligation and prohibition

G ···> STUDENT'S BOOK page 142

5 Underline the correct modal verb.

EXAMPLE: We *must / have to* walk to work now the buses are on strike.

1 You *must / have to* visit us when you're next in Sydney.
2 Paul, you *mustn't / don't have to* touch that machinery – it's dangerous!
3 You *mustn't / don't have to* make a coffee for me – I've just had one.
4 Jo, you *don't have to / mustn't* rush to work this morning – it's Saturday.
5 The manager says we *have to / mustn't* be late on Tuesday.
6 Nurses *have to / mustn't* wear a uniform.
7 Attention! Workers *must / have to* wear a hard hat on this site at all times.
8 When I broke my leg, I *didn't have to / had to* walk with sticks, which was very uncomfortable.

6 Correct these errors made by IELTS candidates (some include *need*).

1 You must to check whether the electricity is switched off before you touch the plug.
2 Everyone need have electricity today.
3 People must working at least eight hours a day to qualify as full-time workers.
4 We hasn't need of any products to help us sleep.
5 We not have to take a nap this afternoon as we're too busy.
6 How much sleep you need must depends on how tired you are.
7 They have not to rest now.
8 You don't must drive when you're tired.

The tourist boom

Reading

1 **Skim the text and answer these questions.**

  1 Where would you find an article like this?
  2 What is the writer's purpose in writing this article?
  3 Is the writer's impression of Antarctica favourable or unfavourable?

⏱ about 575 words

A TRIP TO THE END OF THE WORLD

The pilot's reassuring voice came over the public address system as our Qantas 747 went down the runway at Sydney Airport in Australia: 'We'll be taking off in a southerly direction.' Watch check: 8.20 a.m. Our day trip
5 had begun. We were going to Antarctica. For the first four hours – most of which was a straight line across the ocean – we could have been anywhere, but what makes the outbound journey memorable is the opportunity to study the science and history of the seventh continent as
10 presented by those who have lived and worked there.

There were four specialists on this particular trip: Pat Quilty, geologist and retired chief of the Australian Antarctic programme; Polar Medal-winner Syd Kirkby, who has surveyed more Antarctic territory than any
15 other polar explorer; Di Patterson, the first woman appointed to run an Antarctic research station; and Warren Papworth, who knows more about emperor penguins than the penguins themselves. Instead of in-flight movies, we were entertained, awed and painlessly
20 educated about Antarctica.

Until roughly 160 million years ago, Antarctica was part of the ancient continent of Gondwanaland, before Gondwanaland split up into the continents we know today. A few minutes before noon, the pilot, Captain
25 Dennis, urged us all to take out the compasses we'd been asked to bring. As I placed mine on my knee, the needle moved away from north-south and began to spin wildly. We were passing directly over the South Magnetic Pole. Unlike the geographic pole, it moves
30 about 6km a year.

As I peered through my window at the Southern Ocean below, the outermost ice floes were visible directly beneath the wing, resembling pieces of a vast natural jigsaw. Then came Dumont d'Urville, a base on
35 Antarctica. We continued east along the coast before turning south over the Ross Ice Shelf.

By the end of these middle four hours of the journey, we had seen ice-cliffs, powder ice, amazing blue ice (even the scientists don't know what makes it so), many varieties of glacier and, last but not least, magnificent 40 rivers of ice sliding into the sea. All this grandeur largely offset any disappointment at not glimpsing the penguins which Antarctica is famous for, let alone a colony. The reason was sound enough: to fly low enough to see the penguins clearly would seriously disturb them. 45

We passed the Transantarctic mountains, which Captain Dennis said were 'one of the loveliest mountain ranges on the surface of the Earth'. But for me, the highlight of this unforgettable day trip was Mount Minto, which soars more than 4,000m above the Ross 50 Ice Shelf.

All too soon, it was time to bank around in a half-circle and begin the trip back to Sydney and civilisation. This is one trip that can certainly be recommended to those people who want to do something a bit different. From November 55 to February, the 'season' for doing Antarctica, the weather is remarkably consistent. The outside air temperature is around freezing, but very sunny. Because you won't be putting down anywhere, the journey is classed as a domestic flight, so – sad to say – you won't get an 60 Antarctic stamp in your passport, something which you don't need to carry on this trip. But, by way of compensation, you will receive a commemorative certificate declaring that you have crossed the Antarctic continent, 'thereby joining the exclusive group of travellers 65 who have achieved this feat'.

2 Complete this summary. Choose NO MORE THAN THREE WORDS AND/OR A NUMBER from the passage for each answer. Remember, the words must be in the passage. ⋯▸ TF5

The trip to Antarctica started from **1** .... Airport at 8.20 in the morning. During the first part of the trip, the writer was given some background information on the continent by **2** .... who were accompanying the flight. They explained that Antarctica as we know it had only existed for the last **3** .... Before that, it had been part of Gondwanaland.

The writer discovered that a compass needle was no longer aligned **4** .... when the plane was above the South Magnetic Pole – a pole which changes position by around **5** .... a year. Besides the pole, the writer flew over the **6** .... at Dumont d'Urville. The writer was particularly impressed by the mysterious **7** .... , but was saddened not to have seen any **8** .... However, he understood why this was not possible. What made the trip **9** .... for the writer was seeing Mount Minto, which is 4,000m high.

Anyone can take this trip, which takes place from **10** .... The plane doesn't land, so there is no need for a **11** .... However, a **12** .... is given out to all participants.

Vocabulary

3 Find the ten 'travel' words from Unit 18 in the Student's Book in this wordsearch. (↓ → ↘)

D	B	A	C	K	P	A	C	K	E	R	A
T	E	R	E	Q	B	U	K	G	D	S	B
R	I	S	I	H	N	O	M	X	C	B	R
A	Z	C	T	X	O	N	O	B	R	C	O
V	R	E	I	I	U	T	T	K	U	M	A
E	S	D	V	B	N	L	E	A	I	W	D
L	T	E	C	B	R	A	U	L	S	E	D
L	T	O	U	R	I	S	T	K	E	F	G
E	O	E	R	U	Q	E	R	I	N	V	C
R	W	G	F	K	U	O	E	H	O	D	H
E	S	I	G	H	T	S	E	E	I	N	G
T	R	A	V	E	L	A	G	E	N	T	C

4 Put these words into the correct column of the table below.

cabin   caravan   cash   exchange rate
malaria pills   notes   self-catering apartment
sunscreen   tent   travel-sickness pills
traveller's cheques   vaccination

Accommodation	Health	Money

Grammar

Phrasal verbs

G ⋯▸ STUDENT'S BOOK page 143

5 Complete these sentences using the phrasal verbs in brackets and include a suitable noun, pronoun or verb.

EXAMPLES:
The hotel _takes on extra staff_ every July and August when it is fully booked and more help is needed. (take on)
Your expenses on this trip were quite high – you should try to _keep them down_ in future. (keep down)

1 The flight is overbooked – can anyone .... to this problem? (come up with)

2 Long-haul flights are awful – I find I can no longer .... (put up with)

3 It was hard to understand what the notice said, but in the end they succeeded in .... (make out)

4 My uncle started a travel agency last year – he .... with the help of a bank loan. (set up)

5 We no longer have our hotel – a large American hotel chain .... in June. (take over)

6 Thank you for your letter – I .... you at the travel conference next month. (look forward to)

Reading

⏱ about 575 words

HOW HELICOPTERS WORK

If you have ever flown in a helicopter, you know that it is an exciting experience. Helicopters can fly almost anywhere, because they are the most versatile flying machines in existence today. While virtually all planes can only fly forward, a helicopter is also able to fly backward and sideways. The main characteristic of a helicopter, of course, is that it can hover over one point, and simultaneously either stay motionless in the air, or rotate on its axis, giving the pilot a panoramic view of the ground below. A car or a plane, on the other hand, can only change direction if it is moving.

A helicopter can do a number of interesting tricks, such as rotating through 360 degrees while it travels down a straight line relative to the ground. A helicopter that is flying forward can also stop in mid-air and begin hovering very quickly. Maneuvers like these are impossible in a plane, which must fly forward at all times for its wings to provide lift.

The extra freedom that helicopters offer is what makes them so exciting, but it also makes them complex.

- -

The helicopter is controlled from the cockpit, the small area at the front where the pilot sits and looks out. The controls need to be within reach of the pilot's hands—and feet, as they include pedals.

The word *helicopter* is Greek in origin. *Heliko*—from *helix*—means a spiral, and *pteron* means a wing. To make it possible for the machine to fly upward, the wings have to be in motion, pushing air downward. It is this downward movement which creates the lift that raises the helicopter.

The easiest way to keep wings in continuous motion is to rotate them. This can be done by mounting two or more wings on a drive shaft and spinning the shaft, much like the blades on a ceiling fan. The rotating wings of a helicopter are generally narrow and thin because they must spin so quickly. The helicopter's rotating wing assembly is normally called the main rotor. If this is at a slight angle and the shaft spins, the wings start to push the air down and raise the helicopter. The main rotor is the most important part of the vehicle. As well as lifting it, it allows the helicopter to move laterally, make turns, and change altitude.

In order to spin the shaft with enough force to lift a human being and the helicopter, you need an engine. The engine's drive shaft is connected to the main rotor shaft. This arrangement works really well until the vehicle leaves the ground. At that moment, there is nothing to keep the engine (and therefore the body of the vehicle) from spinning in the opposite direction to the main rotor.

To keep the body from spinning, you need to apply a force to it. This is usually done by attaching another set of rotating wings to the tail boom, which is the section at the back of the helicopter, projecting from the main body. These wings are known as the tail rotor. The tail rotor pushes the air in a sideways direction, counteracting the engine's desire to spin the body, so this keeps the body of the helicopter from spinning.

The proper technique to land a helicopter is to touch down evenly with both landing skids touching the ground at all points at the same time. Otherwise there is a risk of severe vibration that can cause serious damage and possibly destroy the helicopter.

1 The article on page 40 is an American text about helicopters. Read it as far as the dotted line and complete the summary below. Choose NO MORE THAN ONE WORD from the passage for each answer. ⋯⟩ TF5

What makes helicopters so exciting

There is hardly any limit to where helicopters can fly, because they are more **1** .... than planes. Unlike planes, helicopters can fly both **2** .... and **3** .... In addition, they can **4** .... in one position and **5** .... at the same time, giving the pilot a view in any direction. Most planes can only gain **6** .... by flying forward.

2 Read the rest of the article and label the diagram below. Choose NO MORE THAN TWO WORDS from the passage for each answer. ⋯⟩ TF10

1 ....
2 ....
3 ....
   (consisting of wings)
4 ....
5 ....
   (consisting of wings)
6 ....

Grammar

Unreal present and future

G ⋯⟩ STUDENT'S BOOK page 143

3 Correct the mistakes in these sentences, which were written by IELTS candidates. One sentence is correct.

1 I wish creative artists don't do this.
2 I'd rather we drive in my car.
3 I think it is time we should discuss this problem.
4 I wish you should give me half my pay before the weekend, but I don't suppose you will.
5 Some children have paid jobs, but many people would rather they didn't.
6 It is about time students, families and society all realise there is a problem and recognise their own responsibilities!
7 It is high time the government pay women who stay at home to look after their children.

Vocabulary

4 Complete the passage below using words from the box. Notice how the passive is used in this fairly formal description of the light rail system; this is typical of Task 1 of the Academic Writing Module.

accessible	capacity	congestion
conventional	damage	ease	elevated
extension	linked	produce	reliable
seats		

Light**rail**

Light rail is an attractive way of moving large numbers of passengers along busy routes, and town planners are increasingly turning to it to **1** .... the problems of urban traffic **2** ....

A typical two-car unit **3** .... 64 passengers, and with space for many more standing at peak times, they have a far greater **4** .... than a typical bus. Units can also be **5** .... to form longer trains. The vehicles are **6** .... to all, including parents with small children and the elderly or mobility-impaired. In some computer-controlled systems, the train is driverless.

Tracks are set beside or in the middle of streets or on **7** .... bridge sections. Compared with **8** .... trains, there can be more frequent stops. With segregated tracks, there are no traffic jams, and the service is safe and **9** .... Light rail is one of the most environmentally friendly forms of transport. There are no fumes to **10** .... the environment, and vehicles are quiet.

Moving abroad

Reading

This passage comes from a booklet called *Welcome to Australia!*, published by the Australian Government for people who have just moved to the country. It is similar to the passages found in Section 1 of the General Training Reading Module, while the tasks below are found in both Reading Modules.

○ about 425 words

Welcome to Australia!

Apply for a Tax File Number

Everyone who receives any income in Australia needs a Tax File Number. Income includes wages or salary from a job, money earned from investments, and government payments.

Register with Medicare

The Australian Government provides help with medical expenses through a scheme called Medicare. You may be eligible to join Medicare and gain immediate access to health-care services and programs such as free public hospital care, help with the cost of out-of-hospital care and subsidised medicines.

To register with Medicare, you should wait approximately ten working days after your arrival in Australia and then go to a Medicare office, listed in the telephone book, with your passport or travel documents. If you need to see a doctor urgently, you can register with Medicare without waiting ten days.

Medicare has a *Welcome Kit* which is translated into 16 different languages. It explains Medicare and other government health services and the eligibility requirements for benefits and payments. This booklet is available from Medicare offices or you can read it on the Internet.

Open a bank account

People in Australia usually keep their money in a bank, building society or credit union. It is advisable to open a bank account within six weeks of your arrival, as during this time you usually need only your passport as identification. After six weeks, you will need additional identification to open an account.

Register with Centrelink

Newly arrived residents can register with the government agency called Centrelink to get help with looking for work, having overseas skills recognised, and accessing relevant courses. Centrelink also has an application form for Tax File Numbers and can assist you to lodge your application with the Tax Office, so that access to any payments is not delayed.

Register for English classes

English language courses for new arrivals in Australia are provided under the Adult Migrant English Program. As a new resident, you may be entitled to receive free English language tuition of up to 510 hours.

Get a driver's licence

If you are a permanent resident visa holder and have a current driver's licence from another country, in English or with an official translation, you are allowed to drive for your first three months after arrival. After that, if you want to drive, you will need to have the appropriate Australian driver's licence. To get one, you usually need to pass a knowledge test, a practical test, and an eyesight test. Licences from some overseas countries do not require a practical test.

1   Read the passage. Do the statements on page 43 agree with the information given in the passage? ⋯⋗ TF1

    Write

    TRUE   *if the statement agrees with the information*
    FALSE   *if the statement contradicts the information*
    NOT GIVEN *if there is no information on this*

1 A Tax File Number is only required by people who are working.

2 All health-care services are free for people registered with Medicare.

3 In certain cases, it is possible to register with Medicare less than ten days after arriving in Australia.

4 There is a charge for Welcome Kit booklets obtained from Medicare offices.

5 Banks are the most commonly used form of financial institution.

6 If you open a bank account in your first six weeks in Australia, you will probably need fewer documents than later on.

7 Centrelink can help you to get your qualifications accepted officially.

8 Centrelink can lend money to new arrivals if necessary.

9 English language lessons are offered at no cost to all new residents who require them.

10 Whether or not you need to take an Australian practical test for a driver's licence depends on which country you come from.

2 **Complete the sentences below with words taken from the passage. Write NO MORE THAN THREE WORDS AND/OR A NUMBER for each answer.** ⟶ TF3

1 The address of the nearest Medicare office can be found in a ....

2 You can work out from the Medicare *Welcome Kit* whether or not you are entitled to .... from the government.

3 Centrelink can help you with your .... for payments from the Tax Office.

4 The Adult Migrant English Program offers a maximum of .... of English lessons.

5 All foreign driver's licences can be used for .... without taking any part of the Australian driving test.

6 Holders of all foreign driver's licences are required to pass the .... and .... tests.

Vocabulary

3 **The sentences below are about the earliest Inuit and European settlers in Greenland. Most of them contain one of the phrasal verbs from 20.2 in the Student's Book.** ⟶ TF3

Complete each sentence (1–8) with the best ending (a–i) below. There is one ending that you will not need to use.

1 The earliest Inuit settlers (formerly known as Eskimos) had to put up with

2 In such difficult conditions, they had to work at

3 When the climate turned colder, they dealt with

4 Most of the early European settlers had been brought up

5 Many of them had set off

6 Settlers from Iceland were looking forward to

7 Unlike Iceland, however, Greenland failed to live up to

8 The Icelanders arrived in a land that turned out

a a green, fertile island.

b the change by moving south.

c to be very cold and largely covered by glaciers.

d cold weather and very little food.

e making life in Greenland bearable.

f from Iceland to avoid conflicts there.

g during a voyage across the North Atlantic.

h its name.

i in Iceland or Norway.

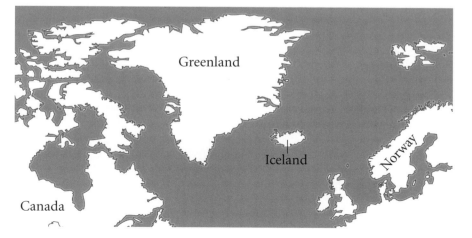

Writing workout 1: Writing letters

General Training Writing Task 1

1 Complete this advice on writing letters by circling the best option in italics.

1 You *must / shouldn't* include an address.
2 You can write *under / just over* 150 words.
3 It is *acceptable / unacceptable* to begin 'Dear Mr Manager'.
4 You *should / don't need to* check your grammar and spelling.
5 You *don't have to / should* split your letter into paragraphs.
6 You *can / shouldn't* end a formal letter with 'Yours faithfully'.
7 A *good / inappropriate* way to end a formal letter is with 'I look forward to hearing from you in the near future'.
8 *Make sure you use / Don't worry about using* appropriate language.

2 The letter below is based on an example from the *Cambridge Learner's Corpus*. It contains some errors that an IELTS candidate has made.

a Read through the letter and decide whether it is successful in following the advice above. Ignore the numbers for the moment.

Hampstead, London

Dear **1** <u>Mr Councillor</u>, I am writing to **2** <u>complaint</u> about two large dogs that run in **3** <u>park</u> every evening. The owner of **4** <u>some</u> dogs, a young man, releases them to play in **5** <u>a</u> park, but I think it is **6** <u>so</u> dangerous **7** <u>to</u> people and animals to share this park. This has been happening **8** <u>since two weeks ago</u>, and I have watched the dogs and the owner from my house. My house is a large detached house in Bedford Drive, and I have lived there for twenty years. The most dangerous thing is that the dogs bark very loudly and **9** <u>running</u> towards people so that they **10** <u>afraid</u> them, especially small **11** <u>kids</u>. In fact, some people, including myself, **12** <u>attempt</u> to talk with the **13** <u>dog's</u> owner, but he seems to ignore what we say. As a **14** <u>mum</u> **15** <u>whose</u> two children, I am naturally worried about their safety. I am sending this letter **16** <u>because</u> a representative of a concerned group of park users. The owner needs to be told to keep his dogs on a leash so that people don't feel **17** <u>scary</u>. I am **18** <u>look</u> forward to **19** <u>hear</u> from you. **20** <u>Best wishes,</u>

(187 words)

b Rewrite the letter, following the advice above and also correcting the underlined words or phrases for 1–20.

3 a Read this General Training Module Task 1 and underline the key words and phrases.

> *You want to sell your bicycle. You think a friend of yours might like to buy it from you.*
>
> *Write a letter to your friend. In your letter*
> - *explain why you are selling*
> - *describe the bicycle*
> - *suggest a date when your friend can come and see the bicycle.*
>
> Write at least 150 words.

b The sample letter below has eight spaces. Complete it by putting a word or phrase from the box in each space.

> asking   brand new   come round
> fine   give you   include   looked at
> make   new   serviced   ship
> take   type   very good condition
> visit   wondering

Dear Alex,

As you know, I'll be going home at the end of term and I've decided that I need to sell my bicycle — it would cost me too much to **1** .... it home to Manila. I was **2** .... if you might be interested in buying it.

It's a mountain bike, four years old now, and it was **3** .... when I bought it. Its green and black with a silver stripe. I have looked after it very well, having it **4** .... every year. The tyres are in **5** .... , and I am happy to **6** .... lights and a cycling helmet in the price. It's a Raleigh bicycle — a very good **7** .... — and I would like to sell it for around £40.

Why don't you **8** .... and have a look sometime? What about next Saturday morning when we don't have lectures?

Give me a ring and let me know.

Best wishes
Alicia

(154 words)

c Underline (an) example(s) of the following in the letter.

1 an explanation
2 a description
3 a suggestion

4 Correct the 12 spelling mistakes in this paragraph.

I'm writing to ask you for a six-month period of leave. I'm very much interested in computers, but unfortunaty I have poor computer skils. Last week, I saw an advertisment for a computer course on the TV. Though the unvirsity is in a diferent province, it is very famous, and the enrolment fee is not expensiv. So I want to attend the course. There I can aquire a lot of knowlege about computers and softwear. The course begins the day after tomorow. When I finnish the course, I will return to my job.

5 Match the purposes (1–6) with the letter extracts (a–f).

1 Suggesting
2 Complaining
3 Inviting
4 Explaining
5 Thanking
6 Apologising

a ... and if you are able to come on Monday evening, you will be very welcome.
b This really can't go on. I am not able to get any sleep at all.
c The reason I have not been able to hand in my work is that ...
d It was really very kind of you ...
e I think it would be a very good idea if we ...
f I promise this will not happen again and am very embarrassed that you had to complain in this way.

6 Do this Task 1.

> *An English-speaking friend is coming to study at your college next year and has written asking for information and advice.*
>
> *Write a letter to your friend. In your letter*
> - *give advice about accommodation in the town*
> - *describe the best thing about the college*
> - *offer to show your friend around the college.*
>
> Write at least 150 words.
>
> You do **NOT** need to write any addresses.
>
> Begin your letter as follows:
>
> **Dear …**

Writing workout 2: Structuring an essay

General Training and Academic Writing Task 2

1 Look at this Task 2 and think about how you might answer it.

> **Below are five popular jobs. State which three you consider to be the most important to society today.**
>
> *doctor*
> *teacher*
> *engineer*
> *computer programmer*
> *journalist*
>
> Give reasons for your answer and include any relevant examples from your own knowledge or experience.
>
> Write at least 250 words.

2 Read the following two essays. Which one do you think would achieve higher marks? Think about:

1 how well the question is answered
2 how the essay is organised
3 if there are relevant examples of personal experience/knowledge
4 the range of vocabulary used
5 if there are examples of complex sentences.

A

Which jobs are the most important to our society today? I believe that of the five jobs mentioned, these three are of the utmost importance: a doctor, a teacher and a journalist.

First of all, I would like to say that just one doctor can make a big difference to the well-being of the inhabitants of a village or town. Let me give you an example. In the past, people were reliant on witch doctors or wise women. Nowadays, thanks to doctors, we all have access to better diagnosis and treatment.

Teachers are also important to our society. If there is no access to education, then a society will remain in the dark ages. People need to learn and understand about themselves and the way that the Earth works. One example is the education of women. It is a well-known fact that when women are educated, the whole of society benefits, as the women will pass their knowledge down to their children.

Finally, I am going to consider the role of journalists in society. A good journalist will find out as much as possible about things which may affect society — for good or bad. Without the journalists who investigated the Watergate affair, for example, we would never have found out about what Nixon had been doing. Consequently, I believe that journalists are important to society.

To sum up, out of the five professions, I believe that doctors, teachers and journalists are more important to society than engineers or computer programmers.

(250 words)

B

In our society today, most jobs require workers to be computer literate, since businesses are now practically run by computers in order to ensure a faster and more efficient output. Technology is developing and the use of computers is increasing. If one does not know how to work with or even use a computer, it will be very difficult for society. That's why I think that computer programmers are essential to society today.

Secondly, in our society, different jobs provide different experiences. Being a doctor is more important than being a teacher, for example. I know this from my experience. My brother is a doctor in a large hospital in my city and he works very hard and has more money and more respect from society than a teacher. Having respect from society is very important, because if your job is valued, then you feel yourself to be valued as well.

Thirdly, engineers and journalists are quite important but not as important as doctors and computer programmers. In fact, they are often not respected professionals. In many countries, journalists lie and often have to go to jail; consequently, this profession would not be essential to society.

In conclusion, I should add that I would like to be a computer programmer and that is why I think like I do. I will be able to help society with the work I do. The company I am going to work for helps people all over the world to have a much better life.

(251 words)

3 What should the writing plan be for this task?

Introduction ....

Paragraph 1 ....

Paragraph 2 ....

Paragraph 3 ....

Conclusion ....

4 Look at the following words and phrases taken from both essays and try to think of other ways you can say them. (See Writing Folders 3 and 8 in the Student's Book.)

1 First of all, I would like to say that …
2 I believe that …
3 Secondly, …
4 One example is …
5 In conclusion, …
6 important

5 Read this example of an IELTS Task 2 answer and punctuate it (add paragraphing, capital letters, full stops, commas and dashes).

should children be allowed to work that is a good question i believe it depends on the age of the child and the type of work that it is asked to do broadly speaking i think that children under the age of 14 should not be allowed to work but from that age on it is permissible if it is regulated first of all children need to learn about the workplace and the pressures that they will face when they finish school secondly children need to understand the relationship between work and money at a fairly young age unless they are from a very rich family they will need to work one way that many children are introduced to work in my country is by way of a newspaper round or a saturday job another example of how children can be introduced to the world of work is by having work experience weeks at their school this can be a very valuable experience as they need to get up early travel to work deal with people and possibly endure total boredom finally although i believe that children should find out about work when they are teenagers i am totally against children younger than 12 working children need to go to school and they also need to have time to play and grow to sum up i believe that when children reach a certain age it is important that they get a job it is part of growing up of learning to be a responsible adult

6 Write about the following topic. You should make a plan first of all.

> *To get a good job today, it is more important for children to study mathematics and foreign languages than art and music.*
>
> *To what extent do you agree or disagree with this opinion?*
>
> Give reasons for your answer and include any relevant examples from your own knowledge or experience.
>
> Write at least 250 words.

Introduction ....

Paragraph 1 ....

Paragraph 2/3 ....

Conclusion ....

Writing workout 3: Graphs and tables

Academic Training Writing Task 1

1 Which of these are important for a good chart/graph/table task?
  Tick the boxes which apply.

  1 at least 150 words in length ☐
  2 mention of all the data ☐
  3 well-organised paragraphs grouping data ☐
  4 a comparison, if asked for ☐
  5 a repetition of the question ☐
  6 a variety of vocabulary and structure ☐
  7 reasons for any change in the data ☐
  8 accurate figures (possibly approximate) ☐

2 Look at the task below and the sentences on the right. Decide whether or not
  each sentence is appropriate in an answer to the question. If it is not, say why.

---

*The bar chart below shows the amount spent on different
types of advertising in the USA in 2003 and 2004. The table
shows the six sectors which spent most on advertising in the
USA in 2003 and 2004.*

*Summarise the information by selecting and reporting the
main features, and make comparisons where relevant.*

Spending on advertising in the USA 2003 and 2004

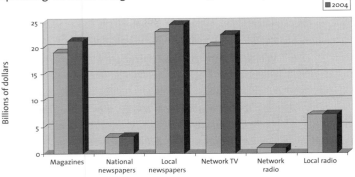

Ranked spending on advertising in the USA in 2003 and 2004

Sector	Rank 2003	Rank 2004
Automotive	1	1
Retail	2	2
Telecom/Internet	3	3
Medicine	4	4
Financial services	6	5
Food, beverages	5	6

---

1 The charts show the amount of
  money spent by the automotive
  industry in 2003 and 2004.
2 Food and beverages rose in
  popularity in 2004 because of the
  increased power of supermarket
  advertising.
3 There was an increase in spending
  on advertising in local newspapers
  in 2004.
4 I think that local newspapers are the
  best way to advertise.
5 Although there was a rise in the
  amount spent on advertising in
  magazines, there was very little
  increase in advertising on local radio.
6 There was a dramatic fall in the
  amount spent on advertising in
  national newspapers in 2004.
7 The bar chart shows the amount
  spent on different types of
  advertising in the USA in 2003 and
  2004.
8 The amount spent on advertising in
  2004 was just over $20 billion in
  magazines, under $5 billion in
  national newspapers, just under $25
  billion in local newspapers, around
  $22 billion on network TV, $1–2
  billion on network radio and finally,
  $6 billion on local radio.

3 Look at the sample answer to the task in exercise 2. Complete the spaces with one of the words from the box.

> accounted   change   fell   followed
> least   ~~overall~~   period   reaching
> rose   showed   whereas

According to the bar chart, there was an **0** _overall_ increase in spending on advertising in the USA in the **1** .... 2003 to 2004. Advertisements in magazines, local newspapers and on network TV **2** .... for the largest increases, **3** .... advertising in national newspapers, network radio and local radio only **4** .... a slight increase. The most favoured forms of advertising were in local newspapers, with the amount spent **5** .... almost $25 billion in 2004, **6** .... by network TV at $23 billion. Network radio was the **7** .... favoured form of advertising at $2 billion in 2004.

There was no **8** .... from 2003 in the top four business sectors when it came to spending on advertising in 2004. The automotive industry ranked number 1, followed by the retail industry. Financial services **9** .... to fifth place in the rankings, taking the place of food and beverages, which **10** .... to sixth place.
(160 words)

4 Correct the mistakes below made by IELTS candidates.

1 From this charts, we can find out about the difference in spending between the UK and the USA.
2 The middle chart it show us the increase in money spent in developing countries.
3 The chart describes the amount spend.
4 Britain spent the highest amount in consumer goods.
5 The third most popular goods was toys.
6 Personal stereos were spent nearly the same amount as TVs.
7 The highest popular consumer item was the camera and the lowest was the personal stereo.
8 Majority of people spent most on films.
9 The graph show that electricity use in winter are much greater than in summer.
10 The use of electricity is shown at a pie chart.
11 The number of units decrease sharply.
12 Several figures is increasing.
13 The demand of electricity then decline until 0800.
14 There is a different of 5.2 between the figures.
15 It's clear that unemployment have decreased.

5 Do this Task 1.

The line graph shows changes in car ownership between 1972 and 2002 in the UK. The table shows the main method of travel to work in the UK in 2002.

Write a report for a university lecturer describing the information in the graph and table.

Write at least 150 words.

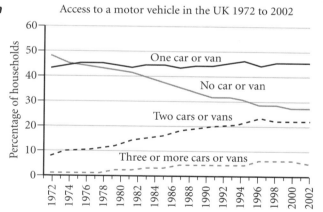

Access to a motor vehicle in the UK 1972 to 2002

Main method of travel to work in the UK, 2002 (% of people)

Country	Car or van	Motorbike or scooter	Bicycle	Bus or coach	Train	Foot	Other
England	70.6	1.3	3	7.5	6.8	10.3	0.5
Wales	80.4	–	1.3	4.5	1.1	11.5	–
Scotland	69.6	–	1.7	11.4	2.9	12.5	1.1
Northern Ireland	79.9	–	–	5.0	–	11.4	1.6

Writing workout 4: Style in essays

General Training and Academic Writing Task 2

1 Which of the following would you **not** expect to find in a formal essay?

    a idioms
    b collocations
    c contractions
    d colloquial language / slang
    e very strong personal opinions / aggressive language
    f abbreviations
    g an impersonal style

2 The following sentences all contain errors of style. Say which errors (a–g) from exercise 1 apply to each. There may be more than one.

    EXAMPLE: I am absolutely against the government <u>putting out</u> <u>ads</u> telling me what to do.
                d (colloquial language: *putting out*)
                g (abbreviations: *ads = advertisements*)

    1 People insist on driving gas guzzlers.
    2 The reason global warming is getting worse is because some countries didn't sign the Kyoto agreement.
    3 We'll soon all be freezing to death if the Gulf Stream changes direction.
    4 We should take advantage of the availability of free resources, e.g. waves and wind.
    5 Some people haven't a clue about the consequences of carbon emissions.
    6 It is no good going by bicycle once in a blue moon; you need to be properly committed to alternative transport.
    7 It's really great that the media are giving this problem so much coverage.
    8 Governments should have a get-together to talk about the problems we face.

3 Rewrite the sentences in exercise 2 using the phrases below. You may need to make changes to the rest of the sentence to make it more formal/appropriate.

    a It is clearly beneficial that
    b have little idea about
    c such as
    d cars which use a great deal of fuel
    e suffering from intense cold
    f It can be argued that
    g high-level discussions
    h occasionally

4 Some of the phrases in exercise 3 are collocations.

clearly beneficial
suffer from cold
intense cold
high-level discussions

Using collocations shows you have a good level of English. Complete the sentences below with the following adverbs to form the correct collocation. There may be more than one answer. Use an English-English dictionary to help you.

clearly	densely	dramatically	heavily
inevitably	repeatedly	seriously	wildly

    1 The minister was .... criticised for not doing enough to promote alternative energy.
    2 The figures for the factory's carbon emissions proved .... inaccurate.
    3 The reasons why the oceans are becoming more acidic are not .... understood.
    4 Experts have .... warned the government and industry of the effects of using carbon-based fuel.
    5 There is no doubt that sea levels will rise ....
    6 Our exploitation of oil .... threatens the environment.
    7 Some cities will suffer more than others, especially ones which are .... populated.
    8 If we continue to drive larger and larger cars, this will .... result in more and more pollution.
    9 The prime minister had .... got his facts wrong.
    10 I have .... written to the government to complain about what is happening.

5   IELTS candidates often find it difficult to know how to start Task 2. Read
    this task and decide which of the four introductions below would gain
    good marks. Give each introduction marks out of 5 and underline any
    words or phrases which are useful for introductions.

> Write about the following topic:
>
> *Governments should make more effort to promote alternative sources of energy.*
> *To what extent do you agree or disagree with this opinion?*
>
> Give reasons for your answer and include any relevant examples from your own knowledge or experience.

A

There is no doubt that the Earth is beginning to suffer the consequences of pollution. People should make more of an effort to recycle and to use public transport. Also to use different sources of energy.

B

It has been suggested in recent months that the government is not doing enough to promote alternative sources of energy. My personal opinion is that they should promote alternative sources of energy.

C

It has been known for some time now that a move towards sources of energy which are not carbon-based is urgently required to stop the effects of global warming. In my view, there are too few governments who seem to be promoting the use of other types of energy – from wind, wave, solar and nuclear sources.

D

First of all, I would like to say that this is a subject that is often discussed. Something needs to change and change quickly. I am in favour of wind power, and indeed in my country we use it a lot.

6   Write a full answer to the task in exercise 5.
    You should write at least 250 words.

General Training and Academic Writing Task 2

1   Read the essay below on role models for young people. Circle the more suitable linking word or phrase in each case.

0 (Firstly) / Well, what is a good role model? **1** Actually / In my opinion, he or she should be hard-working, honest and think of other people besides themselves.
2 Naturally / Unfortunately, many sports stars and celebrities do not have these qualities, possibly **3** because / owing to these are not the qualities that helped them to become famous in the first place.

4 There is no doubt that / As a result, young people today have access to more information about the world than ever before. **5** Consequently / However, much of the information in the media is centred on celebrities and sports stars **6** because / lastly stories about these people, especially scandal, will sell newspapers **7** but / or make people watch television. **8** Whereas / Although much of what young people see or hear is very negative, I believe that most of them are aware that they do not have to copy what a celebrity or sports star does, **9** especially / clearly if it is an example of particularly bad behaviour.

10 Extra / Another point to consider is that there are many people in the community who would make excellent role models. My teacher, for example, raises money to help give children in poor countries an education.

11 At the end / To sum up, I believe that it is not true to say that the only role models young people have are sports stars and celebrities. Young people can think for themselves.
12 Really / Consequently, they are able to see that there are people around them who can fulfil the task of role model rather than relying on people who make the headlines.

2 Each sentence contains an incorrect word. Replace it with the correct one. Use an English-English dictionary to help you.

EXAMPLE: Simon studied ~~Economic~~ at university.
Economics

1 The class spent all yesterday practicing for the marathon.
2 Take my advise, choose a sport which is less competitive than tennis.
3 Salaries of sportsmen and women have raised considerably in the last few years.
4 The team will loose next Saturday.
5 The football court was too hard to play on.
6 The total amount of people who support football in this town exceeds 100,000.
7 You need a coach to give you the knowledges you need to succeed at this sport.
8 Most coaches do more harm than benefit when it comes to training.
9 The standard of life in some countries is very low.
10 My personal assumption is that sport plays an important part in daily life.
11 You will have the possibility to speak to him later.
12 Some sportsmen and women earn a good currency from their sport.
13 I saw an advertising for the Olympics last week on TV.
14 The most popular consumer good is the trainer.
15 The learning of computers should begin at school.
16 She studied in an English-speaking ambience.
17 The least popular homework is washing the windows.
18 She took a part-time work at the local sports centre.
19 I hope you have a good travel to the competition.
20 Youth people today love athletics.
21 Where do you buy your cloths?
22 Don't touch the buttons of the computer.
23 I have no choose in the matter.
24 There are quite a few sports exercises available at the centre.

3 IELTS candidates often have problems with prepositions. Correct the preposition in each sentence below.

1 I'm really grateful for everything they did to me at college.
2 During the period of 1989 and 2001, public services declined.
3 My brother is responsible of training in the company.
4 The government will prevent people to getting jobs without a work permit.
5 I haven't seen you from a long time.
6 The goods won't arrive here since the weekend.
7 The magazine is the least effective medium to communicating news.
8 There is a high demand of electricity in the evenings.
9 Through the Olympics in Greece, everything ran smoothly.
10 There was an advertisement of a job at a local restaurant in the paper.
11 Learning about computers should be compulsory on primary school.
12 I look forward for hearing from you soon.

4 Write out the jumbled text in the correct order. The first part is in **bold**.

1 with a computer every day whether
2 there are undoubted benefits to the use of computers,
3 computers at work, in the home, to pay our bills, to buy books
4 **The computer is an important invention and it**
5 although
6 only that, people who
7 or to plan our holidays. We have dealings
8 has had a huge impact on our lives. We use
9 savings could be deleted. Not
10 bank online are more likely to have
11 we know we are doing so or not. However,
12 that, if something goes wrong, our
13 knows that the banks use computers to
14 process transactions. All our accounts are computerised, with the result
15 their accounts hacked into illegally.
16 there are also some drawbacks. In the first place, everybody

Reading module

Advice on tackling the Reading Module

The Reading Module as a whole

- Spend **60 minutes** on the Reading Module, without any breaks.
- Spend no more than **20 minutes** on each passage. If you spend longer on the first one or two, you won't be able to finish the third.
- You must write your answers on the **Answer Sheet** (see page 64). There is no extra time for doing this. You can write on the Question Paper, but make sure you copy your answers accurately onto the Answer Sheet within the 60 minutes.
- Remember that each question gives you **one mark**, so don't spend a long time on a single question.
- As far as possible, give an **answer to every question**.
- Remember that **you don't need to understand every word**.

Each reading passage

- If there is a headings task, it will appear *before* the passage. Read it quickly before reading the passage.
- Read the **title** and spend about **two to three minutes skimming** the passage. **Mark important information**, such as the main point in each paragraph (often in the first sentence of the paragraph). This will help you to find the relevant part of the passage for each task and question. Ignore details.
- **Don't worry** if you find the passage difficult to understand. You'll probably understand more of it when you try to answer the questions.
- Look at the first task. Read the **instructions** (rubric) carefully and **underline important information**, such as the maximum number of words to give. Advice on each task type is given in the Test folders in the Student's Book.
- If you are not sure of an answer, **write possible answers**, then go on to the other questions in that task. When you have finished the task, go back and choose one answer to each question.
- Check that you have followed the instructions, such as giving only one answer or writing no more than three words.
- If you have spent 20 minutes on the task without finishing it, try and give a possible answer to each question.
- If you have written on the Reading Module, copy your answers onto the Answer Sheet before going on to the next passage.

READING PASSAGE 1

*You should spend about 20 minutes on **Questions 1–13***
which are based on Reading Passage 1 below.

Zheng He

The Chinese admiral-explorer of the 15th century

A Zheng He was born around 1371, to a Muslim family in China's southern Yunan Province, just north of Laos. When he was ten years old, he, along with other children, was captured by the army, and three years later he became a servant in the household of the Chinese emperor's fourth son, Prince Zhu Di.

B He proved himself to be an exceptional servant, becoming skilled in the arts of war and diplomacy and serving as an officer of the prince. Zhu Di became emperor in 1402, and a year later, he appointed Zheng He to the high military position of admiral and ordered him to oversee the construction of a Treasure Fleet to explore the seas surrounding China.

C The first Treasure Fleet comprised 62 ships. The four flagships were huge wooden boats, some of the largest ever built in history: they were approximately 120 metres long and 50 metres wide. The fleet assembled at the capital, Nanjing, on the Yangtze River, and included 100-metre-long horse ships that carried nothing but horses, water ships that carried fresh water for the crew, troop transports, supply ships and war ships for offensive and defensive needs. The ships were filled with thousands of tons of goods to trade with others during the voyage. In the autumn of 1405, the fleet set sail with 27,800 men.

D The fleet used the compass – invented in China in the 11th century – for navigation. Marked sticks of incense were burned to measure time. Latitude was determined by monitoring the North Star in the Northern Hemisphere or the Southern Cross in the Southern Hemisphere. The ships of the Treasure Fleet communicated with one another through the use of flags, lanterns, bells, carrier pigeons, gongs and banners.

E The destination of the first voyage of the Treasure Fleet was Calicut, known as a major trading centre on the south-western coast of India. The fleet reached Sri Lanka and India in 1406, and stayed there for several months, carrying on barter and trade. The following spring, the seasonal change in direction of the monsoon winds enabled the ships to sail towards home. On the return voyage, the Treasure Fleet was forced to battle with pirates near Sumatra for several months. Eventually Zheng He's men managed to capture the pirate leader and take him to the Chinese capital Nanjing, where they arrived in 1407.

F A succession of other voyages followed, back to India and Sri Lanka, to the rich city of Hormuz on the Persian Gulf, and along the east coast of Africa, almost as far south as Mozambique. During each of Zheng He's voyages, he encouraged diplomats from other countries to travel to China, either aboard his ships or on their own vessels.

G Emperor Zhu Di died in 1424 and was succeeded by his son Zhu Gaozhi. The new emperor cancelled the voyages of the Treasure Fleets and ordered shipbuilders and sailors to stop their work and return home. Zheng He was appointed military commander of Nanjing.

H The leadership of Zhu Gaozhi did not last long, as he died in 1426 at the age of 26. His son – and Zhu Di's grandson – Zhu Zhanji became emperor. Zhu Zhanji was much more like his grandfather than his father was, and in 1430, he restarted the Treasure Fleet voyages by ordering Zheng He to resume his duties as admiral and make a seventh voyage, in an attempt to restore peaceful relations with the kingdoms of Malacca and Siam. It took a year to gear up for the voyage, which departed as a large expedition with 100 ships and 27,500 men.

I Zheng He is believed to have died in 1433, on the return trip, although others claim that he died in 1435 after the return to China. Nonetheless, the era of exploration for China was soon over, as the following emperors prohibited trade with foreign countries and even the construction of ocean-going vessels, thus ending an era of trade and exploration.

J It seems likely that a detachment of one of Zheng He's fleets, though not the admiral himself, sailed to northern Australia during one of the seven voyages. The evidence lies both in the Chinese artefacts found there and in the oral history of the native Australians.

Questions 1–5

Reading Passage 1 has ten paragraphs labelled **A–J**. Which paragraph contains the following information?

*Write the correct letter **A–J** in boxes 1–5 on your answer sheet.*

1   a summary of journeys to various places
2   examples of equipment used during voyages
3   speculation concerning a possible destination
4   details of the composition of a fleet of ships
5   how the weather affected the timing of a voyage

Questions 6–9

Complete the sentences below with words taken from Reading Passage 1.
*Use **NO MORE THAN TWO WORDS** for each answer.*
Write your answers in boxes 6–9 on your answer sheet.

The first treasure fleet

6   The ships carried a large quantity of .... which were to be sold.
7   The sailors used the night sky to calculate the ships' ....
8   The fleet sailed to an important .... in India.
9   While returning to China, the fleet was attacked by ....

Questions 10–13

*Complete each sentence with the correct ending **A–G** from the box below.*
*Write the correct letter **A–G** in boxes 10–13 on your answer sheet.*

10   Zhu Di ....
11   Zheng He ....
12   Zhu Gaozhi ....
13   Zhu Zhanji ....

A   travelled to Australia.
B   ended trade with other countries.
C   ended the construction of ships.
D   took children away from their homes.
E   wished to end hostilities between China and certain other countries.
F   made contact with foreign diplomats.
G   ordered ships to be built.

READING PASSAGE 2

You should spend about 20 minutes on **Questions 14–27** which are based on Reading Passage 2 on the following pages.

Questions 14–19

Reading Passage 2 has seven paragraphs **A–G**.

Choose the correct heading for each paragraph from the list of headings below.

Write the correct number **i–x** in boxes 14–19 on your answer sheet.

List of Headings
i   The problem of finding jobs
ii   Outsiders begin to interfere
iii   A lack of homes
iv   Setting off for a new life
v   The community is broken up
vi   A long period of isolation
vii The impact of tourism on island life
viii A struggle to survive
ix   Work has a different function
x   Asking for help

Example Paragraph **A**	*Answer* vi

14	Paragraph **B**
15	Paragraph **C**
16	Paragraph **D**
17	Paragraph **E**
18	Paragraph **F**
19	Paragraph **G**

The evacuation of St Kilda

A St Kilda is a tiny archipelago at the mercy of the storms of the North Atlantic Ocean. The islands are among the most spectacular in Scotland. But the greatest fascination is that, for over a thousand years, people lived there. Cut off from the mainland for most of their history, the islanders had a distinct way of living their lives, mainly eating the tens of thousands of seabirds that returned year after year to breed on the rocks. Their self-sufficiency meant that throughout their history, they possessed a sense of community that was rare in the modern world.

B The St Kildans led a lonely life. They had more in common with the people of other isolated islands, like Tristan da Cunha, than they ever had with fellow Scots living in the cities of Edinburgh or Glasgow. Isolation had a big effect upon their attitudes and ideas. The people sacrificed themselves year in and year out, in a constant battle to secure a livelihood for themselves and the rest of the community. In such harsh conditions, life was only possible because the whole community worked together.

C For centuries, the world outside ignored the people of St Kilda. They were content on the mainland to allow such a remote community to go its own way. As long as the people of St Kilda were so isolated, they were insulated from the forces that wished them to conform. This changed in the 19th century, when St Kilda was subject to pressures from the rest of the country. Education, organised religion and tourism all attempted to throw into doubt the St Kildans' way of life. Help, as interpreted by the articulate spokesmen of the richer and more advanced society on the mainland, was best given by persuading the islanders to give up the struggle.

D In the early 20th century, the strength of the community became weakened as contact with the rest of Britain increased. When disease decimated their numbers, and wind and sea made it difficult to get adequate supplies of food, the St Kildans were forced to turn to the mainland for assistance. However, many on the British mainland, including the government, believed that agreeing to the St Kildans' requests for a nurse and a postal service would be a waste of money. More fundamentally, it was thought that if the St Kildans could not adapt and accept the values of the dominant society, the only solution was to evacuate the islands.

E In 1930, the St Kildans finally agreed to abandon their homes. They settled on the Scottish mainland, not realising that it meant throwing themselves into the 20th century. As adults, they had to accept those values that most Scots are taught to believe in from birth. For instance, the islanders found it difficult to base their existence upon money. They had never lived in a world in which they bought goods and services from each other. They had, of course, accepted gladly the opportunity of making a little money for themselves at the expense of tourists, but that intrusion had never altered the basic relationship one St Kildan had had with another.

F The islanders showed themselves indifferent to the jobs they were given on the mainland. The labours asked of them were unskilled contrasted with the spectacular feats they had once performed in order to kill seabirds. Moreover, while they had been living on the islands, killing birds had directly provided the community with food to survive. On the mainland, on the other hand, the tasks that they were asked to perform did not provide them immediately with what was needed to keep them fed and warm. There was an intermediate step: employment provided money, which in turn made it possible to purchase the necessities of life.

G The history of the St Kildans after the evacuation, of their inability and lack of resolution to fit into urban society, makes sad reading. If St Kilda had been an isolated home, the islanders were to discover that the remote district of Scotland in which they were settled was even more alien. On St Kilda, at least they had formed a tightly-knit community with a common purpose. When they were resettled on the mainland, the St Kildans were forced to live in homes far apart, in a society whose values were unacceptable, if not incomprehensible, to the majority of them. For many, the move was a tragedy.

Questions 20–22

Choose **THREE** letters **A–H**.

Write your answers in boxes 20–22 on your answer sheet.

Which **THREE** points are made about how people used to live on St Kilda?

A The chief source of food was found locally.

B It was essential for people to help each other.

C Very few people had visited mainland Scotland.

D The people had a different religion from the majority of Scottish people.

E The people wanted a more advanced way of life.

F The homes were unsuitable for modern life.

G Money played an insignificant role in life.

H The people disliked visits by tourists.

Questions 23–26

Complete the summary below.

Choose **NO MORE THAN ONE WORD** from the passage for each answer.

Write your answers in boxes 23–26 on your answer sheet.

The twentieth century

In the early 20th century, the islanders had more **23** .... with the rest of Scotland. The number of inhabitants fell because of **24** .... , and bad weather led to shortages of **25** .... Many people on the mainland were unwilling to spend money on a **26** .... or other services for St Kilda.

Question 27

Choose the correct letter, **A**, **B**, **C** or **D**.

Write your answer in box 27 on your answer sheet.

Which of the following is the most suitable subtitle for Reading Passage 2?

A The role of money in modern communities

B How a community adapted to a different form of life

C The destruction of an old-fashioned community

D How a small community resisted government plans

You should spend about 20 minutes on **Questions 28–40** which are based on Reading Passage 3 below.

The Nature of Language

Language is an extraordinary institution, standing in as much need of explanation as any other aspect of human life, possibly more. But to explain it, one has to stop taking it for granted. Virtually all of us are pretty fluent employers of language; we grow up with it as we grow up with the ability to walk or run, and using it seems as easy as those activities. To see how truly remarkable language is, we must, as the psychologist Wolfgang Köhler put it, retreat to a 'psychic distance' from the subject.

Language is the most complex and sophisticated of our possessions. Only very recently, for instance, have grammarians begun to uncover the enormously complicated rules of grammar which underlie our languages, and they still have a long way to go. Computers can be marvellous at dealing with mathematics and playing chess. Yet, at least at present, no computer is at all close to the reproduction of human verbal abilities. Computers are, at best, second-rate users of language, while animals are not users of language at all.

Talking might be seen as the defining characteristic of human beings. No doubt we are also the only creatures who laugh, and have two legs and no feathers – but that is not too interesting. We may be the only creatures who use tools and who organise politically – and this is more interesting. Still, amongst many peoples, political organisation and the use of tools are extremely rudimentary, whereas all known communities have possessed sophisticated languages. Further, it is probably easier to find analogies in the animal world to tools and politics than it is to language.

Many animals, of course, are capable of producing noises which cause their friends or enemies to respond in certain ways, but these noises are so different in kind from human speech that it is, at best, a misleading analogy to speak of such noises being part of a language. First, animals are incapable of organising their noises into sequences beyond the most primitive level, whereas the most salient characteristic of human talkers is their ability to form an infinite number of sequences from a limited stock of noises. As the poet and critic Herbert Read once remarked, 'no difference between man and beast is more important than syntax'. Second, animals produce their noises in direct response to stimuli in their environment, as when a bird squawks at the approach of a cat. Such noises are analogous to human cries of pain or alarm, not to the sentences we produce. Nothing in my environment 'stimulated' me to write down the sentence I just wrote down. In the light of this, it is easier to understand those followers of the French philosopher René Descartes who found it impossible to suppose that animals could be capable of any mental activity. 'If beasts reasoned,' said one of them, 'they would be capable of true speech with its infinite variety.' We might not want to go as far as that, but at least we must admit that speech is one, if not *the*, salient feature of human nature which distinguishes it from any other sort of nature.

Not only is language our most sophisticated, important and unique possession, it is also, remarkably enough, an almost universal human possession. As already mentioned, all known human societies have possessed a language, whatever else each of them may have lacked. Not only that, but whereas there are mathematical geniuses and chess-playing geniuses, when it comes to language, nearly all of us are capable of producing and understanding an infinite number of sentences.

Language is also remarkable in its versatility. By uttering the appropriate noises, in the right circumstances, a single person in a single day can easily do each of the following: inform others of what is happening, ask them to do something, command them, excite them, promise them, insult them, express anger and get married. As some of these examples show, we do not in general utter noises as an activity separate from other activities. We perform actions with words, actions which it would be difficult, inconvenient or even impossible to perform without words. The number of such possible actions is indefinitely large.

Questions 28–33

Do the following statements reflect the claims of the writer in Reading Passage 3?

In boxes 28–33 on your answer sheet write

YES   *if the statement reflects the claims of the writer*
NO   *if the statement contradicts the claims of the writer*
NOT GIVEN   *if it is impossible to say what the writer thinks about this*

28 Grammarians now have a thorough understanding of their subject.
29 Even the least developed communities have complex languages.
30 Certain noises that animals make can be classified as language.
31 Certain human cries have something in common with animal communication.
32 People who are good mathematicians are likely to be good at chess.
33 Talking usually forms part of a wider activity.

Questions 34–37

Complete the notes below.
*Choose **NO MORE THAN ONE WORD** from the passage for each answer.*
Write your answers in boxes 34–37 on your answer sheet.

Characteristics of human beings:

* unlike animals, able to use language and to **34** ....
* far more capable than animals of manipulating **35** .... and organising politically

Characteristics of animals:

* cannot create **36** .... of noises
* only make sounds in reaction to **37** ....

Questions 38–40

Look at the following people (Questions 38–40) and the list of claims below.
Match each person with the claim credited to them.
*Write the correct letter **A–F** on your answer sheet.*

38 Herbert Read
39 Wolfgang Köhler
40 a follower of Descartes

List of Claims

A Attempts to understand the nature of language require objectivity.
B Computers will soon use language as skilfully as human beings.
C More than anything else, grammar distinguishes human beings from animals.
D Speaking can be compared with physical activities such as walking.
E The inability of animals to speak shows that they are unable to think.
F There is no limit to what human beings can say.

Are you: Female? ▭   Male? ▭

Your first language code:

▶ 0 1 2 3 4 5 6 7 8 9	
▶ 0 1 2 3 4 5 6 7 8 9	
▶ 0 1 2 3 4 5 6 7 8 9	

IELTS Reading Answer Sheet

Module taken (shade one box):   Academic ▭   General Training ▭

1		✓ 1 ✗	21		✓ 21 ✗
2		2	22		22
3		3	23		23
4		4	24		24
5		5	25		25
6		6	26		26
7		7	27		27
8		8	28		28
9		9	29		29
10		10	30		30
11		11	31		31
12		12	32		32
13		13	33		33
14		14	34		34
15		15	35		35
16		16	36		36
17		17	37		37
18		18	38		38
19		19	39		39
20		20	40		40

Checker's Initials		Marker's Initials		Band Score		Reading Total	

Answer key

UNIT 1

Reading

1 *Suggested answers*
  1 It's about a parrot that can talk much better than most parrots.
  2 N'Kisi the parrot, his owner Aimee Morgana and Professor Donald Broom.
  3 B It's giving factual information about something happening around now.

2 1 In New York / with Aimee Morgana
  2 He can hold converstaions, use grammar and make sentences.
  3 Jigsaws
  4 About 972
  5 Six years old
  6 Understanding how to make the past tense when using irregular verbs

3 *Suggested answers*
  1 talking about what is happening at the moment
  2 to copy/imitate
  3 inventing
  4 the ability to think
  5 to do/undertake
  6 complicated/difficult
  7 said / added to the conversation
  8 rules of language

Grammar

4 is believed to be (line 10)
  can be taught to (line 20)

5

Infinitive	Past tense	Past participle
send	sent	sent
take	took	taken
teach	taught	taught
make	made	made
form	formed	formed
be	was/were	been
spend	spent	spent
find	found	found
say	said	said
use	used	used
speak	spoke	spoken
give	gave	given

6 1 has recently been made / has been made recently
  2 was spent
  3 is said
  4 is very rarely spoken / is spoken very rarely
  5 can be taught
  6 will be given
  7 is formed
  8 is found / can be found

Vocabulary

7 1 text 2 message 3 talk 4 speech 5 speak
  6 chat 7 hold 8 ring 9 whistle
  (Hidden word: telephone)

8 1 g 2 f 3 a 4 b 5 d 6 h 7 c 8 e

UNIT 2

Reading

2 1 FALSE – *Words and actions are officially laid down, learned by the staff from handbooks and teaching sessions*
  2 TRUE – *Fast-food chains only responded by putting salad on the menu when there was pressure in various countries from doctors and health ministers.*
  3 NOT GIVEN – (*The text says that salad is on the menu, it doesn't say anything about its popularity.*)
  4 NOT GIVEN – *They want … to be thought of as almost inseparable from the idea of everyday food consumed outside the home. They are happy to allow their customers time off for holidays … for which they do not cater.* (*There is no mention of people being too busy to cook.*)
  5 TRUE – *The chains even have very bright lighting to make sure that 'undesirable' people don't want to come in.*
  6 FALSE – *Supplying a hamburger that is perfect in terms of shape, weight, temperature, together with selections from a pre-set list of extras, to a customer who knows what to expect, is a difficult thing to do.*
  7 NOT GIVEN – *The technology involved has meant spending huge sums on research* (*There is no mention of money that needs to be spent in the future.*)

Grammar

3 1 The River Nile is considerably longer than the River Thames.
2 London is far smaller than Mexico City.
3 Fruit is much better for you than sweets.
4 A Rolls-Royce car is a good deal more expensive than a bicycle.
5 Fast food is more convenient than cooking yourself.
6 Australia is far bigger than New Zealand.

4 *Suggested answers*
1 It's the largest desert (in the world).
2 It's the longest wall.
3 He's the richest man.
4 It's the smallest planet.
5 It's the tallest/oldest tree.
6 It's the fastest animal.

5 1 Fast-food outlets are open longer **than** ordinary restaurants.
2 I would rather have a sandwich **than** a pizza.
3 The number of people who eat rice is considerably greater **than** the number who eat potatoes.
4 The amount of meat eaten in the USA is far **greater than that** eaten in China.
OR **Far more** meat **is** eaten in the USA **than** (is eaten in) China.
OR The amount of meat eaten in the USA is far more **than the amount (of meat)** eaten in China.
5 Hamburgers are more popular **than** noodles in Europe.
6 Pizza is not **as** expensive **as** steak.
7 Producing meat is twice **as** expensive in some countries **as** in others.
8 The number of customers we had today was much **smaller than** last night.

Vocabulary

6 1 spicy 2 sour 3 fresh 4 sweets
5 ripe 6 diet 7 chef 8 bland
9 fast food 10 menu

A	L	K	R	E	M	E	N	U	P
S	P	I	C	Y	N	C	S	K	R
N	F	A	S	T	F	O	O	D	I
M	Q	F	W	A	Q	L	T	T	P
L	R	R	D	S	S	O	U	R	E
D	I	E	T	N	W	D	C	V	N
S	H	S	T	Y	E	I	C	D	E
V	H	H	E	Z	E	G	H	H	J
C	M	Q	G	N	T	A	E	F	R
B	L	A	N	D	S	X	F	C	M

7 1 hunger 2 hungrily 3 hunger
4 celebration, celebrity 5 celebrate
6 distinction, distinctiveness 7 distinctively
8 distinguish 9 clean 10 cleanly 11 clean
12 suspicion, suspiciousness, suspect
13 suspiciously 14 suspect 15 warm
16 warmly 17 warm 18 cosy 19 cosily
20 comparison 21 comparative 22 compare
23 politics, politician 24 politically
25 politicise/politicize

UNIT 3

Reading

1 1 D (Istanbul, Turkey)
2 B (Buenos Aires, Argentina)
3 A (Shanghai, China)
4 C (St Petersburg, Russia)

2 1 construction 2 trains 3 grid 4 government
5 tango 6 canals 7 capital 8 paintings
9 continents 10 palace 11 market

3 1 B *… laid out in a grid – that is, most of its streets are straight, like lines drawn on a sheet of paper from top to bottom and from side to side.*

2 A *… a teahouse that may be the model for the well-known 'willow pattern' design, which is used on plates around the world.*

3 D *Topkapi, the magnificent palace, used to have over 50,000 people living and working in its grounds, and even had its own zoo.*

4 C *This city was founded … to increase trade by sea with western Europe.*

5 A *Although there aren't many historic sites to attract tourists …*

6 C *… it is again known by its original name.*

Vocabulary

4 1 boom 2 traditional 3 model 4 founded 5 grid 6 excavated 7 resemble 8 located 9 adopting 10 separating

5 1 amused 2 amazed/astonished/surprised 3 interested (*fascinated* has the right meaning, but is followed by *by*) 4 bored 5 frightened/terrified 6 thrilled 7 fascinated (*interested* has the right meaning, but is followed by *in*) 8 excited

Grammar

6 1 so 2 because of 3 because 4 so 5 so (that) / because 6 because 7 so (that) / because 8 because of 9 so 10 because of

UNIT 4

Grammar

1 1 Service-oriented companies often **give** mobile phones to their sales force.

2 I am writing to tell you that I **have become** a full-time student and started my course last week.

3 Since I was a child, I **have wanted** to be a nurse.

4 The table **shows** that the number of students **has risen** to over five million since 1980.

5 We **haven't seen** each other for a long time, so I want to meet soon.

6 *Correct*

7 In this way, I feel I **am** able to repay the hours and effort that have been spent on me.

8 In the past decade, computers **have become** the most useful tool in offices and factories.

9 This letter is to tell you what I **have been doing / have done** recently.

10 This development **has been happening** for many years.

2 1 have/'ve started 2 am/'m making 3 work 4 don't have / haven't 5 practise 6 belongs 7 play 8 am/'m thinking 9 like 10 are asked 11 have/'ve been practising 12 hope / am/'m hoping 13 has/'s suggested 14 haven't decided 15 depends

3 1 at 2 to 3 about 4 with 5 from 6 about 7 about 8 on

4 1 Writing a project takes a lot of **reading**.

2 Let's talk **about** what you've done.

3 I'm interested **in** finding out about people's jobs.

4 *Correct*

5 How do you feel about **using** a computer?

6 I'm looking forward to **starting** a new project.

7 I'm quite good **at finding** information on the Internet.

8 I enjoy most lessons, apart **from** history.

9 Children are usually better at **learning** foreign languages than adults.

10 Next, we'll look **at** the best way to plan a report.

Reading

6 1 TRUE – *A leaflet containing full details is available on request.*

2 NOT GIVEN – *The College Charter is a series of statements which explain what is being done to promote high standards for people who use College services. It has been designed in accordance with a national framework (There is no mention of consultation.)*

3 FALSE – *… while at the same time being tailored to meet the specific needs of the College.*

4 TRUE – *… the Principal, who will refer each complaint to the appropriate member of staff and then provide a response.*

5 FALSE – *Appeals against external examination bodies must follow their own procedures*

6 TRUE – *Smoking is not permitted inside any part of the building unless specifically authorised.*

7 NOT GIVEN – *All accidents must be reported to Reception (There is no mention of medical help.)*

8 TRUE – *If items are damaged or broken as a result of careless use or failing to follow instructions, the person concerned will be required to cover the cost of repairing or replacing the items.*

9 FALSE – *They must not be taken into any examination room under any circumstances.*

UNIT 5

Vocabulary

1 1 a 2 j 3 f 4 g 5 h 6 i 7 d 8 c 9 e
10 b

2 1 square 2 triangle 3 rectangle 4 cylinder
5 cube 6 sphere

3 1 circle (The others have straight sides.)
2 circle (The others are three dimensional.)
3 tiny (The others mean 'very big'.)
4 minute (The others mean 'not big or small'.)
5 minuscule (The others mean 'very big'.)

4 1 reached 2 carrying out
3 were evaluated/analysed 4 made
5 support(ed) 6 analysing/evaluating
7 performed/carried out 8 put forward

Grammar

5 1 had gone 2 (had) arrived; had eaten / ate
3 were passing; caught 4 didn't enjoy
5 missed 6 was working; saw; had made
7 saw; didn't see; was talking 8 were climbing
9 had made / made 10 was digging; cut

6 **a** It has been known for a long time that the
Ancient Egyptians imported copper from Cyprus.
i What historians had not realised until recently was
the threat posed to these imports by aggressive
tribesmen along the Mediterranean coast.
f New research(,) carried out by a team from
Liverpool University(,) has shown how the
Egyptians built a huge fortress on this coast.
d The fortress was built around 1270 BC by
Rameses II, to protect maritime trade.
e The complex covered five acres and was home to
at least 500 soldiers.
c The men grew their own food and baked bread, but
imported luxury items such as wine and olive oil.
h As well as a bakery and a palace, a temple was also
discovered.
g It was 20 metres long and ten metres wide, with
three central rooms.
b The fortress was only needed for a brief period –
only 50 years or so – and was abandoned in the
13th century BC.

UNIT 6

Reading

1 B

2 1 F 2 B 3 E

3 1 YES – *Both seem a little taken aback by the way
their lives have followed a similar pattern*
2 NOT GIVEN – It is not unusual to find twins
have chosen the same careers, but there is nothing
in the text that says it is unusual for twins to reach
high positions.
3 NO – *Career dynasties … a phenomenon that
occurs in any walk of life.*
4 YES – *a ready-made set of contacts just waiting to
be networked*
5 NO – *Professor Val Dusek is sceptical.*
6 NOT GIVEN – Although the writer refers to job
satisfaction, this is not related to people's
expectations before starting work.

Grammar

4 1 hasn't risen 2 have/'ve been 3 studied; went
4 rang; said; had 5 has never been 6 saw
7 has enjoyed 8 spent

5 1 last saw; ago 2 hasn't worked; for 3 had; ago
4 has been; since 5 taught; ago; didn't enjoy
6 hasn't had; for 7 last went; ago
8 learned/learnt; ago 9 have you been; Since

Vocabulary

6 change, lend, leave, waste, give, pay, invest, spend,
save, make

C	H	A	N	G	E	Z	P
A	L	E	N	D	I	S	A
T	L	S	Q	U	N	P	Y
L	E	A	V	E	V	E	M
Y	S	V	Y	L	E	N	A
T	R	E	M	J	S	D	K
W	A	S	T	E	T	P	E
T	N	F	G	I	V	E	D

UNIT 7

Reading

1 1 C *Lunch and refreshments are provided on both courses at no extra cost.*
2 B *… reliving that age at various public entertainments.*
3 A *… this famous annual competition*
4 C *… you will learn the basic techniques of driving a 60-year-old steam locomotive*
5 D *… a fashion show, which features wedding outfits for brides, grooms, bridesmaids and page boys.*
6 A *… bands, rappers and children's chorus.*
7 C *You are also given one-year membership of the railway society*
8 A *Television crews are invited to use a two-tiered stage 3m from the main stage. The area in front of the main stage is reserved for still photographers and television cameras without tripods.*
9 B *… to re-create the clothing, weapons, tools, jewellery, games, food and furniture of that long-gone period*
10 D *… a wide range of specialists will be on hand to give expert advice on planning your wedding.*

Grammar

2 1 who represent nations from all over the world (A) *Non-defining*
2 which stands at over 50 hot dogs and buns in 12 minutes (A) *Non-defining*
3 that was one of the richest trading centres in the Viking world (B) *Defining*
4 during which you will learn the basic techniques of driving a 60-year-old steam locomotive, under the eye of an experienced instructor. (C) *Non-defining*
5 which gives you the opportunity to become a volunteer on our educational programme. (C) *Non-defining*
6 which features wedding outfits for brides, grooms, bridesmaids and page boys. (D) *Non-defining*

3 1 which/that 2 which 3 whose 4 whom
5 which/that 6 who/that 7 which 8 who/that
9 which

4 The relative pronoun can also be omitted in number 5.

5 Those that can be omitted:
1 which was 2 that was 4 that were

Vocabulary

6 1 like-minded people (B)
2 a first-come-first-served basis (A)
3 one-year membership (C)
4 first-hand experience (C)
5 self-service restaurant (D)
6 all-you-can-eat contest (A)
7 a family-based … society (B)
8 a 60-year-old steam locomotive (C)
9 that long-gone period (B)
The plural noun (*minutes*) becomes singular (*minute*) in front of another noun.
The other example is *60-year-old* (not *60-years-old*).

UNIT 8

Grammar

1 1 are you going to celebrate / are you celebrating
2 're playing 3 won't regret 4 's
5 's going to be 6 starts 7 'm flying 8 leaves
9 'll be 10 'm not going to spend 11 'll be
12 'll send

2 1 *correct* 2 *more likely to be* I'm going to make / I'm making 3 *correct* 4 will begin / is going to begin 5 will/'ll pay 6 *correct* 7 will be used
8 waste (spend *shows that this refers to the present, not the future*) 9 will make 10 *correct*

3 1 There may be another opportunity …
2 … the weather is (very) likely to be fine. /… it is (very) likely to be fine.
3 … they're bound to be there tonight.
4 … you probably won't get tickets.
5 … there's a chance of (our/us) winning … / … there's a chance that we'll win …
6 It's / It is unlikely (that) …
7 There is / There's little chance that we'll …
8 I've no doubt (that) this is …

Reading and grammar

4 1 vii 2 v 3 ii 4 viii 5 iv

5 1 on 2 with 3 By 4 by 5 from 6 of
7 for 8 to 9 for 10 into

UNIT 9

Reading

1 1 1996 2 10cm × 3m 3 Eight
4 about 15,000 years

2 1 TRUE – … *they are at a temperature of –50°C. They are then kept until they reach –20°C when they are ready to be analysed.*

2 NOT GIVEN – *We are told about their levels compared with the past, but not with each other.*

3 NOT GIVEN – *We aren't told why the ice ages happened in the past.*

4 FALSE – *Some people have argued that human-induced global warming is beneficial*

5 TRUE – … *we would have about another 15,000 years to go before the next ice age*

3 1 a **2** b **3** b **4** a **5** a **6** a **7** b

Grammar

4 1 One of the factories near me **is** causing a lot of problems.

2 Many things **worry** me about what **is** happening to the environment.

3 **Everything** in the town **was** hidden in thick smog.

4 There **are** many **advantages** to using solar power.

5 A number of **problems have** arisen recently in low-lying towns.

6 Another thing to mention **is** that we need to plant more trees.

7 Every **country** has **problems / a problem** with a lack of fossil fuel(s).

8 **These things are / This thing is** now being used to make all **kinds** of products.

9 **One** thing to remember **is** that children **need** a safe world to grow up in.

10 All **kinds of problems** will happen if the government **don't / doesn't** do something soon.

5 1 much **2** little **3** little **4** much **5** Few/Many **6** many **7** little **8** much; little **9** Few/Many **10** little

Vocabulary

6 1 endangered species **2** recycling **3** global warming **4** carbon dioxide **5** greenhouse gases **6** ice ages **7** climate change **8** sea level

UNIT 10

Reading

1 1 D whole paragraph

2 F whole paragraph

3 A *ego and grandeur still sometimes play a significant role in the scope of the construction*

4 C *the development of mass iron and steel production*

5 B *the base would take up too much land*

2 1 spread footing **2** (vertical) column **3** cast-iron plate **4** grillage (steel beams) **5** (thick) concrete pad

Vocabulary

3 1 i **2** j **3** k **4** l **5** a **6** h **7** f **8** d **9** e **10** g **11** c **12** b

Grammar

4 1 (in) decorating **2** to share **3** living **4** moving **5** in buying **6** study; do **7** doing **8** getting **9** interviewing; to ask **10** opening **11** working **12** for keeping **13** to leave **14** to move; to get away **15** to give **16** smoking **17** to stay **18** to study **19** to go **20** at fixing

UNIT 11

Grammar

1 D

2 1 – **2** – **3** – **4** the **5** – **6** a **7** a **8** – **9** – **10** the **11** the **12** – **13** The **14** – **15** – **16** an **17** a **18** – **19** the **20** the **21** the/– **22** –

3 1 – **2** – **3** a **4** the **5** – **6** – **7** a **8** the **9** – **10** –

Reading

4 A

5 1 C … *knowledge that will be needed to avoid getting into trouble.*

2 B … *such as knowing who is dominant to whom, who is related to whom, and who has done what to whom in the past.*

3 A … *we can easily tell individuals of our own species apart, and … the same is true of other species of mammals.*

4 D … *the production of milk, allowing baby mammals to have a period of childhood*

5 A *Dolphins have their own signature whistles that act like names*

6 C *All this remembering goes on in a particular part of the brain called the neocortex.*

7 A *When it comes to social behaviour, mammals are far more highly developed than other creatures.*

8 C *This area, though, seems to take a long time to develop fully, and animals in which it is very large take a very long time to grow up to adulthood.*

6 1 birds/fish **2** fish/birds **3** dolphins **4** Elephants **5** information **6** trust **7** neocortex **8** adulthood **9** relationships **10** milk

Vocabulary

7 1 eventually 2 Remarkably 3 respectively
4 simultaneously 5 relatively 6 closely
7 highly

UNIT 12

Reading

1 C *Concepts such as motivation training, and relaxation are the basis for strong mental preparation, whether for a team or an individual sport, for an amateur or a professional …*

2 1 physical 2 goals 3 need 4 routines
5 team; individual

3 A *A good sports psychology consultant can be of great value for a sportsman or woman. However … a large number of these consultants … fail to reach the required standard.*

4 A *in my experience as a sports psychology consultant*

5 1 NOT GIVEN – *They are interviewed in local and national newspapers and heard on radio shows, and a surprising number of professional teams use one. (There is no suggestion that newspapers have created a demand.)*
2 YES – *… too many professionals in this line of work are not worth the money they cost.*
3 NO – *Numerous examples can be given of consultants who have the necessary skills without a certificate from a sports psychology organisation.*
4 YES – *Some sports psychology professionals … are unable to engage in individual counselling for personal, or life, issues, which is an essential aspect of the work.*
5 NO – *I have seen consultants behaving very unprofessionally, for instance by guaranteeing results*
6 NOT GIVEN – *a client's decision to change to another consultant. (There is no reference to the client's reasons for changing.)*
7 YES – *… when choosing a sports psychology consultant, it is important to get information about them, for instance from past or present clients.*

Grammar

6 1 A 2 B 3 A 4 B 5 B

7 1 are taking 2 *correct*
3 should not ~~to~~ be encouraged
4 had better ~~to~~ take
5 ought not to spend 6 *correct*
7 you had/'d better bring

UNIT 13

Grammar

1 1 I can't decide unless you help me.
2 If I don't eat cheese, I don't/won't get fat.
3 If I had gone to Spain, I would have learnt/learned Spanish.
4 I wouldn't be unhappy if I didn't have to make a lot of choices.
5 As long as I go to a good university, I will get a good job.
6 If I learnt to cook, I wouldn't spend so much in restaurants.
7 If I hadn't been to a party last night, I wouldn't have woken up late this morning.
8 Nick can have the job as long as he learns to drive (first).
9 If Susanna were here, she would be able to / could help us.
10 I wouldn't have been unhappy if I hadn't married the wrong man.

Vocabulary

2 1 analysis 2 research/theory/paper 3 process
4 factor 5 paper 6 evidence/analysis 7 theory
8 source

3 1 satisfaction 2 growth 3 ability 4 politician
5 option 6 tendency 7 decision 8 expectation
9 economist 10 difference 11 government
12 recommendation

4

D	T	H	E	O	P	T	I	O	N	R	E	I	S
I	O	N	L	G	O	V	E	R	N	M	E	N	T
F	Y	O	N	E	L	G	S	O	E	D	A	N	D
F	H	E	T	I	I	S	A	O	C	U	R	L	O
E	X	P	E	C	T	A	T	I	O	N	R	G	D
R	J	E	N	S	I	U	I	S	N	C	H	R	I
E	S	T	D	E	C	I	S	I	O	N	H	O	E
N	I	S	E	S	I	O	F	V	M	E	R	W	E
C	I	G	N	N	A	M	A	B	I	L	I	T	Y
E	A	Y	C	H	N	I	C	S	S	W	I	H	L
L	B	E	Y	D	O	N	T	E	T	I	N	H	E
A	V	E	N	A	N	D	I	O	N	E	A	R	T
H	A	M	E	N	C	W	O	B	M	M	V	P	B
R	E	C	O	M	M	E	N	D	A	T	I	O	N

5 1 badly   2 highly   3 perfectly/totally   4 totally
   5 hardly   6 widely   7 highly   8 widely

6 1 total   2 smooth   3 stop   4 soft   5 made a/the

7 1 unanimous   2 obvious   3 snap
   4 given/offered   5 spoilt for

8 1 window shopping   2 bargains   3 half price
   4 (had) cost a fortune   5 reasonable price
   6 try them on   7 keep the receipt   8 refund

UNIT 14

Reading

1
clear	transparent
a consideration	an issue
to create	to make
to extract	to take out
genuine	real

3 1 E … *was so expensive that a law was passed*
   2 A … *wavelengths enter the eye* …
   3 E … *had to be quarried and shipped from Afghanistan*
   4 D … *is not a naturally occurring product. It was made by the ancient Egyptians*
   5 C *shellfish … molluscs … cochineal beetle*
   6 F *slow-drying oil* and *collapsible tin paint-tubes*
   7 B *Linguistic considerations …*
   8 F *oil paint could be built up in layers … different shades of, say, red*
   9 B *The Japanese … green from blue.*
   10 E *cinnabar … was mined in Spain … lapis lazuli stone, which had to be quarried and shipped from Afghanistan.*

Grammar

4 1 I have experience **of/in designing** colour schemes for offices.
   2 Can I suggest **going (you/we go)** to see the science museum?
   3 The interior of the car is designed **to improve** driving.
   4 Leila learned **to use** watercolour paints at college.
   5 Let Pablo **go** into the room first.
   6 He will be under pressure to meet deadlines and **complete** tasks and coursework.
   7 You must ~~to~~ go and see the new colours at the fashion show.
   8 In conclusion, **studying** abroad has fewer advantages than in this country.
   9 To let everyone ~~to~~ know where the talk will be held, there'll be a map.
   10 She intends **going / to go** away after term ends.

11 Pete can't remember **getting** into the car and **driving** to the station.
12 We prevented ~~to~~ him **(from) drawing** on the walls.
13 A lot of time was spent **teaching** them to write.
14 Try **walking / to walk** rather than **driving** everywhere if you want to lose weight.
15 It was years ago, but I'll never forget **seeing** Venice for the first time.
16 You'd better **ring** up your tutor to tell him you'll be late.
17 Elisa's interested **in doing** fashion design next term.
18 Remember **to post** that letter on your way to work.
19 Children often dream **of/about being** football stars.
20 You need **to give** up staying up late watching TV.

Vocabulary

5 1 impatient   2 sensitive   3 appreciative
   4 competent   5 independent   6 cautious
   7 honest   8 impulsive

UNIT 15

Vocabulary

1 1 host   2 complex   3 essential   4 expensive
   5 groceries   6 guest   7 adequate   8 observe
   9 casual   10 resident
Secret word: hospitable

Grammar

2 1 *correct*   2 must have spent   3 must be related
   4 can't be   5 *correct*   6 can't have attended
   7 must be   8 can't be   9 can't be working

Reading

3 1 C … *we create social relations for four main reasons: to enable us to compare ourselves with others, thereby reducing uncertainty; to obtain the reward of stimulating company; to be valued; and to gain emotional support.*
   2 E *Hospital patients facing an operation the next day generally prefer to spend the night with others who have already had the operation and can provide information about the potential danger*
   3 A … *swapping news with your family at the end of the day, … gossiping with your friends about the party you went to last night, … chatting with colleagues at the coffee machine*

4 D *… decide, for instance, whether their fear is justified.*

5 F *… people preferred the company of others in pleasant conditions, … when feeling happy or in the work environment. Company was also preferred in threatening conditions, … In unpleasant conditions … people preferred to be alone, as they did in conditions requiring them to concentrate*

6 E *Just as young children refer to their parents for information in new or ambiguous situations, adults will also seek out someone with more information when in difficulty.*

7 B *From the moment of birth, babies seek to establish an enduring social relationship with their main carer, extending their circle of relationships outwards as skills and circumstances allow. Later, as their social skills improve, children modify their behaviour to others in order to fit in with other people and gain a sense of belonging.*

8 F *In one piece of research, people were asked to specify the conditions under which they would like to be with others.*

9 B *This need for belonging can be observed as the motivation for infants in their earliest interactions with others.*

10 A *Imagining this kind of life is so difficult as to be almost impossible, which neatly illustrates the importance of social relationships in our lives.*

4 **1** value **2** motivation **3** operation
4 belonging **5** hospital **6** need

5 **1** rules **2** behaviour **3** respect **4** consequences
5 discussion **6** appeal **7** interaction

UNIT 16
Reading
1 **1** *Letter Perfect* **2** David Sacks
3 (written) language **4** casual linguists
5 history **6** significance **7** articles
8 information **9** repetition **10** uninteresting
11 unscholarly **12** cover; cover

Vocabulary
2 **1** evolved **2** indicates/indicated **3** abstract
4 modified **5** significant **6** regular
7 representational **8** predecessor

3 to write: (a book,) a book review, a dissertation, an email, an essay, a letter, a report, a thesis
to carry out: an experiment, an investigation, research, a survey, a threat

4 **1** investigation **2** survey
3 research / experiment / investigation
4 thesis / dissertation **5** report **6** review

Grammar
5 *Suggested answers*
1 I recommend that you read this book before writing your assignment about the Roman alphabet.
2 I only managed to finish the book before the deadline by reading it without stopping.
3 Writing a book review is a useful tool for helping you to think carefully about what you have read.
4 I enjoyed reading *Letter Perfect*, despite finding it repetitive in places.
5 After reading *Letter Perfect*, I understood much more about the alphabet.
6 Many readers will be irritated by some parts of the book, while enjoying other parts.
7 Despite being related, the Latin and Arabic alphabets are very different from each other.

UNIT 17
Vocabulary
1 **1** a **2** g **3** e **4** f **5** c **6** d **7** b

2 **1** feel / am feeling **2** 've/have completely lost
3 caught / came down with (*had* is also possible)
4 feel / are/'re feeling **5** came out in **6** had
7 made / has made **8** had **9** to get over
10 lost **11** had come down with / had caught (*had* is also possible) **12** make

3 **1** is/'s doing **2** 're/are making / made / have made
3 make **4** made / makes / has made
5 has/'s never done **6** 'll/will do; make **7** do
8 's/has done **9** make **10** Do; make **11** made
12 do you make

4 **1** regulation **2** regular **3** regulator
4 psychology **5** psychologist **6** consultation
7 consultative **8** consult **9** evolutionary
10 evolve **11** evolutionist **12** variety
13 various, varying **14** communication
15 communicate **16** communicator
17 management **18** manageable, managerial
19 manager **20** destruction **21** destructive
22 destroyer **23** nature **24** naturalist, naturist
25 informative **26** inform **27** informer
28 long **29** lengthen **30** humanity **31** human
32 humanise/humanize

Grammar

5 1 must 2 mustn't 3 don't have to
4 don't have to 5 mustn't 6 have to 7 must
8 had to

6 1 You must ~~to~~ check whether the electricity is switched off before you touch the plug.
2 Everyone **needs (to have)** electricity today.
3 People **must / have to work** at least eight hours a day to qualify as full-time workers.
4 We **don't need** any products to help us sleep.
5 We **mustn't** take a nap this afternoon as we're too busy.
6 How much sleep you need **must depend / depends** on how tired you are.
7 They **don't have to / mustn't** rest now.
8 You **mustn't** drive when you're tired.

UNIT 18

Reading

1 1 In a newspaper/magazine
2 To describe his experience / encourage people to go there / advertise the trip
3 Favourable

2 1 Sydney 2 (four) specialists 3 160 million years
4 north-south 5 6km 6 base 7 blue ice
8 penguins 9 unforgettable
10 November to February 11 passport
12 (commemorative) certificate

Vocabulary

3 backpacker, tourist, sightseeing, travel agent, traveller, cruise, abroad, book, hotel, destination

D	B	A	C	K	P	A	C	K	E	R	A
T	E	R	E	Q	B	U	K	G	D	S	B
R	I	S	I	H	N	O	M	X	C	B	R
A	Z	C	T	X	O	N	O	B	R	C	O
V	R	E	I	I	U	T	T	K	U	M	A
E	S	D	V	B	N	L	E	A	I	W	D
L	T	E	C	B	R	A	U	L	S	E	D
L	T	O	U	R	I	S	T	K	E	F	G
E	O	E	R	U	Q	E	R	I	N	V	C
R	W	G	F	K	U	O	E	H	O	D	H
E	S	I	G	H	T	S	E	E	I	N	G
T	R	A	V	E	L	A	G	E	N	T	C

4

Accommodation	Health	Money
cabin	malaria pills	cash
caravan	sunscreen	exchange rate
self-catering apartment	travel-sickness pills	notes
tent	vaccination	traveller's cheques

Grammar

5 1 come up with a solution / an answer
2 put up with them 3 making it out
4 set it up 5 took it over
6 look / am/'m looking forward to meeting/seeing

UNIT 19

Reading

1 1 versatile 2 backward* / sideways
3 sideways / backward* 4 hover 5 rotate 6 lift
*Note that *backwards* is also possible in British English.

2 1 cockpit 2 drive shaft 3 main rotor
4 tail boom 5 tail rotor 6 landing skid(s)

Grammar

3 1 I wish creative artists **didn't** do this.
2 I'd rather we **drove** in my car.
3 I think it is time we **discussed** this problem.
4 I wish you **would** give me half my pay before the weekend, but I don't suppose you will.
5 *correct*
6 It is about time students, families and society all **realised** there is a problem and **recognised** their own responsibilities!
7 It is high time the government **paid** women who stay at home to look after their children.

Vocabulary

4 1 ease 2 congestion 3 seats 4 capacity
5 linked 6 accessible 7 elevated
8 conventional 9 reliable 10 damage

UNIT 20

Reading

1 **1** FALSE – *Everyone who receives any income … needs a Tax File Number. Income includes wages or salary from a job, money earned from investments, and government payments.*

2 FALSE – *… help with the cost of out-of-hospital care and subsidised medicines.*

3 TRUE – *If you need to see a doctor urgently, you can register with Medicare without waiting ten days.*

4 NOT GIVEN – *This booklet is available from Medicare offices* (There is no mention of any cost.)

5 NOT GIVEN – *People in Australia usually keep their money in a bank, building society or credit union.* (There is no indication of whether banks are used more than building societies and credit unions.)

6 TRUE – *It is advisable to open a bank account within six weeks of your arrival, as during this time you usually need only your passport as identification. After six weeks, you will need additional identification to open an account.*

7 TRUE – *to get help with … having overseas skills recognised*

8 NOT GIVEN – There is no mention of Centrelink lending money.

9 FALSE – *As a new resident, you may be entitled to receive free English language tuition*

10 TRUE – *Licences from some overseas countries do not require a practical test.*

2 **1** telephone book **2** benefits and payments
3 application **4** 510 hours **5** three months
6 knowledge; eyesight

Vocabulary

3 **1** d **2** e **3** b **4** i **5** f **6** a **7** h **8** c

WRITING WORKOUT 1

1 **1** shouldn't **2** just over **3** unacceptable
4 should **5** should **6** can **7** good
8 Make sure you use

2 **a** Problems with the example letter:
   1 There shouldn't be an address.
   2 It is too long.
   3 It needs to begin 'Dear Sir'
   4 Some of the grammar is wrong. The spelling is correct.
   5 It needs paragraphing.
   6 It needs to end with 'Yours faithfully' as it is a formal letter.
   7 'I am looking forward to -ing from you' would be a good ending.
   8 The letter includes some inappropriately informal language.

b *Suggested answer* (Note it has been shortened to just over 150 words.)
Dear **1** *Sir*,
I am writing to **2** *complain* about two large dogs that run in **3** *the park* every evening. The owner of **4** *the* dogs, a young man, releases them to play in **5** *the* park, but I think it is **6** *very* dangerous **7** *for* people and animals to share this park. This has been happening **8** *for the last two weeks*.
The most dangerous thing is that the dogs bark very loudly and **9** *run* towards people so that they **10** *frighten* them, especially small **11** *children*. In fact, some people, including myself, **12** *have attempted* to talk with the **13** *dogs'* owner, but he seems to ignore what we say.
As a **14** *mother* **15** *with/of* two children, I am naturally worried about their safety. I am sending this letter **16** *as* a representative of a concerned group of park users. The owner needs to be told to keep his dogs on a leash so that people don't feel **17** *scared*. I am **18** *looking* forward to **19** *hearing* from you. **20** *Yours faithfully*,
(159 words)

3 **a** You want to sell your bicycle. You think a friend of yours might like to buy it from you.
Write a letter to your friend. In your letter
   • explain why you are selling
   • describe the bicycle
   • suggest a date when your friend can come and see the bicycle
Write at least 150 words.

b **1** ship **2** wondering **3** brand new
4 serviced / looked at **5** very good condition
6 include **7** make **8** come round

c **1** I'll be going home at the end of term and I've decided that I need to sell my bicycle – it would cost me too much to ship it home to Manila.
   2 It's a mountain bike … green and black with a silver stripe.
   3 I was wondering if you might be interested in buying it. / Why don't you come round and have a look sometime? What about next Saturday morning when we don't have lectures?

4 I'm **writing** to ask you for a six-month period of leave. I'm very much interested in computers, but **unfortunately** I have poor computer **skills**. Last week, I saw an **advertisement** for a computer course on the TV. Though the **university** is in a **different** province, it is very famous, and the enrolment fee is not **expensive**. So I want to attend the course. There I can **acquire** a lot of **knowledge** about computers and **software**. The course begins the day after **tomorrow**. When I **finish** the course, I will return to my job.

5 **1** e **2** b **3** a **4** c **5** d **6** f

6 *Suggested answer*

Dear Robert,

I was very pleased to hear that you will be studying at the same college as me. You ask me about accommodation. There are two main choices of accommodation in the town. First of all, there are hostels which are run by the college. These are not expensive, but the study bedrooms are quite small – just a single bed, a wardrobe, desk and chair. There is a shared kitchen and bathroom on each floor. If I were you, I'd try to find a shared flat in the town. It will be about the same price, but you would have a bigger room. There are lots of notices at the college, offering flats to share.

The best thing about the college is the new computer centre. It's huge and has the most up-to-date technology. When you arrive here, give me a ring, and I'll take you on a guided tour of both the college and the town.

Best wishes

(156 words)

WRITING WORKOUT 2

2 Essay A would achieve higher marks.

1 Only essay A answers the question. Essay B mentions all five jobs without discussing three in detail. B has no real introduction, but goes straight into the topic. B has a confused line of argument and gets progressively more muddled.

2 Both are paragraphed, but only A has an organised argument with clear introduction, examples and reasons and a conclusion. B discusses computer programming in paragraph 1, why being a doctor is more important than being a teacher in paragraph 2, why engineers and journalists are not important in paragraph 3 and why the writer wants to be a computer programmer in the conclusion. There is no mention of three professions which the writer thinks are the most important to society today and no real conclusion. There is quite a bit of irrelevancy.

3 A has clear examples of knowledge/own experience for all three jobs.
B has a clear example for a doctor and a computer programmer.

4 A has some repetition of vocabulary – *important* – but both have some good, relevant vocabulary:
A *well-being, reliant on, have access to, pass knowledge down to*
B *computer literate, output, respected professional*

5 Both A and B have complex sentences, for example:
A *Without the journalists who investigated the Watergate affair, for example, we would never have found out about what Nixon had been doing.*
B *Having respect from society is very important, because if your job is valued, then you feel yourself to be valued as well.*

3 *Suggested answer*

Introduction: choose doctor, teacher and journalist; give basic opinion
Paragraph 1: discuss doctor, personal experience/knowledge
Paragraph 2: discuss teacher, personal experience/knowledge
Paragraph 3: discuss journalist, personal experience/knowledge
Conclusion: restate opinion

4 1 The first thing to consider when discussing X is …
There is no doubt that …
One of the main arguments put forward for X is …
Although some people say/believe that …, I believe that …
2 I think that …
In my opinion …
Personally, I believe …
It is clear/obvious to me that …
3 Next …
The second thing I would like to say is that …
The next most important point is …
4 An illustration of this is …
For instance …
An example of this is …
5 To sum up …
I would like to conclude by saying …
Finally …
6 vital, essential, significant, critical, crucial

5 *Suggested answer*

Should children be allowed to work? That is a good question. I believe it depends on the age of the child and the type of work that it is asked to do. Broadly speaking, I think that children under the age of 14 should not be allowed to work, but from that age on, it is permissible if it is regulated.

First of all, children need to learn about the workplace and the pressures that they will face when they finish school. Secondly, children need to understand the relationship between work and money at a fairly young age. Unless they are from a very rich family, they will need to work.

One way that many children are introduced to work in my country is by way of a newspaper round or a Saturday job. Another example of how children can be introduced to the world of work is by having work experience weeks at their school. This can be a very valuable experience as they need to get up early, travel to work, deal with people and, possibly, endure total boredom.

Finally, although I believe that children should find out about work when they are teenagers, I am totally against children younger than 12 working. Children need to go to school and they also need to have time to play and grow.

To sum up, I believe that when children reach a certain age, it is important that they get a job. It is part of growing up – of learning to be a responsible adult.

6 *Suggested plan*

Introduction:	Give personal opinion; agree/disagree or give a balanced opinion
Paragraph 1:	Discuss importance of music and art and give examples from own experience or knowledge
Paragraphs 2/3:	Discuss importance of mathematics and foreign languages and give examples from own experience and knowledge
Conclusion:	Restate opinion/clarify opinion

Suggested answer

There is no doubt that some subjects that are studied at school are felt to be a waste of time when it comes to getting a good job. Among those subjects which often find themselves in this category are music and art. However, I personally believe that students should study a large number of subjects, so that they can make a good decision about their future when they leave school – not everyone is good at mathematics or foreign languages.

Firstly, although many employers today would be looking for someone with a mathematics or a foreign language qualification, I believe that they would also be keen to have someone who knows about art or music. It is good for a child to have an interest in and knowledge about the culture of his or her country. In addition, art and music are essential in helping a child to learn how to express his or herself, and this is a quality that is important in the workplace.

Much depends on what type of job you are applying for. After all, what is a good job? Is it a job which pays well or gives you security? For some people, the salary is not a consideration. It may be easier to find a job where mathematics and a foreign language are important, but there are still jobs, such as in TV, museums and teaching, where art or music would be more appropriate.

In conclusion, I believe that students should study a wide curriculum in order to be able to make an informed decision when they are thinking of a career.
(267 words)

WRITING WORKOUT 3

1 Your answer should include the following: 1, 3, 4, 6, 8

2 1 Inappropriate: not accurate information
  2 Inappropriate: not accurate information + speculation
  3 Appropriate
  4 Inappropriate: personal opinion
  5 Appropriate
  6 Inappropriate: not accurate information
  7 Appropriate
  8 Inappropriate: do not mention every figure – the important thing is to select information showing the main trends

3 1 period **2** accounted **3** whereas **4** showed
  5 reaching **6** followed **7** least **8** change
  9 rose **10** fell

4 1 From **this chart / these charts**, we can find out about the difference in spending between the UK and the USA.
  2 The middle chart ~~it~~ **shows** us the increase in money spent in developing countries.
  3 The chart describes the amount **spent**.
  4 Britain spent the highest amount **on** consumer goods.
  5 The third most popular goods **were** toys.
  6 **Nearly the same amount was spent on personal stereos as on** TVs.
  7 The **most** popular consumer item was the camera and the **least** was the personal stereo.
  8 **The** majority of people spent most on films.
  9 The graph **shows** that the electricity use in winter **was/is** much greater than in summer.
  10 The use of electricity is shown **in** a pie chart.
  11 The number of units **decreases/decreased** sharply.
  12 Several figures **are** increasing.
  13 The demand **for** electricity then **declines/declined** until 0800.
  14 There is a **difference** of 5.2 between the figures.
  15 It's clear that unemployment **has** decreased.

5 *Suggested answer*

According to the graph, the number of households who owned more than one car rose during the period 1972 to 2002. During this period, there was a sharp drop in the numbers of households without a car or van. Numbers who owned one car or van remained steady, and there was a gradual rise in ownership of two cars. By 2002, 45% of households owned one car or van, 22% owned two or more, and 5% owned three or more, with 28% without either a car or a van.

In 2002, the majority of people – 69.6% and above – in the United Kingdom travelled to work by car, with people in Wales and Northern Ireland more likely to do so than people in England or Scotland. In all parts of the United Kingdom, the car was the most popular method, followed by walking, then the bus or coach and finally the train. Few people – less than 3% – used a bicycle or motorbike to get to work.
(165 words)

WRITING WORKOUT 4

1 **a** One idiom used well is fine, but not a large number.

  c Contractions are not normally found in formal writing.

  d Colloquial language / slang is best used in spoken English.

  e Aggressive opinions are not part of a balanced, well-structured essay.

  f Write in full rather than abbreviating.

2 **1** d (*gas guzzlers*)

  2 c (*didn't*) and possibly e

  3 c (*We'll*), a/d (*freezing to death*) and possibly e

  4 f (*e.g.*)

  5 c (*haven't*) and d (*haven't a clue about*)

  6 a (*once in a blue moon*) and possibly e

  7 c (*It's*) and d (*really great*)

  8 d (*have a get-together*)

3 **1** d People insist on driving cars which use a great deal of fuel.

  2 f It can be argued that the reason global warming is getting worse is because some countries did not sign the Kyoto agreement.

  3 e We will soon all be suffering from intense cold if the Gulf Stream changes direction.

  4 c We should take advantage of the availability of free resources such as wave and wind power.

  5 b Some people have little idea about the consequences of carbon emissions.

  6 h It is no good going by bicycle occasionally; you need to be properly committed to alternative transport.

  7 a It is clearly beneficial that the media are giving this problem so much coverage.

  8 g Governments should have high-level discussions about the problems we face.

4 **1** repeatedly/heavily/inevitably

  2 wildly/seriously

  3 clearly

  4 clearly/repeatedly

  5 dramatically

  6 clearly/inevitably/seriously

  7 densely/heavily

  8 clearly/inevitably

  9 clearly/inevitably/repeatedly

  10 repeatedly

5 A *There is no doubt that the Earth is beginning to suffer the consequences of pollution. People should make more of an effort to recycle and to use public transport. Also to use different sources of energy.* This introduction doesn't address the question directly, although the first sentence is acceptable. The last sentence seems rather an after-thought. 3/5

B *It has been suggested in recent months that the government is not doing enough to promote alternative sources of energy. My personal opinion is that they should promote alternative sources of energy.* Repetition of the essay title doesn't gain marks. 2/5

C *It has been known for some time now that a move towards sources of energy which are not carbon-based is urgently required to stop the effects of global warming. In my view, there are too few governments who seem to be promoting the use of other types of energy – from wind, wave, solar and nuclear sources.* A good introduction to the essay. Clear and to the point. 5/5

D *First of all, I would like to say that this is a subject that is often discussed. Something needs to change and change quickly. I am in favour of wind power, and indeed in my country we use it a lot.* Very vague and does not address the question very well. 2/5

6 *Suggested answer*

It has been known for some time now that a move towards sources of energy which are not carbon-based is urgently required to stop the effects of global warming. In my view, there are too few governments who seem to be promoting the use of other types of energy such as wind, wave, solar and nuclear sources of energy.

Governments at present are too reliant on coal, oil and gas. Although some governments are doing research into the use of alternative energy sources, many are not. Energy from the wind, the sea and the sun does not pollute the environment and is an everlasting source of power. Nuclear power is clean, and although it is not totally unproblematic, it would provide a large amount of energy and dramatically improve the environment. Countries such as France have made good use of nuclear power.

My feeling is that more use could be made of wind power. In some countries, there has been a reluctance to use wind turbines, even in areas which are not densely populated, as some people believe they are eyesores. Personally, I believe they are not only useful, but beautiful as well. Governments should spend more time and effort promoting the benefits of this source of energy and trying to make the public understand the reasons for change.

In conclusion, I believe that, if governments forced everyone to have a wind turbine and solar panels on the building they lived in, made more use of wave power and built more nuclear power stations, then they would manage to avert the dangers that are seriously threatening the Earth.

(268 words)

WRITING WORKOUT 5

1 1 In my opinion   2 Unfortunately   3 because
4 There is no doubt that   5 However   6 because
7 or   8 Although   9 especially   10 Another
11 To sum up   12 Consequently

2 1 The class spent all yesterday **practising** for the marathon. (NB *practicing* is correct in US English)
2 Take my **advice**, choose a sport which is less competitive than tennis.
3 Salaries of sportsmen and women have **risen** considerably in the last few years.
4 The team will **lose** next Saturday.
5 The football **pitch** was too hard to play on.
6 The total **number** of people who support football in this town exceeds 100,000.
7 You need a coach to give you the **skills** you need to succeed at this sport.
8 Most coaches do more harm than **good** when it comes to training.
9 The standard of **living** in some countries is very low.
10 My personal **belief/opinion** is that sport plays an important part in daily life.
11 You will have the **opportunity/chance** to speak to him later.
12 Some sportsmen and women earn a good **income/living** from their sport.
13 I saw an **advertisement** for the Olympics last week on TV.
14 The most popular consumer **item/product** is the trainer.
15 The **study** of computers should begin at school.
16 She studied in an English-speaking **environment**.
17 The least popular (**household**) **task/chore** is washing the windows.
18 She took a part-time **job** at the local sports centre.
19 I hope you have a good **journey/trip** to the competition.
20 **Young** people today love athletics.
21 Where do you buy your **clothes**?
22 Don't touch the **keys** of the computer.
23 I have no **choice** in the matter.
24 There are quite a few sports **activities** available at the centre.

3 1 I'm really grateful for everything they did **for** me at college.
2 During the period **between** 1989 and 2001, public services declined.
3 My brother is responsible **for** training in the company.
4 The government will prevent people **from** getting jobs without a work permit.
5 I haven't seen you **for** a long time.
6 The goods won't arrive here **until** the weekend.
7 The magazine is the least effective medium **for** communicating news.
8 There is a high demand **for** electricity in the evenings.
9 **During** the Olympics in Greece, everything ran smoothly.
10 There was an advertisement **for/about** a job at a local restaurant in the paper.
11 Learning about computers should be compulsory **at/in** primary school.
12 I look forward **to** hearing from you soon.

4 4, 8, 3, 7, 1, 11, 5, 2, 16, 13, 14, 12, 9, 6, 10, 15
The computer is an important invention and it has had a huge impact on our lives. We use computers at work, in the home, to pay our bills, to buy books or to plan our holidays. We have dealings with a computer every day whether we know we are doing so or not. However, although there are undoubted benefits to the use of computers, there are also some drawbacks. In the first place, everybody knows that the banks use computers to process transactions. All our accounts are computerised, with the result that, if something goes wrong, our savings could be deleted. Not only that, people who bank online are more likely to have their accounts hacked into illegally.

READING MODULE

Each question correctly answered scores 1 mark.
CORRECT SPELLING NEEDED IN ALL ANSWERS.

Reading passage 1

Questions 1–13

1 F *A succession of other voyages ... to India and Sri Lanka, to ... Hormuz on the Persian Gulf, and along the east coast of Africa, almost as far south as Mozambique.*
2 D *The fleet used the compass ... Marked sticks of incense were burned to measure time ... The ships ... communicated with one another through the use of flags, lanterns, bells, carrier pigeons, gongs and banners.*
3 J *It seems likely that a detachment ... sailed to northern Australia during one of the seven voyages.*
4 C *The first Treasure Fleet comprised 62 ships ... included 100-metre-long horse ships ... water ships ... troop transports, supply ships and war ships*
5 E *The following spring, the seasonal change in direction of the monsoon winds enabled the ships to sail towards home.*

6 goods
7 latitude
8 trading centre/center
9 pirates
10 G *Zhu Di ... ordered him to oversee the construction of a Treasure Fleet to explore the seas surrounding China.*
11 F *During each of Zheng He's voyages, he encouraged diplomats from other countries to travel to China, either aboard his ships or on their own vessels.*
12 C *... Zhu Gaozhi ... ordered shipbuilders and sailors to stop their work and return home.*
13 E *Zhu Zhanji ... restarted the Treasure Fleet voyages ... in an attempt to restore peaceful relations with the kingdoms of Malacca and Siam.*

Reading passage 2

Questions 14–27
14 viii
15 ii
16 x
17 iv
18 ix
19 v
20–22 IN ANY ORDER
        A, B, G
23 contact
24 disease
25 food
26 nurse
27 C

Reading passage 3

Questions 28–40
28 NO – *uncover the enormously complicated rules of grammar which underlie our languages, and they still have a long way to go.*
29 YES – *all known communities have possessed sophisticated languages*
30 NO – *Many animals, of course, are capable of producing noises ... but these noises are so different in kind from human speech that it is, at best, a misleading analogy to speak of such noises being part of a language.*
31 YES – *... animals produce their noises in direct response to stimuli in their environment ... Such noises are analogous to human cries of pain or alarm ...*

32 NOT GIVEN – The article says *there are mathematical geniuses and chess-playing geniuses,* but does not mention any link between them.
33 YES – *... we do not in general utter noises as an activity separate from other activities.*
34 laugh
35 tools
36 sequences
37 stimuli
38 C *... Herbert Read once remarked, 'no difference between man and beast is more important than syntax'.*
39 A *To see how truly remarkable language is, we must, as the psychologist Wolfgang Köhler put it, retreat to a 'psychic distance' from the subject.*
40 E *... those followers of the French philosopher René Descartes who found it impossible to suppose that animals could be capable of any mental activity. 'If beasts reasoned,' said one of them, 'they would be capable of true speech with its infinite variety.'*

OBJECTIVE

IELTS

Michael Black
Wendy Sharp

Workbook with Answers

Intermediate

CAMBRIDGE
UNIVERSITY PRESS

CAMBRIDGE UNIVERSITY PRESS
Cambridge, New York, Melbourne, Madrid, Cape Town, Singapore,
São Paulo, Delhi, Dubai, Tokyo, Mexico City

Cambridge University Press
The Edinburgh Building, Cambridge CB2 8RU, UK

www.cambridge.org
Information on this title: www.cambridge.org/9780521608749

First published 2006
6th printing 2010

Printed in the United Kingdom at the University Press, Cambridge

A catalogue record for this publication is available from the British Library

ISBN 978-0-521-60874-9 Workbook with answers
ISBN 978-0-521-60882-4 Student's Book with CD-ROM
ISBN 978-0-521-60885-5 Self-study Student's Book with CD-ROM
ISBN 978-0-521-60872-5 Teacher's Book
ISBN 978-0-521-60881-7 Audio Cassettes (2)
ISBN 978-0-521-60880-0 Audio CDs (3)
ISBN 978-0-521-60873-2 Workbook

Cover design by Dale Tomlinson

Designed and produced by Kamae Design, Oxford

CAMBRIDGE

New Insight into
IELTS

VANESSA JAKEMAN AND CLARE MCDOWELL

Workbook

WITH ANSWERS

CAMBRIDGE
UNIVERSITY PRESS

CAMBRIDGE UNIVERSITY PRESS

Cambridge, New York, Melbourne, Madrid, Cape Town, Singapore, São Paulo, Delhi

Cambridge University Press
The Edinburgh Building, Cambridge CB2 8RU, UK

www.cambridge.org
Information on this title: www.cambridge.org/9780521680905

First published 2008

Printed in the United Kingdom at the University Press, Cambridge

A catalogue record for this publication is available from the British Library

ISBN 978-0-521-68090-5 Workbook with answers
ISBN 978-0-521-68094-3 Workbook Audio CD
ISBN 978-0-521-68096-7 Workbook Pack
ISBN 978-0-521-68089-9 Student's Book with answers
ISBN 978-0-521-68092-9 Student's Book Audio CD
ISBN 978-0-521-68095-0 Student's Book Pack

Cover design and graphic by Tim Elcock

Produced by Kamae Design, Oxford

Contents

Listening

1 Orientating yourself to the text

Predicting the situation

1 Look at pictures **a–h**, which show people speaking in different situations. Try to imagine what the speakers are saying.

2 🔊 **02** Listen to six short conversations. As you listen, match each conversation to a picture, **a–h**.

Then listen again and complete the rest of the table. If there are two speakers, say whether they know each other or not.

	Picture	Situation	Number of speakers	Key words	Do the speakers know each other?
1	b	Asking for directions on campus	2	I'm looking for, right direction, go along, on your left	No
2					
3					
4					
5					
6					

Predicting the answers from the given information

3 Look at tasks **A** and **B** below and decide what the topic is for each one.

4 Look at the words and layout of the questions in tasks **A** and **B** and decide what information you need to listen out for, e.g. *a place, a number, an adjective*. Complete the 'Type of information' boxes.

A

Complete the form below.
Use **NO MORE THAN TWO WORDS AND/OR A NUMBER** for each answer.

POLICE REPORT

Name: 1 ....

Address: 2 ....
                  Beach Road.

Description of stolen items

• Bag: 3 ....

• Passport No: 4 ....

• Watch: 5 ....

Type of information
1 ....
2 ....
3 ....
4 ....
5 ....

B

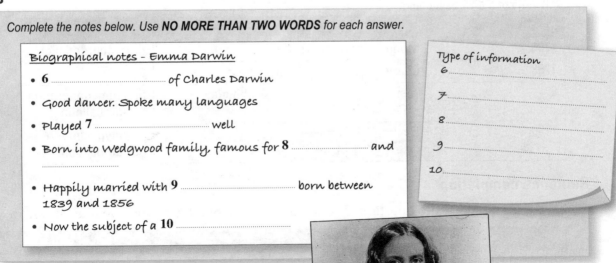

Complete the notes below. Use **NO MORE THAN TWO WORDS** for each answer.

Biographical notes - Emma Darwin

• **6** .... of Charles Darwin

• Good dancer. Spoke many languages

• Played **7** .... well

• Born into Wedgwood family, famous for **8** .... and ....

• Happily married with **9** .... born between 1839 and 1856

• Now the subject of a **10** ....

Type of information
6 ....
7 ....
8 ....
9 ....
10 ....

5 ⊙03 Listen and complete task **A** above.

6 ⊙04 Listen and complete task **B** above.

Now check your answers to see how well you were able to predict the information.

Listening

2 Listening for specific information

Table completion

1 **A** and **B** below are examples of table completion tasks. Study the tables and answer these questions.
  a What is each table about?
  b How do the column headings help you answer the questions?
  c In which direction should you read each table: across or down?
  d What type of word should you listen for in order to do question 1?
  e What type of word will the answer to question 4 be?
  f Why is one part of the second table shaded?

A

Zoo animal	Food consumed in captivity
panda	bamboo
orang utan	1 ....
2	hens' eggs
zebra	3 ....

B History of hot-air ballooning

Date	Balloon created by	Type of gas	Significance
1783	Montgolfier brothers	4	first recorded flight
1783	Charles	hydrogen	5 ....
6	Yost	high altitude gas	first new generation hot-air balloon
1960		7	prototype modern hot-air balloon

Sentence completion

2 Turn the sentences into questions and write what type of information you must listen for.

	Type of information
Example The bus departs at .... *What time does the bus depart?*	*a time*
1 The man wants to study .... at university.	
2 Louis Pasteur was born in ....(2 possible questions)	
3 New Yorkers consume .... of water each day.	
4 Longitude is difficult to calculate at sea without a	
5 .... has a more difficult scoring system than soccer.	
6 Spring rolls are made of .... and vegetables.	

Note taking

3 Look at the task below and answer the questions.
  a What is the topic?
  b Turn the notes into full questions, e.g. *When is the conference?*
  c Make a note about the type of information you expect to hear, e.g. *a number*.

4 (05) Listen and answer questions 1–10.

Complete the notes below. Write **NO MORE THAN THREE WORDS AND/OR A NUMBER** for each answer.

'Architecture 21' conference

Conference dates	1 ....
Conference venue	2 ....
Reservations phone no.	3 ....
Student rate per day	4 ....
Contact person	5 ....

Must act fast!
- Closing date for talks 6 ....
- Summary should have 7 ....
- Maximum length 8 ....
- Also send 9 ....
- email address 10 ....@uniconf.edu.au

Type of information
1 *a number*
2 ....
3 ....
4 ....
5 ....
6 ....
7 ....
8 ....
9 ....
10 ....

5 ⏱ Take 2 minutes to skim the questions and work out what information is missing.

6 (06) Listen and answer questions 1–10.

Questions 1–6
Complete the table. Write **NO MORE THAN THREE WORDS AND/OR A NUMBER** for each answer.

⚓	BLUE HARBOUR CRUISES		
Name of cruise	Highlight Cruise	Noon Cruise	1 .... Cruise
Price per person	$16	3	$25
Departure times	9.30 am	12.00 pm	5 ....
Included in the price	2	4	6 .... and ....

Questions 7–10
Complete the sentences below. Write **NO MORE THAN TWO WORDS** for each answer.
  7 Jetty no. 2 is across the road from the ....
  8 The commentary is in ....
  9 A .... version of the brochure is available.
  10 Passengers are advised to take a ....

Listening

3 Identifying detail

Understanding detailed description

1 Complete the labels on these diagrams with the best word or phrase.

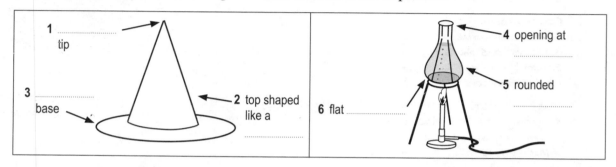

1 .... tip

3 .... base

2 top shaped like a ....

4 opening at ....

5 rounded ....

6 flat ....

2 (07) Listen and decide which picture, **A**, **B** or **C**, matches the description.

3 Complete the text with words you have seen or heard in this unit.

These days children's playgrounds offer a range of attractive equipment. One favourite is a type of climbing **1** .... designed to look like a little house on stilts, with a ladder at the front leading up to an **2** .... where children can get in, and a **3** .... slide at the **4** ...., through which they can get down.

Also popular are the roundabouts, which have a flat **5** .... platform that children stand on, and curved poles for them to hold on to.

Younger children like the sets of interconnecting **6** .... which they can crawl through.

IELTS Listening test practice   **Multiple choice questions**

4 Look at questions 1 and 2 below and say how they differ from each other.
Underline the key words in each question so that you know what to listen for.
⟨08⟩ Listen and answer the questions.

Choose the correct letter, A, B or C.

1 Which lecture did the man attend in the afternoon?
  A psychology
  B sociology
  C history

2 The woman wants to study
  A medicine.
  B medical science.
  C vet science.

5 Look at questions 1–3 below. Read all the options carefully and make sure you understand them.
⟨09⟩ Listen and answer the questions. Then listen again. Were you tempted to tick any of the wrong options? If yes, why?

Questions 1–3
Which **THREE** things does the man recommend bringing on the trip?
*Choose **THREE** letters **A–G**.*

  A camera
  B drinking water
  C food
  D mobile phone
  E radio
  F raincoat
  G sketchbook

6 Listen again and note why the other items in the list are wrong. What does the man say about these items?

Listening

4 Following a description: diagrams, maps and plans

Following directions on a map

1 Study the campus plan below and complete the sentences using a word from the box.

Example

There are *five* blocks.

1 A footpath runs _____ the lake.
2 Block E is _____ to the library.
3 The library is _____ the supermarket.
4 Block A is _____ to Block B than any of the other blocks.
5 A footpath _____ the workshops to the dance studio.
6 The gym is in the _____ corner of the campus.
7 The IT centre is at the _____ end of the campus.
8 The reception is at the entrance, just _____ the roundabout if you're coming from the city.

closer	~~five~~
north-east	links
near	northern
runs	before
opposite	
southern	beside
next	

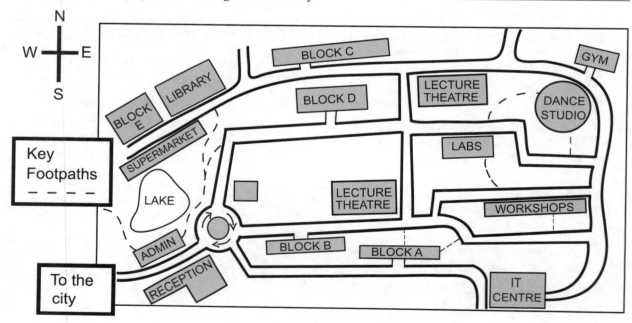

2 (🔊10) Look at the campus plan above and listen to three people giving directions. In each case, which block do the directions lead to?

Speaker 1 is giving directions to Block _____ .
Speaker 2 is giving directions to Block _____ .
Speaker 3 is giving directions to Block _____ .

Vocabulary builder

3   Match these forms of alternative energy to the pictures and say how they work.

bio fuel   solar energy   wave power   hydroelectricity   wind farm

4   Complete the table with the correct form of the word.

Noun	Verb	Adjective
increase		increasing
	to heat	
sun		
	to provide	
representation		representative
type	to typify	
		useful, useless

5   Look at the diagram of a solar heating system and see what parts you will need to label.
🔘 **11** Listen to a talk about solar energy and complete the labels as you listen.

Label the diagram below.
Write **NO MORE THAN THREE WORDS** for each answer.

2 ....

3 liquid: hot ....

Radiation from the Sun

Black surface

Glass

Energy exchanger

1 ....

4 ....

5 ....

Listening

5 Identifying main ideas

1 Look at the ideas related to football below.
Write some questions to find out information about the game of football (soccer).
Write your questions on a piece of paper to refer to later.

Most famous player ever **A**

First football leagues **F**

Example
Who is the most well-known player in the history of the game?

How the game is organised **E**

Origins of the game **B**

International football events **D**

World famous football clubs **C**

2 (🔊12) You will hear four mini-talks on different aspects of the game of football. Match the talks to the main ideas in the thought bubbles above. Write the letter **A–F** in the 'Main ideas' column of the table.

Talk	Main ideas	Details
1	B	*Similar game played in Japan and China. Today women also play.*
2		
3		
4		

3 Listen again and note down the important details in the 'Details' column of the table above. Don't write full sentences.

4 With a partner, ask each other the questions you wrote about football in exercise 1. Answer using information from the recording. Then ask each other questions to find out more.

Vocabulary builder

5 Look at the words and phrases in the box and make sure you know what they mean. Use a good English–English dictionary to check any unfamiliar words.
Then put each word into the correct category in the table.

Books	Assessment	Types of class
on loan		tutorial

on loan   tutorial   lecture
reading list   seminar
out of stock   biography
assignment   set text
dissertation   extension
essay   exam   library
bibliography   pass   fail
non-fiction

IELTS Listening test practice   **Labelling a diagram**

6 **13** You are going to hear four short conversations. Before you listen, read the questions and try to rephrase all the options **A**, **B**, **C** in your own words.
Then listen and answer the questions.

*Choose the correct letter, **A**, **B** or **C**.*

1 The students agree that playing sport is
   A better than studying.   *preferable to having to study*
   B time-consuming.
   C competitive.

2 Why does the man need the library book today?
   A He has always wanted to read it.
   B It is a set text for the course.
   C He is going away on Monday.

3 What problem does the student have?
   A She needs to change her essay topic.
   B She needs better IT material for her essay.
   C She needs more time to write her essay.

4 The student says that he
   A needs to improve his grades.
   B wants to change his main subject.
   C is going to see Dr Pollard that evening.

IELTS Listening test practice   **Matching**

7 **14** Listen and answer the questions.

*Which book is needed for the following purposes? Write a letter **A–F**.*

Purposes
1 course requirement   ....
2 personal study   ....
3 pleasure   ....

Books
A Animal Farm
B Better Writing
C Grammar in Use
D Brighton Rock
E Nelson Mandela
F Pride and Prejudice

Listening

6 Seeing beyond the surface meaning

1 ⊙15 You are going to hear six short conversations. Listen and complete the the first part of the table below with information about the topic, number of speakers and whether they agree with each other or not.

	Topic	Number of speakers	Do they agree?	Words stressed to emphasise meaning	Words used to agree or disagree
1	a movie	2	Yes	really	I thought so too.
2					
3					
4					
5					
6					

2 Now listen to the conversations again and notice how the speakers use stress and intonation to get their meaning across. Complete the rest of the table with the following information.
a Which words do they stress?
b What expression(s) do the speakers use to agree or disagree with each other?

3 ⊙16 Listen to the beginning of five different speaking situations, **A**, **B**, **C**, **D** and **E**, and complete the table below.

	What is the situation?	How many speakers are there?	What is the topic?
A			
B			
C			
D			
E			

4 Look at the questions below and decide what the topic is likely to be.

🔊**17** Listen and answer the questions.

Questions 1–5

*Choose the correct letter, **A**, **B** or **C**.*

1 The introduction of postage stamps
was considered
  A unusual.
  B uneconomical.
  C unnecessary.

2 Before the postage stamp was introduced,
who usually paid for the delivery of a letter?
  A the sender
  B the receiver
  C the post office

3 When was the single rate for a
stamp introduced?
  A 1834
  B 1839
  C 1840

4 Before stamps, the cost of sending a letter
depended on
  A where it was going.
  B how long it took to arrive.
  C how much it weighed.

5 The process of stamp production is
  A expensive.
  B difficult.
  C time-consuming.

Questions 6–9

Complete the notes below.
*Write **NO MORE THAN THREE WORDS** for each answer.*

Stamps must represent aspects of national interest, e.g. pictures of people

from **6** .... , or specific examples of wildlife, such as the Australian

7 .... There are no **8** .... on Australian or

British stamps.

A favourite topic in Britain is **9** ....

Question 10

*Choose the correct letter, **A**, **B** or **C**.*

10 Which picture shows the New Zealand stamp worth $1.50?

A

B

C

Listening

7 Following signpost words

1 Look at the signpost words in the centre of the page and decide what kind of information might follow, e.g. a contradiction, an example, an additional piece of information.

2 Complete each of the speech bubbles with the most appropriate word or words. Then say them out loud, emphasising the signpost words.

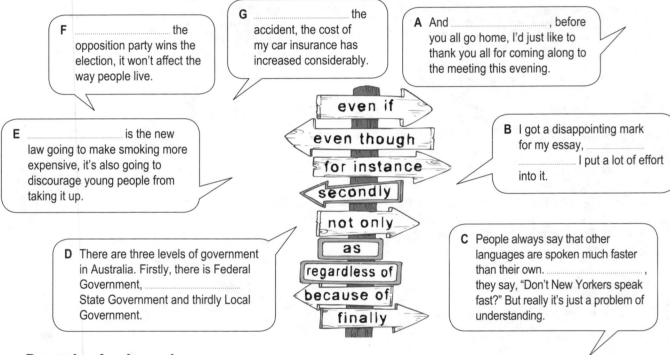

F .... the opposition party wins the election, it won't affect the way people live.

G .... the accident, the cost of my car insurance has increased considerably.

A And ...., before you all go home, I'd just like to thank you all for coming along to the meeting this evening.

E .... is the new law going to make smoking more expensive, it's also going to discourage young people from taking it up.

B I got a disappointing mark for my essay, ... I put a lot of effort into it.

D There are three levels of government in Australia. Firstly, there is Federal Government, ... State Government and thirdly Local Government.

even if
even though
for instance
secondly
not only
as
regardless of
because of
finally

C People always say that other languages are spoken much faster than their own. ...., they say, "Don't New Yorkers speak fast?" But really it's just a problem of understanding.

Preparing for the topic

3 While you are reading through the questions in the Listening test, ask yourself some things about the topic to get prepared for the recording. Note any pictures or graphics.

In the next IELTS test practice you are going to hear about the International Space Station, so try to answer these questions to prepare yourself for the topic.

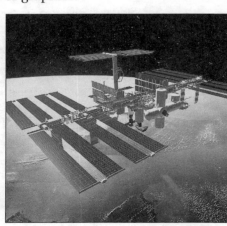

- What do you know about the International Space Station?
- Where is it?
- What happens there?
- Would you like to spend 90 days in space with six other people?
- If so, why? If not, why not?
- What kind of things would you have to prepare yourself for?
- What advice would you give to anyone who was going?
- What do the letters ISS stand for?

4 Read all the questions below (1–3, 4–6, 7–8) and identify the different types of questions. Underline the key words in the stem of each question.

5 ⊛**18** Listen and answer questions 1–3 as you listen.

> *Choose the correct letter, **A**, **B** or **C**.*
>
> **1** How many nations are involved in the ISS?
> **A** 5   **B** 15   **C** 20
>
> **2** How much should the ISS have cost to build?
> **A** $8 billion   **B** $120 billion   **C** $128 billion
>
> **3** How is the water supply maintained on board?
> **A** by using very little   **B** by transporting water from Earth   **C** by recycling all the water

6 Listen again and work out why some of the options are wrong. Use the table below to note down what is said about each option in questions 1–3 above.

5			
15			
20			
$8 billion		using little	
$120 billion		transporting	
$128 billion		recycling	

7 Read questions 4–6 below and think about what words you might hear on the recording. ⊛**19** Listen and answer questions 4–6 as you listen.

> **Questions 4–6**
> *Choose **THREE** letters **A–G**.*
>
> Which **THREE** areas of research will take place on the ISS?
> **A** solar energy   **E** studies in weightlessness
> **B** plant cultivation   **F** psychology
> **C** mapping   **G** nutrition
> **D** weather patterns

What sort of words might I hear?
solar panels

8 Do the same for questions 7–8. ⊛**20** Listen and answer questions 7–8.

> **Questions 7–8**
> *Choose **TWO** letters **A–F**.*
>
> Which **TWO** things do all the astronauts do each day?
> **A** turn on the computers   **D** listen to CDs
> **B** cook meals   **E** take some exercise
> **C** attend a meeting   **F** communicate with family

What sort of words might I hear?

9 Listen to the whole recording again and note the signpost words that you hear.

Listening

8 Following a talk

1 You are going to hear an example and four more mini-talks which contain typical language from IELTS Listening Section 4.

First, look at questions 1–4 and try to rephrase them in your own words, as in the example.

Example

What does the speaker think could (soon become extinct)?

(be endangered / die out)

1 According to the speaker, what is the main purpose of a language?

2 What two things were absent in the period when ballads were popular?

3 In what field of study was John Ray a pioneer?

4 List two more ways in which heat is transferred from one place to another.

Conduction

....

....

🔊 **21** Listen to the example.

> *Recording script*
> In previous lectures in this series we have focused on land conservation. Today we are going to look at the need for marine conservation and in particular the effects of commercial fishing on our oceans … because if we are not very careful, a great <u>many fish</u> are likely to end up on the 'endangered species' list.

Answer: many fish

🔊 **22** Listen to the mini-talks and answer questions 1–4 in **no more than three words** as you listen.

Make a note of the words or structures on the recording which have a similar meaning to the key words in the question.

2 Read questions 1–10 below. What is the topic?
Note how many different types of question there are and make sure you understand the layout.
⊙ **23** Listen and answer questions 1–10.

Questions 1–5
*Choose the correct letter, **A**, **B** or **C**.*

1 What does the speaker compare a computer virus to?
    A a biological organism
    B a corrupt program
    C an irritating person

2 *Core Wars* was designed as
    A a model virus.
    B a form of amusement.
    C a low-cost program.

3 The speaker says that computer viruses are picked up because they can
    A infiltrate programs by themselves.
    B be sold with commercial software.
    C hide in unofficial software.

4 What does the speaker find surprising?
    A the rise in the number of software infections
    B the determination of those who develop viruses
    C the fact that people blame their own computers

5 The worst aspect of a Trojan horse virus is its capacity to
    A delete all the files on your computer.
    B send illegal emails to all your correspondents.
    C perform operations in your name.

Questions 6–9
*List **FOUR** ways of combating viruses.*
*Write **NO MORE THAN THREE WORDS** for each answer.*

6 ....
7 ....
8 ....
9 .... e.g. get anti-virus software

Question 10
*Choose the correct letter, **A**, **B** or **C**.*

10 How does the speaker feel about computer viruses?
    A They are here to stay.
    B They serve no purpose.
    C They can be avoided.

Reading

1 Orientating yourself to the text

Topics and main ideas

1 Read paragraph **A** below, state the topic and underline the main idea.

A

A jet-lagged traveller sleepily lugging his suitcase to the rental car shuttle may well wonder why his brain seems bent upon tormenting his body. If only he could adjust his body clock to his new time-zone he could get the good night's sleep he needs. If his journey has taken him westwards, however, he will probably have an easier time adjusting to his new schedule than if he has travelled east. Some research by Hiroaki Daido of the University of Asaka Prefecture, in Japan, published recently, may help to explain why.

2 Which of the following best summarises the main idea in paragraph **B**?
   A There are more insects than animals to conserve in the world.
   B People are more interested in conserving animals than insects.
   C The conservation of animals has been more successful than the conservation of insects.

B

Although the world is home to tens of millions of animal species, the vast majority are small crawling things with lots of legs. When they are threatened it is difficult for conservationists to stir up much public sympathy. Not so for the big, cute and cuddly animals like orang-utans. People will go to enormous lengths to protect them, their habitats and the other less attractive (but no less important) animals that live with them.

3 What is the topic of paragraph **C**?

C

Our sense of humour is truly perplexing. Surveys show we are ten times more likely to be seen sharing a moment of laughter than any other form of strong emotion. Humour saturates our lives, yet only recently have brain scientists started to turn their scanners and electrodes to the task of examining the flash of amused insight that lies at the heart of understanding a joke. And the findings are not at all what you might think.

4 Which of the following best summarises the main idea in paragraph **C**?
   A Scientists have discovered some unexpected facts about humour.
   B People do not always laugh at the same sort of jokes.
   C Brain scans have failed to explain why people laugh.

Dealing with unfamiliar words

5 Read paragraph **D**. Can you guess the meaning of these words by looking at how they are formed?
   1 guidebook   **2** outdated   **3** shelf-life   **4** backpacker   **5** non-problematic

D

One of the major problems with guidebooks is that they are outdated before they are even published, as it takes, on average, two years from commissioning to publication. And as the shelf-life of most travel books is two years, there may be as many as four years between the original research and a tourist's visit. In extreme cases, this can have serious repercussions, as a young backpacker, Joel Edmond, discovered one autumn. A walk around a border lake described as non-problematic by one travel guide in Asia resulted in him being arrested by soldiers and imprisoned for a month. The guide's author has since apologised to him.

6 Read paragraph **D** again and choose the correct heading from the options **A–C** below.
   A How a tour guide lost his way
   B Why tourist guidebooks may be unreliable
   C Difficulties faced by travellers in Asia

Vocabulary builder

7 The words, phrases and collocations (words often used together) below are taken from paragraphs **A–D**. Try to work out the meaning of any you don't know from the context of the paragraph. Use a dictionary to check.
   Then complete the sentences below with a word, phrase or collocation from the box.

words
adjust (paragraph A)
species (B)
conservationists (B)
perplexing (C)
findings (C)
phrases
go to enormous lengths (B)
lies at the heart of (C)
collocations
vast majority (B)
serious repercussions (D)

1 The .... of people in the world are right-handed.
2 The desire to attract young customers .... most fashion advertising.
3 As we get older, it becomes harder to .... to new work practices.
4 .... believe that we are not doing enough to protect rare .... from extinction.
5 My father had to .... to get a copy of his mother's birth certificate, in order to prove his nationality.
6 The researchers found it .... that their results showed the opposite of what they expected to find.
7 Recent .... show that the burning of fossil fuels has affected the health of the planet.
8 The government's policy on university education has had .... for families on low incomes.

IELTS Reading test practice   **Finding information in paragraphs**

8 ⏱ Read the passage on the next page. Take 8 minutes to do this task.

> The Reading passage has five paragraphs, **A–E**.
> Which paragraph contains the following information?
> **NB** You may use any letter more than once.
>
> 1 reasons why children might be a better target for marketing companies than adults
> 2 examples of some of the first products to be marketed for children
> 3 measures taken by one country to reduce the exposure of children to marketing techniques
> 4 evidence of an increase in children's consumption of goods in one area of the world
> 5 a comparison of the time children spend on different activities
> 6 a common reason for arguments between children in the same family
> 7 an in-store method used by shop owners to encourage consumerism in children

Children and consumerism

Are children in developed countries affected by consumerism?

A In the 18th century, products aimed directly at children, such as toys, games and books, began appearing in shops. However, it was not until the 20th century that children became major
5 consumers in their own right, with the ability to buy items for themselves, or to persuade their parents to buy things for them. Today, children are often conditioned from an early age in the principles of consumerism. A major cause of sibling rivalry is
10 resentment that a brother or sister has a new toy; if children are upset, their parents may try to win back their good mood by buying them a treat.

B There is now a huge range of children's products – from potato crisps and sweets to athletic shoes
15 and video games. Manufacturers and retailers are adept at packaging these items in bright colours so that they catch the eye of children, and at placing these goods on the lower shelves of their stores, so that they are at children's eye level, and within easy
20 reach of their hands. It is assumed that if a child touches a product then there is at least a chance that his or her parents will buy it.

C Children are, in many ways, the ideal consumers, being more susceptible than adults to changes in
25 style and fashion, and providing a ready market for the latest crazes. As a result, a huge amount of money (US$2 billion every year in the USA alone) is spent on advertising to children, and last year, children's

direct
30 influence on parental purchases in the USA was estimated at
35 US$188 billion (as opposed to US$5 billion in the 1960s).

D Television advertising is seen as a major reason for
40 the rise in children's consumerism. It is estimated, in Western countries, that children aged between two and 17 watch between 15,000 and 18,000 hours of television, compared to just 12,000 hours spent in school. Commercials
45 showing children having fun using products like video games can convey several messages, such as 'this product is cool' and 'you are inferior if you do not have this product'.

E The European Union is considering regulating
50 advertising aimed at children, and the Scandinavian country of Sweden has already banned such advertisements from primetime children's television programmes. This decision was taken after research showed that children
55 under ten were unable to differentiate between a commercial and a programme.

Paraphrasing

9 Rephrase these ideas from the passage in your own words.

Example in their own right (line 5) themselves

1 a major cause of (line 9)
2 a huge range of (line 13)
3 catch the eye (line 17)
4 at children's eye level (line 19)
5 within easy reach (lines 19–20)
6 in many ways (line 23)
7 the latest crazes (line 26)
8 differentiate (line 55)

Star phrase 'being more **susceptible** than adults **to**'

1 Guess the meaning from context.

2 Answer the question.

3 Complete the sentence using the star phrase and the words in brackets.

How susceptible are you to changes in fashion?

Many consumers ....

(promises / advertisements)

Reading

2 Scanning for a specific detail and skimming for general understanding

Scanning

1 ⏱ Before you read the following text for meaning, practise your scanning skills by moving your eyes down the lines of the passage very quickly in order to find, and underline, the following. Take about 15 seconds for each.

1 a US state
2 an American soil researcher
3 a company
4 a country other than the US
5 a fruit or vegetable

Fruitful Drinking   *It's what tomatoes everywhere have been thirsting after*

A smart irrigation sensor that gives plants only as much to drink as they need can increase tomato yields by more than 40 per cent. The sensor has been developed by Yehoshua Sharon and Ben-ami Bravdo at the Hebrew University of Jerusalem's Faculty of Agriculture in Rehovot, Israel. The researchers say that their system not only increases the yield of crops, but it also dramatically reduces water usage – by up to 60 per cent for some crops.

At the heart of the system is an electronic sensor that clips onto a plant leaf and measures its thickness to an accuracy of 1 micrometre. 'A leaf's thickness is dependent on the amount of water in a plant,' says Sharon. 'A healthy leaf is 60 per cent water.' A thin leaf is a sure sign that the plant is suffering stress because it is thirsty, and stress is bad for yields.

The sensor consists of two plates, one fixed and the other spring-loaded, which together grip the leaf. The moving plate is connected to a small computer that regulates the voltage in an electrical circuit. As the leaf's thickness changes, the plate moves, causing a change in the voltage. This signal is fed to a processor that adjusts the plant's water supply.

Unlike conventional irrigation systems, which water crops periodically, the Israeli system waters the plants continuously, but adjusts the flow to the plant's needs. 'The idea is to give the plant the proper amount of water at the correct time, according to what the plant requires,' says Sharon.

Field studies show the system increases the yields of several crops while reducing consumption of water. Yields of grapefruit increased by 15 per cent while needing 40 per cent less water. For peppers, the yield rose by 5 per cent while water usage fell by 60 per cent. Tomato plants yielded 40 per cent more fruit while consuming 35 per cent less water.

'It is an interesting idea,' says John Sadler, a soil scientist at the US government's Agricultural Research Service in Florence, South Carolina. 'Other researchers have measured stress by measuring a plant's temperature or stem thickness. But I haven't heard of anyone doing irrigation at such a refined level,' he says.

But Sadler is a little surprised by the figures for water savings. 'They would depend on the technique you're comparing these results with,' he says. Sharon says the savings are based on comparisons with the Israeli government's recommendations for irrigating crops.

He admits that the system has to be very reliable if it is to be effective. 'Because the plants are watered continuously they are more susceptible to sudden changes in water supply,' he says. 'This means our system has to operate very reliably.'

The researchers have founded a company called Leafsen to sell the new irrigation system, and they hope to start marketing it within the next few months.

New Scientist

Paraphrasing

2 Skim the passage for words or phrases that have the following meaning and underline them.

1 the amount (of fruit) produced *yield*
2 the quantity of water used
3 plants grown by farmers
4 clear indication
5 traditional
6 method of watering
7 at regular times
8 the amount (of water) used by (plants)
9 the main stalk of a plant
10 reserves (of water) that result from using less

3 🕑 Take 12 minutes to answer the questions below.

Questions 1–7

Choose **NO MORE THAN THREE WORDS AND/OR A NUMBER** *from the passage for each answer.*

1 What is the main part of the researchers' irrigation system?
2 How often do traditional irrigation systems water plants?
3 Which crop showed the highest increase in yield during field studies?
4 How much less water did the peppers take up?
5 & 6 What two features of plants have previous researchers used to assess stress?
7 From which organisation will farmers be able to buy the new system?

Questions 8–11

Label the diagram below.

Choose **NO MORE THAN ONE WORD** *from the passage for each answer.*

11 .... – controls water supply to plants

10 .... – monitors electrical circuit

8 .... used to calculate 9 .... of leaf

Vocabulary builder

4 You need to be able to use and recognise words in their different forms.
Complete the sentences below using a **different form** of the words in the box. You may need to add or delete a prefix or suffix.

irrigation	consumption
yields	measure
agriculture	recommend
rely	operate
health	fruit
adjust	marketing

1 The article describes recent _agricultural_ studies that have taken place in Israel.

2 Farmers are always keen to ensure that their crops .... more fruit.

3 How soil is .... depends upon the available technology and local water supplies.

4 Some plants .... more water during growth than others.

5 If a plant has thin leaves, it is probably stressed and ....

6 The processor in the system makes small .... to the plants' water supply.

7 Temperature .... have been used in the past to assess a plant's stress levels.

8 The Israeli government makes .... about how much water can be used on crops.

9 The system has to be .... because sudden changes in water supply could harm the plants.

10 The system will shortly go into ....

11 The success of the product will depend on how well it is ....

12 All in all, the research done on irrigation has proved to be very ....

Star phrase 'A leaf's thickness **is dependent on** the amount of water in the plant.'

1 Guess the meaning from context.

2 Answer the question.

3 Complete the sentence using the star phrase and the words in brackets.

Are you financially dependent on anyone?

Young animals ....

(their parents / food and shelter)

Reading

3 Identifying main and supporting ideas

Main ideas

1 The sentence containing the main idea has been removed from the following two paragraphs. Read each paragraph carefully and then write an opening sentence for each.
Then compare your sentences with the key to see how well you understood the main themes.

Talk about REM

1 ....

This is according to a preliminary study presented in Surfer's Paradise. Sarah Loughran of Swinburne University of Technology in Melbourne left a mobile phone transmitting beside the right hemisphere of participants' brains for half an hour before they went to sleep. They showed more alpha-wave activity in the first period of non-REM* sleep, and started REM or deep sleep about 17 minutes sooner, than on nights they were not exposed to the phones. Loughran thinks electromagnetic radiation is the cause, but it's not yet clear whether this could have harmful effects.

*REM sleep = rapid eye movement sleep – the period when we sleep deeply but do not dream

---

Spice up your Nights

2 ....

Andrew Davies of the University of Tasmania in Launceston and his team placed 25 people on a diet containing 30 grams of chopped chilli a day for four weeks. On average, the volunteers went to bed two hours later and slept for 20 minutes less than in the previous four weeks, when their diet had been chilli free. But they were also less active in their sleep and seemed to sleep more deeply, Davies told the Australasion Sleep Association conference held in Surfer's Paradise, Queensland. The participants also reported feeling more alert the next day and were more physically active. The researchers have yet to pinpoint which ingredients in chilli are responsible.

---

2 How are the above paragraphs similar in terms of a) their structure and b) their content?

Paragraph structure

3 Complete the labels on the paragraph, using words or phrases from the box.

> topic   main idea
> further support

1 [   ]

In the 1930s, the French philosopher, Pierre Teilhard de Chardin predicted the emergence of a noosphere, a network linking mankind at the mental rather than the physical level. Teilhard was a sociologist, a scientist and a Jesuit theologian; *he described this noosphere partly in physical terms, as an information network, and partly in spiritual and philosophical language, as a force which would act to unify society. One of the many metaphors which he used to put the concept across was that of a 'halo of thinking energy' encircling the planet.* Today, the same combination of technical, sociological and philosophical terminology is used to describe the Internet.

2 [   ]   **3** [   ]

4 What main point is the writer making in this paragraph about Pierre Teilhard?

    A He tried to build an early version of the Internet.
    B He forecast the problems surrounding the Internet.
    C He understood the principles underlying the function of the Internet.

Vocabulary builder: compound nouns

5 A noun and adjective are often put together to make a compound noun phrase. This can be done to avoid using a longer relative clause. For example:
cities that are underground = *subterranean cities*

Skim the passage below for noun phrases that have these meanings.

    1 people who are walking in city streets
    2 large numbers of ants that are moving around together
    3 movement that is difficult because of a lot of traffic
    4 regulations that relate to traffic
    5 structures that are on fire
    6 large groups of people who are shopping
    7 vehicles that are moving in both directions
    8 a bridge that splits and goes in two directions

Ants show us the way forward

They march in their thousands along narrow trails that wind across the countryside. Often their traffic is two-way as they seek vital supplies to haul back to their subterranean cities. Scientists say that if the mysteries of how ants manage their traffic problems can be unravelled, the secrets could be applied to human travel, making life easier for urban pedestrians.

Recently, the Australian Research Council announced a $244,000 grant for a three-year study of ant traffic. It is one of 1214 research projects costing $370 million to be funded between 2006 and 2010.

'Ants meet their transportation needs without traffic congestion or complex centralised control,' said Martin Burd, a Monash University biologist. 'They have no traffic laws, no traffic lights and no traffic police and yet they are able to organise themselves.' Dr Burd, who will work with a French researcher, Dr Audrey Dussutour, believes ant transport models could help humans cope with everything from dashing through airports or fleeing burning buildings to negotiating shopping crowds.

One surprise is that ants move faster on trails involving two-way traffic. 'With no left and right lanes, that's not what you would expect,' Dr Burd said. They appeared to avoid congestion by separating heavily laden ants, thus avoiding convoys of slow-moving traffic.

Dr Dussutour has investigated how ants organised traffic over a forked bridge set up in a laboratory. She found that ants pushed each other at the fork to avoid bottlenecks forming. 'You wouldn't think pushing would ever be good,' said Dr Burd, who conceded the technique could never be employed to smooth out human jams.

6 🕐 Take 8 minutes to do the following task based on the passage on page 27.

> Do the following statements agree with the information in the passage?
> *Write*
>
> **TRUE**   *if the statement agrees with the information*
> **FALSE**   *if the statement contradicts the information*
> **NOT GIVEN**   *if there is no information on this*
>
> **1** Ant territory is easier to find in Australia than in other countries.
> **2** The Australian Research Council is funding three studies over a four-year period.
> **3** Some ants obviously have special duties related to traffic movement.
> **4** Ants move in both directions in single lanes.
> **5** Ants operate a primitive traffic management system.
> **6** Ants sometimes construct simple bridges.
> **7** Force is sometimes used by ants to get rid of congestion.

Paraphrasing

7 Find verbs in the passage that match these meanings.

Example   walk or stride *march*

1 search for	**4** financed	**7** finding your way through
2 solved (a problem)	**5** fulfil (needs)	**8** studied
3 stated publicly	**6** rushing	**9** accepted (an argument)

Star phrase 'ant transport models could help humans **cope with** everything from ...'

1 Guess the meaning from context.

2 Answer the question.

3 Complete the sentence using the star phrase and the words in brackets.

> Could you cope with studying at the same time as doing a full-time job?
>
> I'd like to go .... more often but
> I ....
> (the gym / different types of equipment)

Reading

4 Improving global reading skills

1 ⏱ Take 12 minutes to do the following task.

The Reading passage has nine paragraphs, **A–I**.
*Choose the correct heading for paragraphs **B–I** from the list of headings below.*

List of Headings

i An unexpected preference for modern items
ii Two distinct reasons for selection in one type of museum
iii The growing cost of housing museum exhibits
iv The growing importance of collections for research purposes
v The global 'size' of the problem
vi A place where some collections are unsafe
vii The need to show as much as possible to visitors
viii How unexpected items are dealt with
ix The decision-making difficulties of one museum worker
x The two roles of museums
xi A lengthy, but necessary task

Example	*Answer*
Paragraph **A**	**xi**

1 Paragraph **B** ....
2 Paragraph **C** ....
3 Paragraph **D** ....
4 Paragraph **E** ....
5 Paragraph **F** ....
6 Paragraph **G** ....
7 Paragraph **H** ....
8 Paragraph **I** ....

Behind the scenes at the museum

With more and more of what museums own ending up behind locked doors, curators are hatching plans to widen access to their collections.

A When, in 1938, the Smithsonian National Museum of Natural History, in Washington, DC, decided it had run out of space, it began transferring part of its collection from the cramped attic and basement rooms where the specimens had been languishing to an out-of-town warehouse. Restoring those specimens to pristine condition was a monumental task. One member of staff, for example, spent six months doing nothing but gluing the legs back on to crane flies. But 30 million items and seven years later, the job was done.

B At least for the moment. For the Smithsonian owns 130 million plants, animals, rocks and fossils and that number is growing at over 2 per cent a year. On an international scale, however, such numbers are not exceptional. The Natural History Museum in London has 80 million specimens. And, in a slightly different scientific context, the Science Museum next door to it has 300,000 objects recording the history of science and technology. Deciding what to do with these huge accumulations of things is becoming a pressing problem. They cannot be thrown away, but only a tiny fraction can be put on display.

C The huge, invisible collections behind the scenes at science and natural history museums are the result of the dual functions of these institutions. On the one hand, they are places for the public to go and look at things. On the other, they are places of research – and researchers are not interested merely in the big, showy things that curators like to reveal to the public.

D Blythe House in West London, the Science Museum's principal storage facility, has, as might be expected, cabinets full of early astronomical instruments such as astrolabes and celestial globes. The museum is also custodian to things that are dangerous. It holds a lot of equipment of Sir William Crookes, a 19th century scientist who built the first cathode-ray tubes, experimented with radium and also discovered thallium – an extremely poisonous element. He was a sloppy worker. All his equipment was contaminated with radioactive materials but he worked in an age when nobody knew about the malevolent effects of radioactivity.

E Neil Brown is the senior curator for classical physics, time and microscopes at the Science Museum. He spends his professional life looking for objects that illustrate some aspect of scientific and technological development. Collections of computers, and domestic appliances such as television sets and washing machines, are growing especially fast. But the rapid pace of technological change, and the volume of new objects, makes it increasingly hard to identify what future generations will regard as significant. There were originally, for example, three different versions of the videocassette recorder and nobody knew at the time, which was going to win. And who, in the 1970s, would have realised the enormous effect the computer would have by the turn of the century?

F The public is often surprised at the Science Museum's interest in recent objects. Mr Brown says he frequently turns down antique brass and mahogany electrical instruments on the grounds that they already have enough of them, but he is happy to receive objects such as the Atomic domestic coffee maker, and a 114-piece Do-It-Yourself toolkit with canvas case, and a green beer bottle.

G Natural history museums collect for a different purpose. Their accumulations are part of attempts to identify and understand the natural world. Some of the plants and animals they hold are 'type specimens'. In other words, they are the standard reference unit, like a reference weight or length, for the species in question. Other specimens are valuable because of their age. One of the most famous demonstrations of natural selection in action was made using museum specimens. A study of moths collected over a long period of time showed that their wings became darker (which made them less visible to insectivorous birds) as the industrial revolution made Britain more polluted.

H Year after year, the value of such collections quietly and reliably increases, as scientists find uses that would have been inconceivable to those who started them a century or two ago. Genetic analysis, pharmaceutical development, bio-mimetrics (engineering that mimics nature to produce new designs) and bio-diversity mapping are all developments that would have been unimaginable to the museums' founders.

I But as the collections grow older, they grow bigger. Insects may be small, but there are millions of them and entomologists would like to catalogue every one. And when the reference material is a pair of giraffes or a blue whale, space becomes a problem. That is why museums such as the Smithsonian are increasingly forced to turn to out-of-town storage facilities. But museums that show the public only a small fraction of their material risk losing the goodwill of governments and the public, which they need to keep running. Hence the determination of so many museums to make their back room collections more widely available.

Using context to guess the meaning of words

2 Scan the passage and underline these words and phrases. Use the information, ideas and reference words around them to help you decide on their meaning, in the passage.

1 pristine	**4** custodian to	**7** 'type specimens'
2 not exceptional	**5** sloppy	**8** entomologists
3 dual	**6** domestic appliances	

Using word form to guess the meaning of words

3 Scan the passage for these words. Examine how they are formed and use this information to help you work out what they mean, as they are used in the passage.

Example

word	**part of speech + how it is formed**	**meaning**
collection	noun *collect* + *ion*	group of items that have been put together

1 pressing	**4** increasingly	**7** unimaginable
2 storage	**5** valuable	**8** catalogue
3 sloppy	**6** polluted	**9** goodwill

IELTS Reading test practice   **Sentence completion**

4 ⏲ Take 10 minutes to answer questions 1–8.

> *Complete the sentences below.*
> *Choose **NO MORE THAN THREE WORDS AND/OR A NUMBER** from the passage for each answer.*
>
> **1** It took staff as long as .... to make the items in the Smithsonian collection look as good as new.
> **2** The size of the collection at the Smithsonian Museum is increasing annually by about ....
> **3** As well as putting items on display, science and natural history museums also have a .... function.
> **4** As a result of his carelessness, Sir William Crookes' tools show traces of ....
> **5** Both household equipment and the number of .... are increasing particularly rapidly in Neil Brown's collection.
> **6** At natural history museums, either the .... or the typical features of an item can make it important.
> **7** Pollution caused by the .... in Britain affected the colour of moths' wings.
> **8** .... want to keep a record of every insect, no matter how small it might be.

Star phrase 'Mr Brown says he frequently turns down antique brass and mahogany electrical instruments **on the grounds that** they already have enough of them.'

1 Guess the meaning from context.

2 Answer the question.

3 Complete the sentence using the star phrase and the words in brackets.

I feel that all zoos should be closed on the grounds that animals shouldn't be kept in cages. Do you agree?

The authorities are planning to

....

....

(introduce / road charges / too many cars)

31

Reading

5 Summarising

Paraphrasing

1 Sentences 1–5 are paraphrases of ideas in the passage below. For each paraphrase, underline the words in the passage.

1 There are plenty of reasons why chocolate is popular.

2 The chocolate industry is becoming a global phenomenon.

3 More money is spent advertising sweets and chocolate than any other similar product.

4 Although well-known products achieve the highest sales, new ones are also important.

5 The short-term availability of a new product provides consumers with an interesting and reliable change.

Soft centres – hard profits

Are you being seduced by the sweet industry?

If chocolate were found to be seriously addictive, then the UK would need major therapy to kick the habit. The British lead the world in their love of the cocoa-based treat. As a product, chocolate has a lot going for it, appealing to all ages, both sexes and all income brackets. In 1997, the value of the total UK confectionery market increased by 3% to a staggering £5.2bn, with chocolate sales accounting 5 for 70%, at £3.6bn, and sugar confectionery the remaining £1.6bn.

The UK market has shown consistent growth – increasing over the last decade by around 16%. 'Chocolate confectionery is a market that seems to be remarkably resilient,' says Pamela Langworthy, marketing director for Thorntons, the luxury chocolate producer and retailer. It also increasingly 10 transcends national boundaries. In 1997, Swiss Nestlé, the largest confectioner, exported over a quarter of its production to more than 100 countries. Nestlé has recorded particularly fast growth in confectionery sales in Asia, with the expansion of KitKat into several countries in the region. Eastern Europe 15 provides another promising market. But few markets challenge the UK in terms of current confectionery consumption. In the US, the land associated with excess, each American devours a mere 10kg of confectionery per person a year, whereas UK consumers each manage 16kg. In Europe, where the chocolate 20 market is estimated to be worth over £12bn ($18.5bn), the UK accounts for almost a third of that total, followed some way behind by Germany, France and Italy.

Around 60% of all confectionery is bought on impulse, which makes its availability a key determinant of sales. Impulse buying also makes the development of a strong brand image vital, and large, long-established brands control the market. Building up these brands costs serious money. Media expenditure on confectionery exceeds that for any other impulse market. The Cadbury & Trebor Bassett 1997 Confectionery Review reveals that in 1996 media expenditure on chocolate reached £94m, compared with £69m spent on soft drinks, £31m on the lottery and £23m on crisps and snacks.

Innovation is also essential for ongoing success, despite the chocolate market being dominated by 'consistent performers'. In 1996 the chocolate company Mars launched 'Flyte', claiming to be the first mainstream brand to address the demand for lower fat products. At 98 calories a bar, Flyte is designed to appeal to weight-conscious women. Another 1997 Mars launch, 'Celebrations', is claimed by the company's annual review to be showing signs of 'revolutionising the boxed chocolates market by attracting new, younger customers'. 'Traditionally, the boxed chocolates market hasn't changed very much. People who buy the products tend to be older and female. With Celebrations, we are finding that younger people and men are buying because the chocolates don't come in the traditional-shaped box – they look different. Products such as Flyte and Celebrations are attempts to introduce a different product category and increase sales for retailers, rather than just shifting market share,' a Mars spokesman says.

One feature of the chocolate industry in recent years has been the emergence of special editions. The concept was a marketing triumph. Producers believe that special editions offer the consumer a new and exciting variation of a product, while suggesting the same consistent quality they associate with familiar brands. Since special editions are only available for a few weeks while stocks last, they also have a unique quality about them. Far from denting sales of the straight version, limited editions appear to simply boost overall sales.

IELTS Reading test practice   **Summary completion**

2   Read the summary below. First decide what type of answers you need to look for and complete the table on the right. Then take 5 minutes to complete the summary.

*Choose **NO MORE THAN TWO WORDS AND/OR A NUMBER** from the passage for each answer.*

Chocolate – the figures
The chocolate market in the UK in 1997 was worth 1 ...., having shown a steady increase during the preceding ten-year period. Overall the manufacturer Swiss Nestlé supplies chocolate to over 2 .... and the company has seen rapid sales increases in the markets in 3 .... Nevertheless the UK market remains the biggest – surprisingly, British people eat more than 4 .... consumers. Within the European market their consumption amounts to 5 .... of the total revenue.

Type of answer
1 amount of money
2 ....
3 ....
4 ....
5 ....

3 Check your answers to exercise 2 by completing the following table.

	Find place in passage by scanning for	Word(s) in passage	Rewording in summary
1	UK, 1997	value decade	worth ten-year period
2			supplies over
3			rapid sales increases
4			eat more than (comparison)
5			amounts to

4 Take 6 minutes to complete this summary.

Complete the summary below using words from the box.

The Chocolate Market

The chocolate market is dominated by **1** .... brands. For this reason, confectioners spend large sums of money on **2** .... advertisements. In fact, in 1996, the amount spent totalled £94m.

However, it is also important for companies to allocate resources to developing **3** .... ideas. Examples of these are the 'Flyte' bar and 'Celebrations'. Chocolate producers try to increase sales by changing their customers' **4** .... habits. For example, if a product has an **5** .... image, it may be necessary to alter this.

A **6** .... increase in sales can be achieved by introducing 'special editions' on to the market. These are successful because they have **7** .... value.

A purchasing	**E** impulse	**I** novelty	**M** new
B low-fat	**F** similar	**J** unsuccessful	**N** children's
C selection	**G** eating	**K** well-known	**O** lasting
D media	**H** outdated	**L** international	**P** temporary

Referencing

5 Find the following words and phrases in the passage and state what they refer to.

1 the cocoa-based treat (lines 2–3)
2 the remaining (line 6)
3 It (line 10)
4 the region (line 15)

5 that total (line 22)
6 which (line 24)
7 these brands (line 27)
8 the products (line 39)

Vocabulary builder

6 This passage contains a lot of vocabulary that is used in the subject of economics. Use the text and a dictionary to help you complete this table.

Noun	Verb	The person	Related phrases
product	produce	producer, manufacturer	mass production
market			
sales			
growth			
retail			
brand			
industry			
stocks			
launch			

Star phrase 'with chocolate sales **accounting for** 70% of ...'

1 Guess the meaning from context.

2 Answer the question.

3 Complete the sentence using the star phrase and the words in brackets.

What accounts for the largest part of your personal spending?

The improvements that were made in

....

....

(curriculum / excellent exam pass rates)

Reading

6 Understanding argument

Predicting the content

1 ⏱ Read the title and sub-heading of the passage below and answer these questions.

 a What do you think the verb *ape* means?
 b How do you think the article might be organised?

2 ⏱ Take 5 minutes to read the passage and answer these questions.

 a What did the scientists who wrote this passage want to find out?
 b How did they do this?
 c What two conclusions did the scientists form?

Do apes ape?

Recent studies by two famous scientists investigate whether chimpanzees and other apes can learn by imitation

The notion that the great apes – chimpanzees, gorillas, orang-utans and gibbons – can imitate one another might seem unsurprising to anyone who has watched these animals playing at the zoo. But in
5 scientific circles, the question of whether apes really do 'ape' has become controversial.

Consider a young chimpanzee watching his mother crack open a coula nut, as has been observed in the Taï Forest of West Africa. In most cases, the youth
10 will eventually take up the practice himself. Was this because he imitated his mother? Sceptics think perhaps not. They argue that the mother's attention to the nuts encouraged the youngster to focus on them as well. Once his attention had been drawn
15 to the food, the young chimpanzee learned how to open the nut by trial and error, not by imitating his mother.

Such a distinction has important implications for any
20 discussion of chimpanzee cultures. Some scientists define a cultural trait as one that is passed down not by genetic inheritance but instead when the younger generation copies adult behaviour. If cracking open a coula nut is something that chimpanzees can simply figure out how to do on their own once they hold

25 a hammer stone, then it can't be considered part of their culture. Furthermore, if these animals learn exclusively by trial and error, then chimpanzees must, in a sense, reinvent the wheel each time they tackle a new skill. No cumulative culture can ever develop.

The clearest way to establish how chimpanzees learn is through laboratory experiments. One of us (Whiten), in collaboration with Deborah M. Custance of Goldsmith's College, University of London, constructed artificial fruits to serve as analogues of those the animals must deal with in the wild. In a typical experiment, one group of chimpanzees watched a complex technique for opening one of the fruits, while a second group observed a very different method; we then recorded the extent to which the chimpanzees had been influenced by the method they observed. We also conducted similar experiments with three-year-old children as subjects. Our results demonstrate that six-year-old chimpanzees show imitative behaviour that is markedly like that seen in the children, although the accuracy of their copying tends to be poorer.

In a different kind of experiment, one of us (Boesch), along with some co-workers, gave chimpanzees in the Zurich Zoo in Switzerland hammers and nuts similar to those available in the wild. We then monitored the repertoire of behaviors displayed by the captive chimpanzees. As it turned out, the chimpanzees in the zoo exhibited a greater range of activities than the more limited and focused set of actions we had seen in the wild. We interpreted this to mean that a wild chimpanzee's cultural environment channelled the behavior of youngsters, steering them in the direction of the most useful skills. In the zoo, without the benefit of existing traditions, the chimpanzees experimented with a host of less useful actions.

In our view, these findings taken together suggest that apes do ape and that this ability forms one strand in cultural transmission. Indeed, it is difficult to imagine how chimpanzees could develop certain geographic variations in activities such as ant-dipping and parasite-handling without copying established traditions. They must be imitating other members of their group.

We should note, however, that – just as is the case with humans – certain cultural traits are no doubt passed on by a combination of imitation and simpler kinds of social learning, such as having one's attention drawn to useful tools. Either way, learning from elders is crucial to growing up as a competent wild chimpanzee.

3 🕐 Take 5 minutes to do this task.

> **Questions 1–3**
> Which **THREE** of the following arguments are stated in the passage?
>
> **A** Scientists are in agreement on the copying behaviour of apes.
>
> **B** Young chimpanzees work out how to open nuts by experimenting.
>
> **C** Chimpanzee behaviour is best understood by observing them in their natural habitat.
>
> **D** Children are better imitators than chimpanzees.
>
> **E** Chimpanzees in zoos try out fewer actions than those in the wild.
>
> **F** Activities such as ant-dipping are more rare among chimpanzees these days.
>
> **G** Chimpanzees' observation of parent behaviour is vital to their development.

4 Underline the parts of the passage where the three answers can be found.

5 Underline the parts of the passage that relate to the other options and explain why they are wrong.

6 ⏲ Take 8 minutes to do the following task. Use the grid below to help you.

Classify the following as being a feature of

  A *Whiten's experiment*
  B *Boesch's experiment*
  C *both experiments*
  D *neither research project*

Write the correct letter, **A**, **B**, **C** *or* **D**.

1 Two different groups of chimpanzees were observed.
2 Some of the food items in the experiment were not real.
3 The experiment was conducted on humans.
4 The chimpanzees were not shown how to do anything.
5 Rewards were used for successful behaviour.

	Question	A	B	Answer
1	Two different groups of chimpanzees were observed.			
2	Some of the food items in the experiment were not real.			
3	The experiment was conducted on humans.			
4	The chimpanzees were not shown how to do anything.			
5	Rewards were used for successful behaviour.			

Vocabulary builder

7 The following words are commonly found in research-based texts. Scan the passage for the words, and then try to work out their meaning, as used in the passage. Use a dictionary if you need one to help you decide on the correct meaning. Do you know any other forms of the same word?

Word	Meaning	Other forms? (if any)
notion	*idea*	*notional (based on a notion)*
controversial		
implications		
collaboration		
recorded		
subjects		
monitored		
exhibited		
interpreted		
findings		

Collocations

8 Complete the following sentences using the best word or phrase **A–D**.

1 The newspaper article on language development proved to be .... controversial.
  A highly   **B** greatly   **C** totally   **D** wildly

2 The researchers .... their experiment in an old school gym.
  A put up   **B** set up   **C** built   **D** raised

3 In the second part of the TV documentary, the focus had .... from family life to the community.
  A shifted   **B** gone   **C** slipped   **D** transferred

4 The scientist .... the results of the soil experiment on television.
  A uncovered   **B** offered   **C** presented   **D** exhibited

5 Police .... monitored the traffic for speed.
  A entirely   **B** totally   **C** thoroughly   **D** carefully

6 The planning authorities .... the implications of the proposed new building and decided against it.
  A considered   **B** calculated   **C** estimated   **D** added up

7 It was agreed that organising the project should be a collaborative ....
  A co-operation   **B** co-ordination   **C** process   **D** preparation

Star phrase 'we then recorded **the extent to which** the chimpanzees had been influenced by the method they observed ...'

1 Guess the meaning from context.

2 Answer the question.

3 Complete the sentence using the star phrase and the words in brackets.

To what extent has the DVD market affected the film industry?

People often fail to realise ....
....

(bad language / have influence on children)

Reading

7 Identifying the writer's views and claims

1 Read each of the following texts and then answer the questions.

A

For those people without a family crest and signet ring, there is a place a few inches above the finger where social standing can still be displayed – the wrist. With its ticking heartbeat, the mechanical wristwatch is alive and never felt better. And for most people, the very definition of a luxury watch is a Rolex. It has a mystical aura of high fashion, high quality and high price. It is the most popular high-end watch, with an estimated 750,000 sold annually, and even more changing hands each year in the second-hand market.

A1 Does the writer approve of status symbols?

A2 What words in the text paraphrase *status*?

A3 Which claim is YES, which is NO and which is NOT GIVEN?

    a More people buy Rolex watches new than second-hand.
    b Watches are as popular now as they have ever been.
    c The Rolex is less expensive than it used to be.

B

Big publishing businesses do not really understand books. They are good at marketing bestsellers, but they are incapable of nurturing authors whose books are not immediately profitable. In their obsession with profit margins, they neglect writing that might shore up their companies once the bestsellers have long been forgotten.

B1 What is the writer suggesting?

B2 Can you guess the meaning of *shore up*?

B3 Which opinion is YES, which is NO and which is NOT GIVEN?

    a Publishers should focus more on long-term gains.
    b More effort needs to be put into advertising bestsellers.
    c Consumers are showing a preference for big bookstores.

B4 Which word in the text has a similar meaning to *popular books*?

C

Scientists have scant idea of why we sleep, and find dreaming an even bigger mystery. Theories range from the brain clearing its memory of junk to the liberation of suppressed subconscious urges. The reason for their ignorance lies in the astonishing design of the brain. The most complex known object in the universe, it contains as many nerve cells – neurons – as there are stars in the Milky Way; about 100 billion of them. Each communicates with thousands of its neighbours, generating an unimaginable chatter.

C1 How confident is the writer in the theories of scientists on this subject?

C2 Can you guess the meaning of *scant* and *generating*?

C3 What word in the text means difficult to understand?

C4 Which claim is YES, which is NO and which is NOT GIVEN?

    a There are well-researched reasons why people need to sleep.
    b We know more about how the brain works than we used to.
    c A comparison can be drawn between nerve cells and stars.

D

> Ten years ago, few people appreciated the effect of wide biodiversity on ecosystems. But it is not hard to grasp the case for keeping more species. Having more species in an ecosystem gives it more stability, allows it to retain more nutrients and makes it more productive. Some ecologists reckon that the rate at which species are being lost is so high that, if it continues, palaeontologists of the future will look at the fossil record now being laid down and liken it to earlier mass extinctions such as the one that killed the dinosaurs. Those previous extinctions are thought to have been triggered by external shocks such as an asteroid impact or a huge volcanic eruption. But it is not known how much of each previous extinction – in which at least 95% of all species were lost – was caused directly by the shock and how much by a subsequent unravelling of the ecosystem due to the loss of specific habitats and species. What seems certain is that finding out by repeating the experience will be risky and unpleasant for everyone.

D1 What is the writer's view of current attitudes to this topic?

D2 Can you guess the meaning of *biodiversity*, and *triggered by*?

D3 Which claim is YES, which is NO and which is NOT GIVEN?

    a More species are being lost in some areas of the world than in others.
    b Scientists of the future will see clear differences between our era and that of the dinosaurs.
    c The arguments in favour of conservation are easy to appreciate.

D4 What does 'the experience' in the penultimate line refer to?

E

> Fingerprints, the touchstone of forensic science, have never been subjected to proper scientific scrutiny. For most of the century since it made its courtroom debut, fingerprinting has enjoyed an impeccable reputation for identifying criminals. What jury would acquit a suspect if his prints matched those found at the scene of a crime? It was thus understandable that when a speaker at a recent meeting on Science and the Law held in San Diego by America's Justice Department hinted that the technique might not deserve its aura of infallibility, an FBI agent in the audience was later overheard calling him a rude name. Understandable, but not, says the speaker, Simon Cole, justified. For he is one of a small group of people that has started looking at the technique which, above all others, gave forensic science its scientific status. And, surprisingly, he has found it is scientifically and statistically wanting.

E1 What does the writer think about the FBI agent's comment?

E2 Can you guess the meaning of *scrutiny*, *acquit* and *wanting*?

E3 Which opinion is YES, which is NO and which is NOT GIVEN?

    a Juries used to expect more evidence than fingerprint matches.
    b We may have placed too much trust in fingerprints.
    c Simon Cole is a better judge of fingerprints than many others.

2 ⏱ Take 6 minutes to read the passage and answer the questions below.

Herbal Medicine

Herbal remedies are more popular than ever. Estimates vary, but the global market has grown rapidly in the past decade, and according to the European Herbal Practitioners Association, the European Union market is worth 6.8 billion euros a year.

No one doubts that herbs are full of medicinal chemicals – after all, plants are the source of half the pharmaceuticals in our modern medicine cabinet. Most of the top seven sellers, such as Ginseng and Garlic powder, seem to have something going for them. But why take a risk by swallowing something as unpredictable as plant material when modern science can isolate the active ingredient and serve it to you straight?

Herbalists claim it is because mixtures are better than pure chemicals. They say the dozens of biologically active compounds in a plant work together to produce a greater effect than any one chemical on its own. It sounds like New Age hokum, but scientists are finding that the herbalists are sometimes right.

In fact, herbs could point us towards a whole new generation of drugs. Modern medicine is hooked on the idea of the 'magic bullet' – the pure drug molecule, like aspirin or penicillin. Even multi-drug approaches such as combination therapy for HIV are just more of the same. Each ingredient in the cocktail is a magic bullet in its own right.

Revolutionary though modern medicine has been, there are a host of illnesses, from depression to multiple sclerosis, for which there is no magic bullet. Some respond better to the kind of mixtures found in herbs. Is it time for a rethink?

Do the following statements agree with the claims of the writer in the Reading passage?

Write
YES   *if the statement agrees with the claims of the writer*
NO   *if the statement contradicts the claims of the writer*
NOT GIVEN   *if it is impossible to say what the writer thinks about this*

1 More herbal remedies are sold in the European Union than anywhere else in the world.
2 It is widely known that herbal medicines lack proper chemical ingredients.
3 The risks associated with herbal medicine are well documented.
4 Research has provided some evidence for the effectiveness of herbal ingredients.
5 Combination therapy is based on the same concept as herbal medicine.
6 Some current illnesses are more effectively treated by herbal remedies than by modern medicine.

⭐ **Star phrase** 'But it is not hard to grasp **the case for** keeping
more species.'

1 Guess the meaning from context.

2 Answer the question.

3 Complete the sentence using the star phrase and the words in brackets.

> Do you think there is a case for refusing medical treatment to people who smoke?

Do the effects of global warming mean

....

.... (restrict / air travel)

Reading

1   Look at the texts on this page and answer these questions.

   a What is similar about the two texts?
   b Who are these texts written for?

2   Answer the questions below.

*Choose **NO MORE THAN THREE WORDS** from the texts for each answer.*

PICASSO MUSEUM
Château Grimaldi, Antibes, France

The Picasso Museum of Antibes is housed in a beautiful old villa built on ground that was once occupied by the ancient Greeks and later by the Romans. Picasso himself lived in the house and painted there in 1946.

Guided tours can be organised on request. There are several programmes for children (ages 4–11) and workshop visits for school groups on Wednesdays and holidays.

June 1 – September 30 10am – 6pm
October 1 – May 31 10am – noon and 2 – 6pm

Closed Mondays and holidays

NATIONAL MARITIME MUSEUM

WHAT'S ON TODAY?
- Enjoy the display of Tall Ships on the harbour
- Watch two tug boats guide a cruise ship into port
- Experience the conditions on board The Vampire submarine
- Learn about Captain Cook's original sailing ship The Endeavour – short film in theatre

CAFÉ
Refreshments with views of the harbour

MUSEUM SHOP
Crammed with books and unusual souvenirs

VOLUNTEERS
Opportunities exist for interested people to donate their time by becoming tour guides at the museum. Enquire at the Volunteers' desk.

PHOTOGRAPHY
Use of flash not permitted inside the museum.

HOURS
10am – 5pm daily, except Christmas Day

1   Where is the Picasso Museum?
2   Who once lived in the villa?
3   When are there special programmes for schoolchildren?
4   Which months is it open all day?
5   Which of the boats can you visit at the Maritime Museum?
6   What can you see from the café?
7   Where can you find out about showing people around the museum?
8   What should you not do in the museum?
9   When is the Maritime Museum not open to the public?

Group activity

3 Get into small groups and select one of the following topics.
English language courses   jobs   travel   films   restaurants

- Cut out some adverts from magazines on your chosen topic and bring them to class.
- In groups, pick the six most interesting adverts and paste them onto an A4 sheet of paper.
- Write some 'short answer questions' on your set of adverts. Make sure they can be answered in three words.
- Exchange sets of adverts and questions with another group and answer the questions.

4 Read the leaflet below and answer these questions.

a What does the heading tell the reader?
b Who is most likely to read this leaflet?
c How many parts are there to the leaflet and how do they differ in style?
d Underline any unfamiliar words and try to guess their meaning from their position in the text.

PHYSIOTHERAPY AND SPORTS INJURIES

Sport is a vital part of our lives. It provides exercise, social contact, relaxation, competition and promotes well-being. It may also cause injuries, many of which can be prevented. Most sports injuries can be effectively treated by your physiotherapist, enabling you to return to your sporting activities as soon as possible.

COMMON INJURIES
- Bruises
- Sprains and tears
- Muscle strains
- Overuse injuries
- Stress fractures

HOW YOU CAN PREVENT THEM
- Correct warm-up and warm-down exercises
- Proper stretching exercises
- Protective strapping in some cases
- Correct footwear
- Good general fitness

+ Family Pharmacy Health Tips +

---

5 Read the leaflet again and answer these questions.

1 The information is
   A aimed at professional sportsmen and women.
   B offered as part of a training course.
   C designed for physiotherapy students.
   D intended for anyone who does sport.

2 What does the leaflet say about sports injuries?
   A They are often avoidable.
   B Some are worse than others.
   C They can happen easily.
   D They can put people off sport.

Vocabulary builder

6 Find a single word in the *Physiotherapy and Sports Injuries* leaflet which has the same meaning as the following phrases.

1 extremely important ....
2 good health ....
3 make something happen ....
4 stopped from occurring ....
5 using something too much ....
6 making it possible

7 ⏲ Read the information leaflet about Australia and take 10 minutes to answer questions 1–10.

Welcome to Australia!
Essential Information for Travellers

The great outdoors
Australia is the world's oldest continent and indigenous Australians have one of the world's oldest cultures.

In Australia you will see some of the most beautiful scenery in the world. Many parks have information centres offering advice on where to go, what to see and, most importantly, how to see it. Pick up some leaflets, for both your personal safety and to protect our unique plants and animals.

Banks and money matters
Banks are generally open between 9.30am and 4.00pm on Monday to Thursday and between 9.30am and 5.00pm on Friday.

Foreign currency or traveller's cheques can be changed at all banks and some of the larger hotels. There are currency exchange facilities at all international airports.

The sun
Take care! Our sunlight is very strong and you can get sunburnt.

For best sun protection, it is advisable to wear:

★ broad brimmed hat   ★ shirt with collar and sleeves   ★ sun screen with high protection factor

Swimming
We have so many beautiful places to swim – beaches, lakes, rivers and creeks.

★ Many of our waters are safe for swimming, but if you have any doubts, ask before entering the water.

★ Most of our popular ocean beaches have patrols with a lifesaving service. Red and yellow flags mark the area that you are advised to swim within. Blue flags often indicate danger.

★ If there are no flags and no lifeguards on the beach, talk to local people about the best areas to swim.

Staying safe on the roads
★ Australians drive on the LEFT hand side of the road.

★ For safety, everyone in the car, including children, must wear a seatbelt.

★ Motor cyclists and bicyclists are required by law to wear a helmet.

★ Watch out for native animals crossing the roads, especially at night.

Questions 1–6
Write   **TRUE**   *if the statement agrees with the information*
       FALSE   *if the statement contradicts the information*
       NOT GIVEN *if there is no information on this*

1 Written guidance on caring for the environment is often provided.
2 You can always change money at the hotels.
3 You run the greatest risk of sunburn at the beach.
4 You can only swim if there are lifeguards on the beach.
5 It is illegal to ride a bicycle without wearing a helmet.
6 Many native animals are killed on the roads at night.

Questions 7–10
Write **NO MORE THAN THREE WORDS AND/OR A NUMBER** for each answer.

7 Banks have longer opening hours on ....
8 Clothes and strong .... are recommended in hot weather.
9 Flags indicating where it is safe to swim are coloured ....
10 It is obligatory for car passengers to ....

Reading

Understanding paraphrase

1 Read the short text below and underline the words which have the same meaning as the words or phrases (1–8) in the box.

Ideas that make a difference

A series of public lectures by prominent international speakers will be held in Sydney throughout the year. Guaranteed to stimulate discussion and debate, this is a unique opportunity to learn about everything from politics and sociology to science and religion. The first speaker in the series is Prof. Frank Furedi, a sociologist from the University of Kent in the UK. He is in Australia as a guest of the Queensland government for the 'Ideas Festival' taking place in Brisbane in April.

1 the study of society
2 encourage or generate
3 conversation
4 well-known or famous
5 someone who has been invited to do something
6 talks
7 around the world
8 lecturer

2 Read the text in exercise 1 again and complete each of the following statements with the best ending **A–H**.

1 The lecturers come from ....
2 The series of talks will take place in ....
3 The talks should generate ....
4 Prof. Furedi has been invited by ....

A the government of Queensland
B Brisbane
C scientific research
D Sydney
E around the world
F heated conversation
G interest in sociology
H the University of Kent

3 Look at the paragraph headings **i–x** below, which relate to the text *College Services* on page 47.
Match the idea contained in each heading to the alternative expressions 1–10. The first one has been done for you.

List of Headings

i Cultural events
ii Exchange programmes
iii Formal means of assessment
iv Getting around the campus
v Financial assistance
vi Special consideration
vii College regulations
viii Personal identification
ix Study skills workshops
x Writing skills

Alternative expressions

1 rules governing the way things are done
2 arrangements for studying abroad
3 artistic activities such as concerts or theatre
4 funding provided by the college
5 ability to produce a written paper or assignment
6 particular attention because of a problem
7 something which shows who you are
8 ways of measuring your performance
9 special classes to help improve your learning strategies
10 moving around the college grounds

4 🕐 Take 8 minutes to do questions 1–6.

*The text below has seven paragraphs **A–G**.*
*Choose the correct heading (**i–x**) from the list of headings on the previous page.*

Example   *Answer*
Paragraph **A**   **x**

1 Paragraph **B** ....   **4** Paragraph **E** ....
2 Paragraph **C** ....   **5** Paragraph **F** ....
3 Paragraph **D** ....   **6** Paragraph **G** ....

COLLEGE SERVICES
Essential information for students

A For many courses at our College, your marks will be based on two pieces of written work so you need to develop your skills as a writer. You will also be asked to produce some practical work to demonstrate your grasp of the subject. Most departments offer advice and guidelines on how to present your work but the requirements may vary from one department to another.

B There are two examination periods each year at the end of each semester. The first period is in June and the second in November. Additionally, individual departments may have tests at other times, using various methods such as "take-home" exams or assignments.

C If you feel your performance in an examination has been affected by illness or a personal problem, you should talk to the Course Co-ordinator in your department and complete a special form. Each case is judged on its own merits depending on individual circumstances.

D The College has arrangements with similar institutions in North America, Europe and Asia. The schemes are open to all students and allow you to complete a semester or a year of your course overseas. The results you gain are credited towards your final certificate. This offers an exciting chance to broaden your horizons and enrich your learning experience in a different environment and culture.

E Youth Allowance payments or government funding may be available to full-time students. Reimbursement of travel costs may also be available in some cases. Scholarships are also on offer, but these are competitive and the closing date for applications is 31 October in the year before the one for which the funds are sought.

F Your student card, which you get on completion of enrolment, is proof that you are enrolled. Please take special care of it and carry it with you when you are at the college. It is proof of who you are and you may be asked to show it to staff at any time. This card is also your discount card for the canteen as well as allowing you access to the library.

G The Students' Club provides opportunities for a wide range of activities, including the production of films, plays and concerts, as well as art and photo exhibitions of work done by the students. If you have a creative idea in mind, pick up a form from the office on Level 3 of the Administration Building.

5 Read the text on page 47 again and answer questions 1–5 below.

Answer the questions below.

Use **NO MORE THAN THREE WORDS** *from the passage for each answer.*

1 In addition to written work, what must most students prepare in order to receive their course marks?
2 At which time of the year are examinations held?
3 What expenses can some students claim back?
4 Where can you get reductions using your student card?
5 Which body organises displays of students' work?

Vocabulary builder

6 Read the text again and find words which have the same meaning as these definitions.

Example   one of the sections of a school or college   *department*

1 a piece of work set by your teacher, often with a deadline
2 a set of rules which tell you how to do something
3 a division of the academic year
4 someone who organises a course
5 money which is given back to you
6 a document proving who you are
7 to register at a college for a course
8 a reduction in price
9 a display of artwork

7 Using words you found in exercise 6, complete the notes below.
Use one word only for each space.

Advice for new students

When you first arrive at college, you will need to **1** .... in the subjects that you have chosen to study. For each course there is a **2** .... , who is responsible for organising the programme, and you should make sure that you introduce your-self to him or her early in the **3** .... In that way, if you need to make any changes to your programme, you will know who to speak to. The form of assessment for each course varies from one **4** .... to another, but most will use a combination of examinations and **5** .... and there will be a set of **6** .... explaining how this works.

Your **7** .... is an important document as it provides proof of your identity, so keep it on you at all times. It enables you to borrow books from the library and also entitles you to a **8** .... in the cafeteria.

Reading

Understanding paraphrase

1 Quickly skim the full text on the next page and say what it is about.

2 Read paragraphs **A–D** again and find words or expressions which mean the same as these.

1 playing sport for a living
2 scientists investigating a topic
3 speed
4 think / consider
5 tired
6 employees

7 in the lead / leading
8 natural aptitude
9 sportsmen and women
10 equivalent (thing or person) in another country
11 where research takes place outside the laboratory
12 observation

| **IELTS Reading test practice** | **Finding information in paragraphs** |

3 ⏱ Read paragraphs **A–H** on the next page and take 8 minutes to answer these questions. The words which will help you to identify the type of information you are looking for have been underlined.

> Which paragraph contains the following information?
> **NB** *You may use any letter more than once.*
>
> 1 <u>the idea that</u> athletes can predict their opponents' actions
>
> 2 <u>a description</u> of a virtual sports environment
>
> 3 <u>two areas</u> where the AIS has previously excelled
>
> 4 <u>an example</u> of what a specially designed item of footwear can do
>
> 5 <u>a description</u> of an exercise designed to promote concentration
>
> 6 <u>reference</u> to a study which is highly regarded by another nation

4 Scan the text again to find where these people are first mentioned and say what role each of them has.

	Paragraph	Role
1 Michelle Wilkins	....	....
2 Damien Farrow	....	....
3 Jana Pittman	....	....
4 Allan Hahn	....	....
5 Eddie Jones	....	....

Creating the champions

A coach's tool used to consist of a stopwatch, a whistle and an ear-shattering voice, but science is changing that

A In the heart of the Australian Institute of Sport (AIS) a scientist holds up a shoe that looks exactly like those worn by every professional football team in the country. Except this one is special. Champion hurdler Jana Pittman has been helping researchers test a running version of this shoe which can measure the amount of time feet are in contact with the ground, and the degree of their power and velocity.

B Scientists reckon they can use this information to monitor not only the physiology of specific feet and how people run, but to locate the point at which athletes become fatigued. Researchers need to find the exact moment when fatigue sets in, so that training and competition days are maximised. Eddie Jones, who coached the Australian rugby team for many years, worked out that he could use such foot technology to determine the strength of his team.

C At the AIS pool, Olympic medallists wear matchbox-sized gadgets on their backs, which relay incredible detail about every stroke they make during each training lap. Jones has his eye on this, too. "We are looking at the technology to accelerate our performance," he explains. "It's all in the margins, but I can see the benefits already after 12 months."

D Being ahead of the game is the aim of AIS staff in developing new sports technologies. In the past they have been at the forefront of global sports science in areas such as talent identification and some altitude-training techniques. But Professor Allan Hahn, the institute's Head of Physiology for the past 21 years, is most excited by two streams of emerging technology. "These will ensure that our athletes maintain their edge over our international counterparts." One stream concerns the way athletes learn their skills; the other takes the laboratory into the field to allow continuous monitoring of performances using micro-technology.

E Damien Farrow is a skills acquisition specialist at the AIS and has already brought about changes to the way athletes learn their skills in team sports such as netball, basketball, cricket, tennis, hockey and water polo. He does this by videoing the games at very close range and using the footage as part of the training. Everyone knows that the truly talented athletes have an innate ability to "read the play". But can everyone learn this? Farrow believes – and his research bears this out – that the truly great players can anticipate exactly what is going to happen. And he thinks this can be taught.

F In one of the rooms of the AIS, the windows have been blacked out with cardboard. The room is filled with the sound of crowds jeering, the olfactory senses are overloaded with the odour of sweat and liniment, and an elite netball player puts on 3-D glasses to study a screen displaying sections of a game from the previous weekend. At a certain point the image is blanked and the player has to make an instant decision where to throw the ball. Once she has improved her decision-making response time, she will have to repeat the exercise, this time distracted by annoying beeps, or by having to sing a song, or by having the tape of the game sped up.

G AIS netball coach Michelle Wilkins says such training makes her players more self-aware and because they react like lightning, they have more time to execute the play. "They become conscious of where they should be in relation to their fellow players and they are now far more analytical about their game," she says.

H Farrow says the speed and/or accuracy of responses increases 5 to 10 per cent doing these exercises. He has had great success with football goalkeepers – to the extent that Italian football authorities want to buy his research. What Farrow has found is that the cue to read where the ball is headed is not the foot or the ankle, nor can you tell by reading the shooter's eyes. "The foot can disguise the shot easily and the best players do that all the time," says Farrow. Instead, the goalkeepers are trained to look at the angle and rotation of the hips and the pelvis, and he knows this because high-tech skeletal images of footballers show the hips never lie.

5   Read paragraphs **A–H** again and take 10 minutes to answer the questions.

Look at the following statements (questions 1–6) and the list of people.

Match each statement with the correct person.
NB *You may use any letter more than once.*

1   Using simulation can greatly improve an athlete's responses.
2   Knowing when players get tired could help assess a team's potential.
3   The new coaching techniques will guarantee a leading position worldwide for Australian sports people.
4   Becoming more responsive leads to better teamwork.
5   Talented sports people know how to trick their opponents.
6   Monitoring performance electronically can achieve results within a year.

List of People

A   Eddie Jones
B   Allan Hahn
C   Damien Farrow
D   Michelle Wilkins

6   Read the last two paragraphs of the text and then take 8 minutes to complete the summary below so that the original meaning is unchanged.

Alongside advances in the way athletes learn skills, one of the most radical developments in training has been the use of micro-technology, coupled with Bluetooth or GPSW satellite transmission to send intricate data back to coaches, such as the stroke rate in rowing or swimming. The idea is to have every training session monitored in the field, rather than haul in athletes at regular intervals to train under simulated conditions. It is a direct and less intrusive way of collecting masses more information.

In the future sports with more subjective judging criteria such as snowboarding, will be able to use technology to improve the objectivity of scoring. The devices will record the length of time a snowboarder is in the air, the altitude, and spin speed and height, for instance. Judges will only need to decide how spectacular they thought the performance looked. And, of course, all of that data will provide some nifty graphics for the TV camera.

Complete the summary below using words from the box.

As well as improving how sportsmen and women acquire
1 .... , it is possible to transmit detailed
2 .... direct to the trainers from the track, field or pool.
This has made a significant difference to how athletes train. It is envisaged
that all training will soon be **3** .... in this manner as
opposed to monitoring the athletes in **4** .... conditions.
And sports which are scored by a group of **5** .... will no
longer have to rely on the **6** .... of this panel, thanks to
the introduction of the technology.

A expertise	**J** lawyers
B messages	**K** statistics
C observed	**L** done
D talent	**M** indoor
E unusual	**N** experts
F opinions	**O** conducted
G instructions	**P** graphics
H artificial	**Q** altered
I coaches	**R** players

Writing

Interpreting charts, tables, graphs and diagrams

Vocabulary: choosing the right words

⊙ The **Cambridge Learner Corpus** tells us that IELTS candidates often make errors such as these:

A large <u>amount of people</u> enjoy snow sports. ✗
The <u>quantity of men</u> looking after children at home is growing. ✗

Get it right!

number is used with countable nouns: *A small **number** of cars are still made by hand.* ✓
amount is used with uncountable nouns: *The desert contains a large **amount** of sand.* ✓
quantity is often used for things that can be measured: *The world consumes a large **quantity** of oil.* ✓
Often the plural form is used: *Elephants consume large **quantities** of vegetation.* ✓

Some uncountable nouns go better with *level* than *amount*: *The **level** of carbon dioxide in the atmosphere is rising.* ✓
A phrase is often formed by putting *level(s)* after the noun: *crime levels* ✓

All these words are used with the preposition *of* when they come before the noun.

NB *Figure(s)* is sometimes used to replace *numbers* when describing data, e.g. though we say *number of people in a country*, we refer to *population figures*.

1 Complete these sentences using one of the words in the box. You may have to form a plural.

quantity (of)	number (of)	amount (of)	level (of)	figure

Example
The _number of_ female managers in companies has increased.

1 There has been a decrease in the .... fruit consumed by children in the last twenty years.
2 The graph shows the .... tourists who visited Brazil between 2000 and 2006 and the .... money they spent.
3 Pollution .... in industrialised countries increased rapidly during the last century.
4 The population .... for developing countries are predicted to decrease over the next 50 years.
5 In summer the .... ultraviolet in sunlight is higher than in winter.
6 Large .... palm oil are being produced in Brunei.
7 Solar panels and wind farms can generate a large .... power.
8 Increasing .... schoolchildren are being educated to the age of 16 and beyond.

Vocabulary: choosing words that go well together

⊙ The **Cambridge Learner Corpus** tells us that IELTS candidates often make errors such as these:

a <u>big</u> amount ✗
the <u>great</u> level ✗
<u>More number of people</u> watch television in the evening than during the day. ✗

Get it right!

Use *huge/great/large/small* with *number, amount* and *quantity*: *a large amount* ✓
Use *high/low* with *level* and *figures*: *a high level* ✓; *low inflation figures* ✓
Be careful with comparatives and superlatives:
A greater number of people / More people watch television in the evening than during the day. ✓

2 Correct the highlighted phrases.

Example
There is a low number of computers in primary schools in Africa.
There is a small number of computers in primary schools in Africa.

1 Vegetable soup contains a low quantity of fat.
2 The company has ordered a high number of IT equipment.
3 Some planes carry a very great amount of passengers.
4 Smog levels were large in the middle of the day.
5 The reptile museum receives a little quantity of visitors during the day.
6 A high number of chocolate is made in Belgium.
7 Cholesterol levels are small in Asian countries.
8 Planes produce more amount of pollution than cars.

3 Write a one-sentence introduction to each chart below, then complete the gaps in the sentences.

1 The .... fish caught in the Pacific Ocean is .... that caught in the other two oceans.

2 The .... fish is caught in the Indian Ocean.

3 .... fish is caught in the Atlantic Ocean than the Indian Ocean.

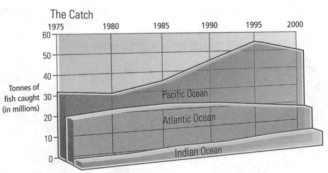

4 Between 2000 and 2040, the population figures for China are predicted to be .... than those for India.

5 In 2050, it is predicted that .... people will be living in India than in China.

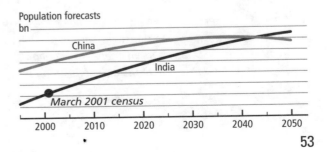

53

Writing

2 Describing trends

Grammar: using correct verb forms

> ⊙ The **Cambridge Learner Corpus** tells us that IELTS candidates often make errors such as this:
>
> *Then in 1992, the number of storms <u>rised up</u> to ten.* ✗
>
> ### Get it right!
>
> *Then in 1992, the number of storms **rose to** ten.* ✓
>
> Learn these verb forms:
> *rise – rose – has/have risen   fall – fell – has/have fallen*
>
> When adding the data and using *to*, you must not use *down* or *up* with these verbs.
>
> **NB** Use a *rise/fall **in*** + noun: *There was a significant **fall in** the number of animals in the park.* ✓

1 Read the box above and then correct the highlighted words in the following sentences.

   1 In some countries, unemployment is raising fast.
   2 At 3 p.m. each day audience figures are expected to rise up to about 45,000.
   3 Pollution levels rised since 1997 at 60 parts per million.
   4 Spending falls down in 2003 into approximately US$ 33 billion and then raise steadily in the next two years.
   5 In the next ten years, average literacy levels are going to raise to record levels worldwide but the number of graduates fell down during the same period.

Grammar: forming noun phrases

> ⊙ The **Cambridge Learner Corpus** tells us that IELTS candidates often make errors such as this:
>
> *There was a <u>slightly increased</u> in the number of fires in the dry season.* ✗
>
> ### Get it right!
>
> The noun forms are *increase/decrease* and both are used with the preposition *in*:
> *There was a slight increase in the number of fires in the dry season.* ✓
>
> *Increasing/decreasing* can be used as adjectives with *number, amount* and *levels*.
> The noun *trend* goes with *downward* or *upward* NOT *increasing*.
> *Japan has an increasing trend of ageing population.* ✗
> *There is **an upward trend in** the age of the population in Japan.* ✓
>
> **NB** *Increased* and *decreased* are past participles. *Increasement* is not a word.

2 Read the box on the previous page and then correct the highlighted parts of the following sentences. Add any necessary words.

Example
The graph shows a huge increased trend of people working from home.
The graph shows an upward trend in the number of people working from home.

1 There was a decrease of demand for sportswear in winter. *in the number*
2 There is an increased figure for paper used in offices.
3 The chart predicts a slight decreased birth rate.
4 Between 1995 and 2005, a decreased trend of crime took place.
5 After 2009, a steady increasement in the population is predicted.

Vocabulary: using precise words

3 Fill the gaps in the summary of this graph with an appropriate word or phrase. Use adjectives and adverbs to make the description as precise as possible and add any necessary prepositions. Some words are given to help you.

Demand for electricity during a televised World Cup football match

Before the match begins, demand for electricity is **1** _constant_ at about 28,500 units. There is a **2** (fall) _slight fall_ in demand during the first half of the match but then demand **3** (rise) _____ a peak of 29,000 units during half time. At the start of the second half, the demand for electricity **4** (drop) _____ and hits its **5** (point) _____ at 26,000 units.

In the thirty minutes before full time, the graph shows a **6** (rise) _____ just over 28,000 units. However, at the beginning of extra time there is another **7** (fall) _____ and a levelling off for a short period, before demand **8** (return) _____ normal.

Content: providing an overview of the information

4 Add the introduction and overview to the summary above.

5 Write an introduction and overview to the table below.

Percentage of Japanese school-leavers going to university					
	1960	1970	1980	1990	2000
Boys	15	25	40	33	42
Girls	3	8	12	15	25
Total	18	33	52	48	67

Coherence: linking ideas

6 Write the rest of the answer for the table above. Try to use words or phrases from the box to link your ideas. Compare your answer with the key, underlining the linkers in both.

but then	although	but	even though	generally	
however	overall	this	which	while	with

55

Writing

3 Summarising information

Grammar: using prepositions correctly

1 Complete the text about this chart using prepositions from the box.

at	by	from	in	over	to	to

Some changes took place, **1** _____ a two-year period, in the way the farmland was used. While the area devoted to some crops increased **2** _____ size, less land was used for others.

The area of land used to grow vegetables increased **3** _____ two **4** _____ three hectares. However, the area of land used for fruit cultivation fell **5** _____ half a hectare **6** _____ one hectare. The uncultivated area remained the same **7** _____ two hectares.

Grammar: making predictions

> ◉ The **Cambridge Learner Corpus** tells us that IELTS candidates often make errors such as this:
>
> *It is <u>predict</u> the population will grow.* ✗
>
> #### Get it right!
>
> We usually use verbs like *predict, forecast* and *estimate* in the passive when describing data:
> *It is **predicted/forecast/estimated** that the population will grow.* ✓
> *Crime levels **are predicted/forecast/estimated** to rise.* ✓
> **NB** The past participle of *forecast* is irregular.
>
> If you want to use the active voice, you must include a subject:
> ***Experts / The chart(s)** predict(s)/forecast(s)/estimate(s) that crime levels will rise.*

2 Make complete sentences using the words given. You may need to change the form of some words and add other words.

Example
Estimate / *people* / *world* / reach / 11 billion / 2200
It is estimated that the number of people in the world will reach 11 billion by the year 2200.

1 Forecast / *popularity* / *science subjects* / *at university* / fall / sharp / next ten years
2 Estimate / *pollution levels* / *the 1900s* / higher than / today
3 Forecast / *global population figures* / reach / 10 billion / 2050
4 Predict / *more children* / *adults* / obese / 2030
5 Predict / *number* / *hours* / *people spend* / *watch TV* / fall / while / amount time / using technology / rise
6 Estimate / *average person* / *Britain* / consume / 74,802 cups of tea / in their lifetime

3 Rewrite each sentence in exercise 2, starting with the words in italics.

Example
The number of people in the world is estimated to reach 11 billion by the year 2200.

Grammar: forming complex sentences

You need to use some complex sentences to have a chance of scoring Band 5 or above for Grammar. Sometimes you can join two simple sentences together to make a complex sentence by using an *-ing* form.

You can often do this when adding more information about a trend or when describing trends that hit a low, reach a peak or stabilise:
*The number of households rose in Canada, **reaching** 11.8 million in 2004.*

NB Remember to put a comma before the *-ing* clause.

4 Join these sentence pairs together to make one complex sentence. First, underline the verb that will change to the *-ing* form.

Example
In 2005, crime levels rose again. They <u>reached</u> a peak of 225 cases per week.
In 2005, crime levels rose again, reaching a peak of 225 cases per week.

1 Between 2005 and 2006 the amount of rainfall decreased. It hit a low of 2mm per month in the summer of 2006.
2 Standards in hospitals rose in the 1960s. They showed a 20% improvement over the previous decade.
3 The average number of hours children spend on computers is predicted to increase over the next five years. It will reach a peak of ten hours a day.
4 Sales figures for 2007 fluctuated. They were high at the beginning of the year and low at the end.

Writing

4 Comparing and grouping information

Coherence: using reference words and nouns to avoid repetition

1 Reference words like *this, these* and *their* can be used to link ideas. Complete these sentences by adding an appropriate noun from the box after each reference word. You may have to form a plural.

> ~~activity~~   facility   feature   figure   industry   popularity
> product   resource   significance   use

Example
Forty-five per cent of girls say they enjoy sewing, painting and dancing. However, *these* _activities_ are less popular among boys.

1 Tunnels and caves are sometimes found in limestone rock. *These* _product_ are produced by acid rain.

2 Mobile phones are used by many people around the world but *their* _popularity_ has grown at different rates in different countries.

3 Mexico spends over $2,000 million on imports of oil and natural gas, as it doesn't have enough of *these important* _resource_ to meet demand.

4 In 1995 skateboarding was enjoyed by 65 per cent of boys. Since then, *this* _figure_ has fallen.

5 Air travel produces a lot of greenhouse gases and the level of emissions from *this* _____ is rising every year.

Coherence: using linkers and comparatives

2 Fill gaps 1–9 in the paragraphs below using linkers and comparatives.

The table compares top performance between men and women in five major running events.

Running event	Men	Women	% difference
100 metre sprint	9.95 secs	10.49 secs	6.1
1500 metre sprint	2 min, 27.37 secs	3 mins 50.45 secs	10
Marathon	2 hrs, 6 mins, 50 secs	2 hrs, 21 mins, 6 secs	10
24-hours	178 miles	154 miles	15.6
6-days	640 miles	548 miles	16.8

The table provides information about speed and distance for men and women in different major running events. Looking at the figures overall, it can be seen that men are generally **1** _brightest_ than women in these races, but the gap is greatest in the long-distance races and it is **2** _____ in the sprints.

In the long-distance events, men can run up to 640 miles in six days, **3** _whereas_ women can only manage 548 miles. This amounts to a difference of 16.8 per cent.

4 _____ in the 100-metre sprint, the percentage difference is much

58

5 _____ , at 6.1 per cent.

In between these two extremes, there is a ten per cent difference in speed for **6** _____ the 1500-metre sprint and the marathon and a **7** _____ per cent difference in the distances that men and women can cover in the 24-hour event. For this event, the fastest men can run 178 miles **8** _____ 154 miles for women, which marks the second **9** _____ significant difference in performance.

Grammar: using correct tense and voice

The diagram below shows how cocoa beans are prepared for export to countries that make chocolate.

3 Complete the gaps in the following description by changing the verbs in brackets into the correct form, where necessary.

Cocoa beans have to undergo a number of different processes, so that they lose their bitter taste and are ready to **1** _be manufactured_ (manufacture) into chocolate.

Initially they **2** _____ (ferment). Once a pod is ripe, it is cut open and the beans and pulp **3** _____ (remove) and heaped onto a layer of banana leaves. Here, they **4** _____ (leave) under the hot sun for six days to ferment. During this time, they **5** _____ (turn) from purple to brown.

When the beans have been fermented, they **6** _____ (spread out) on raised mats and left to dry for ten to twenty days. After this, the farmers **7** _____ (pour) the dry cocoa beans into sacks, which are then **8** _____ (take) to the local agent. He or she weighs the beans and checks that they are good quality before **9** _____ (buy) them from the farmers.

Finally, the sacks of beans are transported to a port and **10** _____ (load) onto a ship for export. Eventually they will **11** _____ (make) into chocolate and **12** _____ (eat) by consumers.

Writing

5 Planning a letter

Content: covering the task fully

1 Read this example of a General Training Writing task and complete the first table below with some realistic information that you could use in a letter.

> You recently took a part-time job working for a local company.
> After a few weeks you realised there were some problems with the job.
>
> Write a letter to the manager of the company. In your letter
> - explain why you took the job
> - describe the problems that you experienced
> - suggest what could be done about them

Job	Why I took it	Problems I had	Suggestions
telesales	good hours / reasonable money		

2 Look at the table below which gives five possible writing tasks, **a–e**. Choose three tasks and note down some realistic ideas for each point.

a Letter to travel company about a holiday you booked with them	b Letter to a friend about a museum or gallery you visited recently	c Letter to a transport company about a method of transport	d Letter to a tutor about something that happened in a lecture that concerned you	e Letter to a friend about your new accommodation
• details of the holiday	• why you went to the museum or gallery	• when and why you use this method of transport	• details of the course and lecture	• why you have moved
• good and bad points about the holiday	• what you saw	• criticisms of the transport service	• what happened during the lecture	• a description of the new accommodation and its location
• request for information on a future holiday	• why you do / do not recommend it	• suggestions regarding how the service could be improved	• how this has affected you / your work	• an invitation to your friend to visit you

3 ⏱ Pick one of the topics **a–e** above and write a letter in 15 minutes. Use the three points in the column as the framework for your letter. Remember to use the correct level of formality.

Coherence: organising your points logically and clearly

4 Read this example of a GT Writing task and the sample paragraph below. There are two reasons why this paragraph would lose marks, even though it contains no grammatical mistakes. What are they?

> *Last week you went to a musical concert. You were very impressed with the performance.*
>
> *Write a letter to a friend about the concert. In your letter*
> - *say what the concert was and why you went*
> - *describe the performance*
> - *suggest why he/she should go to the concert*

> Last week I went to see a musical concert and I was very impressed with the performance. It was a group from South Africa. Their name was "The Swing Band". My mother came. It was her birthday.

5 Rewrite the paragraph so that you would not lose marks.

6 Here is a different answer to the same task. What notes did the writer work with? Complete the notes below.

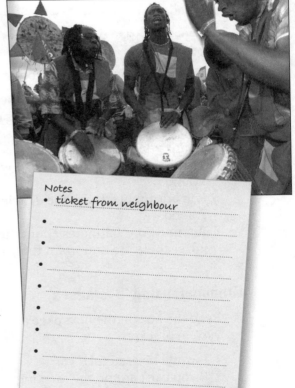

> Dear Katy,
> I must tell you about the concert that I went to see last Monday. I didn't know about the event but my neighbour came round the night before with a spare ticket for an African percussion band called 'Jangle Jive'.
> As I had nothing planned for the evening, I agreed to go and the whole evening was amazing. The players wore the most beautiful, brightly coloured clothes and the scenery changed as the evening progressed from sunrise, at the start, to sunset at the end of the show. As for the music, the most memorable part was a fifteen-minute number called 'Jungle Rhythms', which included lots of animal sounds that were made using drums and many other weird and wonderful instruments.
> I'm pretty sure they will be playing in your town next month and I really recommend that you go. You may think drums are loud and boring but wait till you hear this! Even you will say it's a great sound!
> Take care,
> May

Notes
- ticket from neighbour
- ....
- ....
- ....
- ....
- ....
- ....
- ....
- ....

7 Underline the words and expressions that the writer uses to introduce and link the points together.

Writing

 Communicating your message

Vocabulary: using appropriate expressions

1 Match the opening sentences 1–5 to the situations **A–E** in the box. Underline the words that help you decide.

> 1 I would like to enquire about the Stock Market seminar advertised in your latest newsletter.
>
> 2 Two years ago we stayed at your lovely hotel in Delhi, and I would like to book two rooms for the first week of October for a group of six people.
>
> 3 Further to our phone conversations, we now enclose the signed documents you sent us. It is disappointing that the Bank has taken so long to respond as …
>
> 4 Thanks so much for your email and lovely holiday photos. We've just come back from two weeks in New Zealand ourselves, which were absolutely fantastic, and I'm attaching the details as I know you'd love it there.
>
> 5 I am writing to explain why I wasn't able to attend the school reunion last week. I'm so sorry because I was really looking forward to it.

> **GT Task 1 Situations**
>
> **A** making a complaint
> **B** recommending something
> **C** apologising for something
> **D** seeking information
> **E** making a reservation

2 Write one or two sentences about each of these situations.

> 1 Your next-door neighbour always puts his rubbish out for collection on the wrong day. Give him a reason for not doing this (e.g. rubbish sits on the pavement all week).
> 2 Apologise to a colleague for missing a meeting this morning. Say what happened.
> 3 Thank your friend Alison for lending you her car. You've filled the tank.
> 4 Write to your grandparents about a family celebration you are organising. Invite them to attend.
> 5 You are annoyed with the dry cleaners where you sent your best suit. The trousers are ruined.
> 6 Remind your flatmates about the meeting with the landlord on Friday. Encourage them to go, as there are important things to discuss.

Grammar: using 'if' clauses

3 Read the box on the next page and complete these sentences using the correct form of the verb in brackets.

> 1 I would be grateful if you _____ (can) give me a call.
> 2 If you can't attend the meeting, I _____ (go) in your place.
> 3 I _____ (appreciate) it if you could have the desk repaired.
> 4 If your plane _____ (arrive) after 9 p.m. I would come to get you at the airport, but I'm afraid I can't be there in the afternoon.
> 5 If you come to my office before 8 a.m., the building _____ (not be) open.
> 6 I _____ (be) delighted if we _____ (can) meet up to exchange ideas.

62

Get it right!

Conditional 1 (used to talk about likely events/situations in the future and to make offers)
will in main clause + present tense in 'if' clause:
I'll call you on your mobile, if I'm running late.
If you want tickets for the concert on Saturday, I'll buy them for you.

Conditional 2 (used to talk about unlikely events/situations in the future and for polite requests)
would in main clause + past tense in 'if' clause:
David would be very happy if he passed his driving test this week.
It would be helpful if you could reply as soon as possible.

Grammar: using *suggest*

4 Read the box below and complete these sentences by using the words in brackets in their correct form. You may need to add some words of your own.

1 In order to make sure that your customers are not inconvenienced like this again,
.... (suggest / employ more staff)

2 If you want to know more about living and studying in London,
.... (suggest / look / this website)

3 As you haven't understood the assignment properly, ...
.... (suggest / take another week to complete it)

4 To avoid this happening again, ...
.... (suggest / salespeople / check all
the boxes)

5 I would like to see the apartment early next week. ....
.... (Can / suggest / convenient time?)

Get it right!

Suggest needs to be followed by a clause or a gerund: *I suggest looking on the Internet.* ✓
Suggest is never followed by an infinitive: *I suggest (that) you change your appointment.* ✓
Suggest is never used with an indirect object: *Can you suggest/recommend a good English course?* ✓

Writing

7 Approaching the task

Content: covering the task fully

1 Analyse each of the two tasks below by:

  a deciding on the topic
  b turning it into a question
  c deciding how many parts to write about
  d selecting 2–4 main ideas to write about

Task A

> *In achieving personal happiness, our relationships with other people (family, friends, colleagues) are the most important factor.*
>
> *Do you agree or disagree?*

Task B

> *Some people argue that there are no basic differences between the way men and women approach academic study. Others insist that there are big differences in areas such as organisation, attitude and ambition.*
>
> *Discuss both these views and give your opinion.*

Content: adding support to main ideas

2 Read this paragraph from an essay on Task B and write the main idea and supporting points in the box below.

> It also seems to me that men organise their study time in a different way from women. In my experience, men are more likely to study on their own, whereas women prefer to work in groups. This is because women like to talk about their assignments before they do them. Men, on the other hand, do not seem to need this type of support.

Main idea	Supporting points
....	1 .... 2 ....

3 Do the same with another paragraph from a different essay on the same topic.

> In my view the differences between how students manage their study time depends on the type of person they are, rather than on whether they are male or female. Although many men may seem to leave things to the last minute, there are plenty of women who do the same thing. Similarly, there are people of both sexes who make sure that they use aids such as diaries and wall plans to help them meet deadlines comfortably.

Main idea	Supporting points
....	1 ....
....	2 ....

Coherence: writing a well organised paragraph

4 Underline these words and phrases in the paragraphs in exercises 2 and 3 and look at how they are used to link ideas.

> | also | on the other hand | similarly | whereas |
> |------|-------------------|-----------|---------|
> | rather than | such as | this is because | although |

5 Select an appropriate word or phrase from above to link the ideas in the paragraph below.

1 .... it is true that our families, friends and workmates are important to our well-being, there must be other factors that contribute to happiness. In my view, money is **2** .... important. Experts argue that money doesn't lead to happiness but if you are starving and looking for food **3** .... cooking a nice meal, it must make a difference. **4** .... good health means a lot to people. **5** .... there are many things that you cannot enjoy if your health is poor, **6** .... sports and other independent activities.

6 Read this paragraph from an essay on Task A and answer these questions.

a What is the main idea of the paragraph?
b Are there any supporting points?
c What do you notice about the structure of the paragraph?

> In my opinion, my friends are the most important people in my life. This is because my friends are more important to me than anyone else and they help me in my life. Actually I have a lot of friends and I feel very lucky to have so many friends. Other people may not have good friends but I would not be happy without my friends around me. Even if I am ill, I still need my friends and no-one else can take their place. As a consequence, I value them very highly.

7 Now rewrite the above paragraph. Make a small plan first, and then take no more than 15 minutes to write two paragraphs about the topic.

Writing

8 Planning your essay

Content: showing a clear line of development

1 Read the following task and the sample answer, then do questions **a–f** below.

> *People who have original ideas (e.g. people who invent or discover things) are of greater value to society than people who are simply able to copy the ideas of others well.*
>
> *To what extent do you agree or disagree?*

> *Sample answer*
>
> I certainly agree that people who come up with new ideas are terribly important to our society. However, I also think there is a role in society for good imitators.
>
> No one would deny that certain individuals must be thanked for providing us with facilities that we use every day. Where would we be, for example, without basic items such as the washing machine, the computer and, more recently, digital cameras and mobile phones? These inventions are now used so regularly that we tend to take them for granted.
>
> In fact, the society we live in today has become increasingly consumer-oriented and, while it may be possible to constantly update and improve consumer goods, not everyone in my country can afford them. Furthermore, not everyone lives in an area that has access to the latest models on the market. For these reasons, it is useful if someone can provide good copies of expensive products.
>
> Having said that, certain innovations have a more serious impact on our lives than others and cannot easily be replicated. Vital medicines like penicillin and vaccines against dangerous diseases also exist because people made continual efforts to develop them. Scientific ideas such as these enable us to live longer and avoid illness.
>
> Undoubtedly, scientists and engineers work extremely hard to make life better for us. In some areas, their work just adds comfort to our lives, and if people copy their ideas, it allows a wider population to benefit from them. However, in other areas, their contribution is unique, cannot be copied and without it we would be unlikely to survive or move forward.

  a Underline the words in the opening paragraph that paraphrase the task.
  b What is the writer's position?
  c Underline the main ideas in paragraphs 2, 3 and 4.
  d Underline a supporting point in each paragraph.
  e How does the writer use paragraphing to develop the answer?
  f What does the writer do in the conclusion?

Content: making a plan

2 Read this task and the ideas in the plan on the next page. Then think of some more supporting points to complete the plan.

> *In order to be able to study well, students need an attractive, clean learning environment. Universities and colleges should make efforts to provide this.*
>
> *Discuss both statements above and give your opinion.*

	Main idea	Supporting points
Paragraph 2	Why might a clean environment help?	a *assists clear thinking* b c
Paragraph 3	Compare education with other areas of life	d *businesses* e f
Paragraph 4	Is it the responsibility of the educational institution?	g *funding problems* h i

Content: introducing and concluding the essay

3 Read this task and the sample introductions and conclusions. Say whether **a**, **b**, **c** and **d** are introductions or conclusions.

> *Crime is nearly always related to the environment in which it occurs. For this reason, international laws and international law courts are unrealistic and will not succeed in reducing crime levels in different countries.*
>
> *Do you agree or disagree?*

a Initially the argument seems reasonable, but in order to prove this, a closer examination of the causes of crime is needed.	**b** Taking all the arguments into account, it seems that there is substantial evidence of a link between crime and the location in which it occurs and this link cannot be addressed internationally.
c So, while the idea of establishing international laws is basically good, it seems to me that such a system would be unlikely to work in practice.	**d** Is there a relationship between crime and the environment? If there is, is it justifiable to say that international laws will not work?

4 Practise writing some introductory sentences. Look at the task in exercise 2 and write one or two sentences that …

    a generally agree with the statement
    b express some doubt about the statement
    c express a mixed view on the statement
    d question the definition of 'study well'
    e explain what you understand by 'environment'.

5 Write an answer to the following task in 40 minutes. Take 5 minutes to map out some ideas and then write an answer to the task in 30 minutes. Use the last 5 minutes to check your work.

> *In some cultures the parents arrange marriages for their children but in others people choose their own marriage partner.*
>
> *What are the advantages and disadvantages of each system?*

Writing

9 Turning your ideas into written arguments

Content: presenting ideas

1 Match statements **1–6** with the ways of introducing arguments **a–f**.

1 *In my view* human nature is fundamentally good.
2 *While I appreciate* the importance of computers, *I still think* we rely too heavily on them nowadays.
3 *By* 'professional expertise' *I am referring to* the skill with which people do their jobs.
4 *I am not convinced that* goal setting is an important aspect of personal fulfilment.
5 *People have a tendency to* resist change.
6 *Ultimately* there are stronger arguments in favour of marriage than against it.

a	making a concession
b	making a generalisation
c	explaining / defining
d	refuting an argument
e	drawing a conclusion
f	giving a personal opinion

2 Correct the expressions used to present ideas in these sentences written by IELTS candidates.

1 I am really disagree this view.
2 As far as I concern, it is better to have a long holiday.
3 In my opinion, I strongly agree that children should wear school uniforms.
4 Even there are disadvantages to studying in another country, many students choose to do this.
5 In my point of view, poor nations need more financial support.
6 I think is good rich nations support poorer nations.
7 In conclude, I find there are merits to both of the views.
8 To sum up my opinion, I would support my child going overseas to study.

3 Read these seven extracts from candidates' essays. Use the prompts to improve the way the main idea is presented and to build a complex sentence.

Example   We have a tendency to accept new technology, regardless of its effect on our health.

		Prompts
Ex	We just accept new technology and don't think about its effect on health.	*have a tendency to / regardless of*
1	Parents should not choose to have a boy or a girl baby.	*my view / unethical for*
2	A lot of steps have been taken to help old people but it's not enough.	*Despite the fact that / we still / do more*
3	Antibiotics will probably become ineffective one day.	*doubtful whether / continue / long term*
4	People say that fat is bad for you but it isn't true.	*little evidence to support / view that*
5	Students get tired but still stay up late.	*although / get tired / stay up late*
6	I don't think tourism helps poor countries.	*unconvinced / tourism / benefits poor nations*
7	Most people think animal testing is OK.	*generally believed / animal testing / justifiable*

Vocabulary: using words correctly

◉ The **Cambridge Learner Corpus** tells us that IELTS candidates often make errors such as this:

Basically some workers consider that they can do anything they want. ✗

Get it right!

Consider is followed by the object + *to be*.
*I **consider** online bookshops **to be** very useful.* ✓   *I **consider** pride **to be** a good quality in a person.* ✓

Think is followed by the object + the correct form of the verb.
*I **think** (that) pride **is** a good quality in a person.* ✓

NB Do not confuse *consider* with *concerned*.
As far as <u>my opinion is considered</u>, online bookshops are very useful. ✗
*As far as **I am concerned**, online bookshops are very useful.* ✓

NB Do not use *about* with *consider*.
*We do not **consider where** our food comes from.* ✓   *We need to **think about where** our rubbish goes.* ✓

4 Rewrite these sentences using the word *consider*.

Example   I think that taxes are too high.   *I consider taxes to be too high.*

1 Some people think that money is the most important aspect of life.
2 Many conservationists think that humans are responsible for the loss of wildlife.
3 Teachers are not thought to be as important as doctors.
4 My grandparents thought education was very important.
5 In Europe, bread is thought of as a staple food.
6 Have you thought about your future?

Writing practice

5   Fill the gaps in the paragraphs below with one or two words.

One of the main arguments **1** .... of school uniforms is that they cover up any obvious socio-economic differences. By this **2** .... that they make all schoolchildren within one school look the same, and thus prevent children from feeling embarrassed about the clothes they wear. I consider this **3** .... very important because children should be concentrating on their studies, **4** .... worrying about their appearance.

5 .... it is not ideal to take away people's freedom of choice by imposing a uniform, I **6** .... whether children think about this. Neither do I **7** .... that paying for uniforms places a financial burden on families. **8** .... they would spend less on a uniform than they would on brand-name clothes that would inevitably be popular if children could wear what they wanted.

Writing

10 Linking your ideas

Coherence: using appropriate linking words

1 Read the following task and a paragraph from a student essay. Then answer the questions.

> *It has been suggested that in the not-too-distant future people will take their holidays on the moon. How realistic do you think this is? What type of holidays do you think people will take in the future?*

a Are the linking devices appropriate?

b Identify three ways the student could improve on this paragraph.

> I would predict that it is unlikely that people will choose to go to the moon for their holiday in the future. Who would want to travel to the moon? Actually, it would be very expensive to do this and some people can't afford it. As well, there are a lot of dangerous aspects to it and people may be afraid. On the other hand, the facilities would be limited and people would prefer to be at home.

2 Read this next paragraph, which would receive very good marks despite one or two mistakes. Then answer questions **a–d** to analyse why it is successful.

> According to space experts, some people will soon be so eager to try something new that they will happily check into a moon hotel – assuming it ⟶ one
> is available. As far as I am concerned, this is a rather far-fetched idea.
> To begin with, the cost of travelling to the moon is likely to be so high
> that only the extremely wealthy can afford it. Secondly, though it is argued ⟶ will be able to
> that tourists are looking for a challenge, the dangers involved in just
> getting to the moon are well known and these will surely put a lot of
> people off the idea. Besides, even if you do manage to get up there in one
> piece, you still have to survive in an alien environment for the time of the ⟶ duration
> holiday. And lastly, what will tourists do in space? Can you imagine playing
> space football, for example?

a Why is the opening sentence effective?

b Underline the linking words/phrases and reference words.

c What does 'besides' mean? What is it used to link?

d Why does the writer choose to use a rhetorical question at the end?

Vocabulary: using precise and varied expressions

3 Find the following expressions in the paragraph above.

1 an adjective that means 'really wanting to'
2 a phrasal verb that means 'stay at' a hotel
3 an adjective that means 'silly'
4 a phrase that means 'very rich'

5 a phrasal verb that means 'discourage'
6 an idiom that means 'arrive safely'
7 a phrase that means 'strange place'

70

4 This sentence, with the underlined noun phrase, is from the paragraph in exercise 2. It refers to the idea put forward in the previous sentence of the paragraph.

As far as I am concerned, this is <u>a rather far-fetched idea</u>.

Make some more noun phrases to describe the views below, by selecting a word from each of the boxes. Begin with the structure provided.

Adverbs		**Adjectives**			**Nouns**	
very		unhealthy	one-sided		proposal	development
rather	**+**	cruel	positive	**+**	claim	attitude
particularly		unrealistic	inevitable		activity	approach
		uncharitable			outcome	

Example   Mobile phones should be banned on trains and buses. *In my view …*
    In my view, this is a rather unrealistic proposal.

1 Brazilians are the best footballers in the world.	*I tend to think this …*
2 You should not give money to beggars.	*Surely this …*
3 Children have become more independent.	*I think this …*
4 Animals are used to test drugs.	*In my view, this …*
5 Smoking cigarettes stops you from overeating.	*I feel this is …*

Vocabulary: choosing the 'best' word(s)

5 Read this sample answer on Energy Options and improve it by replacing the underlined words with more precise words or expressions. Use the notes to help you.

ENERGY OPTIONS

The debate about the best way to **1** <u>make</u> electricity is back on the agenda. The most common **2** <u>ways</u> are by burning coal, building dams or using nuclear power. However, many people think that nuclear power is **3** <u>danger</u>, and when you consider the **4** <u>experiment</u> of Chernobyl in the Ukraine 20 years ago, you can see why.

Countries such as France, however, get about 80% of their electricity from nuclear power plants, and **5** <u>the scientists in favour of nuclear power</u> argue that it is actually much cleaner than burning fossil fuels, which **6** <u>contribute</u> global warming.

Others argue that it is better to get electricity from sustainable **7** <u>things</u>, such as the wind, the sea and the sun. Although this sounds like a **8** <u>fantastic</u> idea, they are not **9** <u>rely</u> enough to maintain a constant supply of power. For instance, you cannot make solar energy at night.

10 <u>Really</u>, we need a source of energy that will not **11** <u>run away</u> and if it cannot be hydro electricity or coal-fired energy, it will have to be nuclear. Finding a way of **12** <u>assuring</u> that nuclear power is safe and cannot be misused is the real challenge.

Notes
1 a verb which goes with *electricity*
2 be more precise
3 use the correct word form
4 use the correct noun
5 make a noun phrase using the adjective *pro-nuclear*
6 include a preposition
7 be more precise
8 more appropriate adjective needed
9 use the correct word form
10 use the adverb from *basic*
11 use the correct phrasal verb
12 use the correct verb

Speaking

1 Responding to personal questions

Vocabulary: using a range of words related to the topic

1 **a** What are the key words in questions 1 and 2 below?
   b What is significant about the words in **bold** in the responses?

> **A** Well … I really like **rock music** and these days you can download a lot of **good songs** from the **Internet**. And that's great!

> **1** What kind of music do you like?

> **C** Actually, my **favourite** kind of music is **film music**. I enjoy listening to the **sound tracks** of **movies** – especially when I've enjoyed the film and I want to remember it.

> **B** Well, in fact I really only listen to **classical** music and **opera**. To be honest with you, I find **modern music** quite **boring**. It's just a terrible **noise** as far as I'm concerned.

> **2** What is the best way to learn how to use a new mobile phone?

> **D** I suppose you could read the **instruction manual**, but I think it's better to **get your friends to help you**.

> **E** Um ... well, using a mobile phone seems to come naturally to young people. But most older people seem to need some kind of actual **lesson**. So I think the **salesperson** at the shop should show you **the basic features** when you buy the **phone**.

> **F** Personally, I'm not very good at **learning from watching** other people. So I think the best way is to **sit down** with the **manual**, and **read it carefully**. At least that's what I'd do.

Pronunciation: using word stress to assist meaning

2 (24) Listen to each speaker's response and underline the words that are pronounced more strongly than others.

3 Listen again. Why might the speakers have chosen to stress these words?

	Words/phrases that are stressed	Reason for stress
Speaker **A**	really like these days	to emphasise how much to compare with the past
Speaker **B**		
Speaker **C**		
Speaker **D**		
Speaker **E**		
Speaker **F**		

Grammar: using the right tense

4 Read questions 1–10 and underline the main verbs in each question.

1 How do you like to spend your spare time?

2 What sort of TV programmes do you enjoy watching?

3 When you were at school, did you play any team sports?

4 What do you want to do when you finish this course?

5 What is your favourite meal of the day?

6 What is the best way to learn how to use a computer?

7 How do the clothes you wear compare with the clothes your grandparents used to wear when they were young?

8 Would you rather get an email message or a letter? Why?

9 Do you prefer to study in a library or at home?

10 Why are you studying English?

5 Complete the table about the questions 1–10 above.

	Verbs	Tense needed for answer	Type of vocabulary needed
1	do you like to spend	present simple, e.g. I like ...ing	leisure activities, sports, shopping
2			
3			
4			
5			
6			
7			
8			
9			
10			

With a partner

6 Ask and answer the questions above.
As you listen to each other's answers, complete the checklist below.

What topic vocabulary did your partner use? ....
Which tense did he/she use? ....
Was it the right tense? ....
Which words did he/she stress? ....
Did the use of stress help you understand? ....

Speaking

2 Becoming more fluent

Fluency: linking ideas

1 Match these questions to the responses **A–J**.

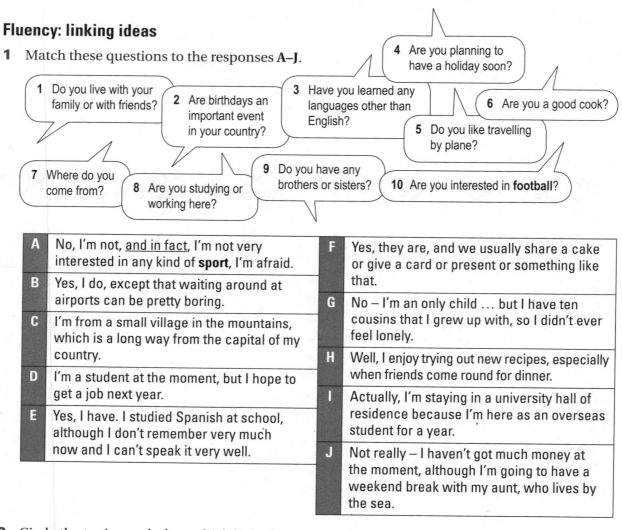

1 Do you live with your family or with friends?

2 Are birthdays an important event in your country?

3 Have you learned any languages other than English?

4 Are you planning to have a holiday soon?

6 Are you a good cook?

5 Do you like travelling by plane?

7 Where do you come from?

8 Are you studying or working here?

9 Do you have any brothers or sisters?

10 Are you interested in **football**?

A	No, I'm not, <u>and in fact</u>, I'm not very interested in any kind of **sport**, I'm afraid.	**F**	Yes, they are, and we usually share a cake or give a card or present or something like that.
B	Yes, I do, except that waiting around at airports can be pretty boring.	**G**	No – I'm an only child … but I have ten cousins that I grew up with, so I didn't ever feel lonely.
C	I'm from a small village in the mountains, which is a long way from the capital of my country.	**H**	Well, I enjoy trying out new recipes, especially when friends come round for dinner.
D	I'm a student at the moment, but I hope to get a job next year.	**I**	Actually, I'm staying in a university hall of residence because I'm here as an overseas student for a year.
E	Yes, I have. I studied Spanish at school, although I don't remember very much now and I can't speak it very well.	**J**	Not really – I haven't got much money at the moment, although I'm going to have a weekend break with my aunt, who lives by the sea.

2 Circle the topic vocabulary which links the ideas in responses **A–J** with the questions.

Example   A – sport and *10 – football*

3 Now underline the linking words which join the ideas grammatically and make a list of them.

Example   A – and in fact

4 Link the ideas in these answers to a set of Part 1 questions using one of the linking words and expressions from above.

EXAMINER: Where do you usually go shopping for food?
STUDENT: I tend to go to the supermarket ___because___ it's very convenient ___and___ you can find everything you want there.

74

EXAMINER: Do you think large department stores are better than markets?

STUDENT: No, 1 _____ I prefer the markets. They're much more colourful 2 _____ things are a lot cheaper there, 3 _____ is good if you don't have much money.

EXAMINER: Have the shops in your area changed since you were a child?

STUDENT: Yes, they have, 4 _____ in the city centre. When I was a child there were only small shops there 5 _____ now it's totally different – there are high-rise buildings everywhere!

EXAMINER: When do you prefer to go shopping for clothes?

STUDENT: I guess the weekend's the best time. 6 _____ I don't think I ever go shopping during the week – oh, 7 _____ when I'm on holiday.

EXAMINER: Do you think people will always enjoy shopping?

STUDENT: I don't know. These days people shop on the Internet a lot, 8 _____ you can't try things on if you shop online 9 _____ it isn't as much fun, 10 _____ I guess shopping will always be popular.

Fluency: being able to keep going

5 **25** Listen to a student answering these questions. As you listen, read the notes below.

Where do you come from?

What is the best thing about _____ ?

Is it famous for anything in particular?

	Main information	Additional information	Linking words, fillers
Name of place	Victoria Vancouver Island	Capital of British Columbia, Canada – Vancouver not on Vancouver Island	well, which, actually, but, although
Good points	Good climate Lovely architecture	Better than Eastern Canada	you know, with, and, once
Famous for	Eco-tourism – whale watching. Butchart gardens	Best from May to Sept. Clean and safe	these days, in particular, so, you know, even if

6 **26** Make a table similar to the one above. Then listen and complete it with the information you hear.

Pronunciation: saying words clearly and correctly

7 **25** and **26** Listen to both recordings again and listen out for these words and phrases. Note which syllables the speaker stresses. Practise repeating the words to yourself.

Recording 1		Recording 2	
island	eco-tourism	beautiful	public transport
climate	tourists	avenues	traffic
certainly	predominantly	competition	European
architecture	friendly	serious	

With a partner

8 Take it in turns to ask and answer the three questions in exercise 5 about the place where you grew up. Try to give the information, followed by a supporting point. While your partner is talking, complete a table similar to the one in exercise 5.

Speaking

3 Preparing your talk

Vocabulary: using appropriate words

1   Read the following Part 2 task. A candidate has underlined the key words and written some notes for her talk.

> <u>Describe</u> a <u>zoo</u> or a <u>wildlife park</u> you have visited that has <u>impressed</u> you.
>
> You should say:
> • where it is situated
> • when you went there
> • how you felt about it
> and explain what impressed you about it.

I have a clear memory of my visit and what I saw

Notes
Key words: describe, zoo, impressed
Melbourne Zoo – Australia
large – near city centre
during school holidays
not many fences and cages
many different species
animals appear to be free – open areas
best zoo in world

🎧 27 Listen to the candidate giving her talk and answer these questions.

a Did she mention all the points from her notes?
b Did she include anything new? If so, what?
c Which tense is used most? Why?
d What, did you feel, was the speaker's main point?

2   🎧 28 Listen to someone talking about a visit to an African wildlife park. As you listen, complete the table below. You can listen as many times as necessary.

Key words used	*South Africa, wildlife park*
Adjectives used to express feelings	
Main tense used	
Speaker's main point	

Using the table, try to create the notes that the speaker made before he gave his talk.

Grammar: using articles correctly – zero article (no article) / a (an) / the

3   The 'zero' article (no article) carries meaning, so you can only omit it in these situations.

an abstract noun	**an uncountable noun**	**a plural noun (non-specific)**
Time is money	**Sugar** is sweet	**Butterflies** have wings

Look at these abstract nouns and think of some more to add to the list.
a time   b life   c health   d love   e beauty

4   Use each of the above words in their abstract sense (without an article) and then in a more concrete sense (with a definite article).

Example   *abstract*   **Time** *flies!*
              concrete   *Remember* **the time** *when we got lost at the zoo?*

5 Add an appropriate article (*a/an, the*) or no article to the talk below.

I've never been to **1** _____ zoo, but I have seen animals at the circus, which is similar, I suppose. Bertrams's Circus used to come to town every summer and I still have **2** _____ vivid memories of it all. They would set up their big tent near **3** _____ centre of town, surrounded by lots of **4** _____ trucks and **5** _____ equipment. I used to go and watch **6** _____ acrobats performing in **7** _____ open air to anyone who wandered by. And there were lots of **8** _____ animals to see too: **9** _____ elephants, **10** _____ lions, all sorts. One year, one of **11** _____ big cats escaped from its cage and they had to get **12** _____ vet to help catch it. **13** _____ life with the circus looked pretty exotic then, but now I think it would be **14** _____ very hard life, and of course you don't often find **15** _____ animals in circuses now.

Coherence: introducing points in a natural way

6 The expressions below are all useful to introduce ideas.
Complete the sentences, adding information in the right-hand column.

What I like about (*city*) _____ Perth _____ **is**	**(that)** *it's not a very crowded city.*
The reason I don't like (*film*) _____ **is**	**(that)**
One of the problems with (*university*) _____ **is**	**(that)**
One of the (good) things about (*activity, e.g. riding a bicycle*) _____ **is**	**(that)**
What I enjoy about (*sport or hobby*) _____ **is**	**(that)**

With a partner

7 Work with a partner to create an 'ideas bank'.
Look at the topics **1–6** below. For each topic, see how many ideas come into your head – nouns, verbs, adjectives, proper nouns like places, people, etc. and write them down. Don't worry if some of them seem unusual! If they flow from the topic for you, and you can explain that relationship, then they belong in your 'ideas bank'.
Decide whether you would use the present, the past or the future to talk about topics **1–6**.

1 A sportsman or woman that you admire	**2** A TV programme that you enjoy watching regularly	**3** A place that you plan to visit
4 A film you have seen in English that impressed you	**5** A subject you would like to study	**6** An invention that has benefited humanity

8 Use some of the expressions from exercise 6 to make some statements about topics **1–6** above.

Example   *One of the amazing things about Roger Federer is …*

Speaking

4 Giving your talk

Vocabulary: using words in the correct form

1   Complete the second sentence so that it has a similar meaning to the first sentence, using a noun and any other words necessary. Say the new sentence out loud and emphasise the feeling.

  Example   I really admire my father.
          I have great admiration for my father.

  1 He used to enjoy his work.
     He used to get a lot of ....
  2 I am pleased with what I have achieved at college.
     I am pleased with my ....
  3 I believe that to succeed you need to work hard.
     I believe that .... comes from ....
  4 I respected the way my colleagues handled the problem.
     I had great ....
  5 Most people benefit tremendously from taking regular exercise.
     Regular exercise has ....
  6 I recorded the observations we made on our geography field trip in great detail.
     I made a ....
  7 Improved transport systems should reduce the amount of time people spend in their cars.
     Improved transport systems should lead to a ....
  8 We should find ways of improving the health system in our country.
     We need to make some ....
  9 After his illness, my grandfather was not able to speak properly.
     My grandfather lost the ....

Vocabulary: choosing words that go well together

2   Complete each sentence using the best word (adjective or adverb form) from the box.

  Example   It is .... *highly* .... unlikely that I will go back to live in my home town.

  1 My maths teacher had a .... influence on me when I was at school.
  2 We used to do all the .... things that children get up to!
  3 My father and I see each other on a .... basis.
  4 When you live with someone you discover their .... character.
  5 When I didn't get into my preferred course, I was .... disappointed.
  6 It is a .... mistake to think that you can study and work at the same time.
  7 My trip to Macao was great fun and full of .... surprises.
  8 In Paris, we parked in a no-standing zone and got a .... fine.
  9 To be a vet, you'd need to have a .... affection for animals.

  | usual(ly) |
  | wonderful(ly) |
  | heavy (ily) |
  | genuine(ly) |
  | regular(ly) |
  | common(ly) |
  | strong(ly) |
  | true(ly) |
  | bitter(ly) |
  | high(ly) |

Grammar: expressing a future plan

Conditional 1 Definite plan	If I <u>get</u> a student visa, I <u>will</u> definitely <u>go</u> to New Zealand.	*if* clause – present tense main clause – *will*
	My plan <u>is</u> to travel across Russia on the Trans-Siberian railway, if I <u>can get</u> a ticket.	main clause – present tense *if* clause – present tense
	The picnic <u>will be</u> in the park on Saturday afternoon unless it <u>rains</u>.	main clause – *will* *unless* (= *if not*) – present tense
Conditional 2 Possible, improbable or unreal outcome	My English <u>would improve</u> a lot faster, if I <u>spent</u> time in an English speaking country.	*if* clause – past simple main clause – *would*
	If I <u>had</u> enough money, I <u>would like to visit</u> South America.	
	If you <u>were</u> a bird, you <u>would be able</u> to fly.	

3 Read the examples above, then complete these 'plans' with a suitable clause.

  1 Ultimately I'd love to work overseas for a year, if ....
  2 If I get the opportunity to study abroad, I ....
  3 My aim is to study medicine, if I ....
  4 I'd like to go to Hong Kong to learn about acupuncture, if ....
  5 If I don't pass my driving test, I ....
  6 If I'm lucky, I .... a scholarship to fund my studies.
  7 I hope to live and study in Canada for a year, unless ....

4 Read this Part 2 task and say how the tenses you will use will be different from those used for the task about the zoo on page 76.

> Talk about a subject (a hobby, a skill or an academic subject) that you would like to study at some time in the future.
>
> You should say
> • what subject you would choose
> • where you could study it
> • how well you think you would do at it
> and say why you would choose this subject.

> **Useful phrases**
> Ultimately
> In a couple of years' time
> After I've done … I'd like to …
> In the long term
> Down the track

On your own

5 Give a talk on the task above and, if possible, record it. Check your timing. Play the talk back and complete the table below.

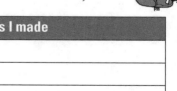

	Things I did well	Mistakes I made
Fluency		
Vocabulary		
Grammar & accuracy		
Pronunciation		

How did you introduce each point?
Was your talk interesting?

Speaking

5 Understanding abstract and analytical questions

Fluency: giving a full, coherent answer

I need to tell the examiner what I think are the good things about keeping animals in a zoo.

What do you think are the benefits of keeping animals in a zoo?

1 Read six responses to the above question. Which speakers answer the question by giving the benefits of keeping animals in a zoo?

A I think there are lots of good reasons for keeping animals in a zoo. One is that you can see animals from other parts of the world that you'd never see in the wild. And they're great for children, too.

B Personally, I don't like zoos. I can't see the point of them. You can see animals on the TV if that's what you want.

C I can see a number of advantages. They give us a chance to observe animal behaviour, and they also help to protect some species of animal, such as the panda bear, which are in danger of extinction. I think they're really important because they're a kind of scientific laboratory.

D I'm afraid I can't see any real benefits in old-fashioned zoos. Wildlife parks, on the other hand, where the animals are living in their natural environment, are a bit different. There the animals are protected from, you know, people who want to kill them for their hides or their ivory, for instance.

E Um … I'm not really sure, but I can't really see any benefits for the animals in a zoo. I mean, would you want to be stuck in a cage all day?

F Um … One of the main pluses of zoos is that we can see animals such as lions and kangaroos, which you wouldn't normally see. Well, not where I come from anyway. But, then again, some people think it's really cruel and they may have a point.

2 Which speaker
   a gives an argument against zoos, as well as a benefit of zoos?
   b doesn't answer the question?
   c looks at the question from the animals' point of view?
   d supports the answer with lots of examples?
   e makes a comparison between types of zoos?

Vocabulary: using paraphrase effectively

3 If you can't think of the correct word or phrase for something, you have to 'paraphrase' what you want to say. This means finding an alternative way of saying it. For example, if you can't think of the expression 'looking for prey', you might say that an animal is 'hunting for food'. Find a word or expression in responses **A–F** in exercise 1 which matches each paraphrase below.

1 in a natural place like a jungle or a forest ....
2 good things ....
3 what animals typically do ....
4 may all die out soon ....
5 place where you can study animals indoors ....
6 in the place where the animals are born and belong ....
7 area which stops animals escaping ....
8 very unkind ....

Pronunciation: grouping words to produce connected speech

4 ⊚29 Listen to response **A** from exercise 1 and notice how the words are grouped.

> I think // there are lots of good reasons // for keeping animals // in a zoo. // One is // that // you can see animals // from other parts of the world // that you'd never see in the wild. // And they're great for children // too.

Now mark possible word groupings in responses **B–F** and then read them aloud.

With a partner

5 Look at the list of Part 2 topics (**1–7**) in the box. Read the two Part 3 questions below and say which of the topics they are exploring.

> **A** Some people spend more time watching sport than playing it. What are the benefits, if any, of watching sport or supporting a special team?

> **B** How important is it to keep things like photos and books from your past?

Part 2 topics
1 A sportsman or woman that you admire
2 A TV programme that you enjoy watching regularly
3 A place that you plan to visit
4 A film you have seen in English that impressed you
5 A souvenir of someone or something that is important to you
6 A subject you would like to study
7 An invention that has benefited humanity

6 Now write a Part 3 question to go with each of the other topics.
Ask your partner each of your questions turn.
Make a note of the reasons he/she gives for each answer.

Speaking

6 Giving a reasoned response

Vocabulary: using appropriate language to fit the question

1 Read questions 1–5 below and match each one with what the question asks you to do (**a–e**). (See Student's Book Unit 6.) Underline the words which tell you this. Then answer the questions.

a give a reason	**b** give an opinion	**c** make a suggestion
d compare two things	**e** look ahead	

1 Can you say whether you would prefer to live in a house or an apartment?

2 You mentioned that you often use the Internet but that your parents don't. Why do you think older people find it difficult to adopt this new technology?

3 Smoking is known to be very harmful to our health. How do you think we can stop young people from taking up smoking?

4 What do you think our cities will look like by the year 2020?

5 Some people say we are born the way we are and we can't change ourselves. Other people say we learn from our experiences and our environment. Do you think people are born naturally 'good at music' or 'good at maths'?

Fluency: using adverbs to express an opinion

2 Rephrase these sentences using the adverb in brackets to emphasise the point.

Example   It is clear that there's been a mistake. (Clearly)
    Clearly, there's been a mistake.

1 From what I've read recently, the government is planning to remove the tax on imported cars, which, I think, is a very bad policy. (Apparently)
2 To be absolutely frank, I think the idea of the monarchy is completely out of date. (Frankly)
3 I am not in favour of sports like fox-hunting or even horse-racing, but that's just my opinion. (Personally)
4 It's a great shame that we still have no cure for some forms of cancer. (Regrettably)
5 Some people must enjoy horror movies, because otherwise the film studios wouldn't keep making them. (Obviously)
6 A free national health service is a wonderful idea in theory, but in practice it's almost impossible to sustain without private backing. (Theoretically)
7 The government spends thousands of dollars on anti-smoking campaigns, so we hope to see a change in people's smoking habits. (hopefully)
8 In my sincere view, we should be doing everything possible to reduce world poverty. (seriously)

Vocabulary: using idiomatic language

3 It is a good idea to learn a few idiomatic expressions and try to use these when you answer questions. Fill the gaps with one of the idiomatic expressions from the box.

A I'd like to spend more time with my family but ....*5*.... when I have so many other things to do.

B .... I don't really have time to do any sports.

C I'm quite happy with my accommodation. It's not very close to town but .... I think it's value for money.

1 think nothing of
2 to be honest
3 I can see your point
4 get along well
5 that's easier said than done
6 go along with the idea
7 the pros and cons
8 cold feet
9 on the whole
10 in the end

D I always drive everywhere, but my uncle would .... walking ten miles to see a good friend.

E It's good to make changes but I think you have to weigh up .... first.

F I used to order things online, but now I've got .... because there is so much Internet crime.

G The students in my class are from many different backgrounds but we ....

H ...., but I believe that people should be paid more money for working at the weekend.

I I can't really .... that people should have to retire at 65 just because they've reached this age.

J People can give you all sorts of advice on what career to choose, but .... you have to make the decision for yourself.

With a partner

4 🔊 **30** Listen to responses **A–D** below and notice how the speakers stress certain words to emphasise their meaning.

- Circle the adverb which supports the opinion.
- Practise saying the responses out loud, emphasising words as on the recording.
- Write a suitable Part 3 question for each response.
- Look carefully at how each response begins, and make sure your question fits the meaning and the grammar.

A I don't think we should waste money on trying to build a colony in space because, frankly, I think we have enough problems on Earth which we need to fix first.

B Personally, I believe museums still have an important role to play in our society. I think it would be a great shame if the government stopped providing the funds to keep them open.

C That's a hard question! On balance, I think single-sex schools are probably better. They say that girls do much better at single-sex schools, you know, but apparently, boys don't do so well.

D Well, no, I don't think so, because people should be allowed to make their own choices. So, no ... I'm not really in favour of compulsory seat-belts in cars, but obviously we have to have other road rules, such as speed limits.

Practice test: Listening

Questions 1–6

Complete the form below.

Write **NO MORE THAN THREE WORDS AND/OR A NUMBER** *for each answer.*

PATIENT RECORD

Time of appointment	*Example* ...10.00 am........................
Given names	Simon **1** ....
Family name	Lee
Date of birth	**2** 1989
Address	**3** .... ,
	Adams Terrace, Wellington.
Phone no.	0211 558809
Name of insurance company	**4** ....
Date of last eye test	**5** ....
Patient's observations	**6** Problems seeing ....

Questions 7–10

Answer the questions below.

Write **NO MORE THAN THREE WORDS** *for each answer.*

7 When must Simon wear his glasses? ....

8 What type of glasses are the least expensive? ....

9 What is good about the glasses Simon chooses? ....

10 How does Simon decide to pay? ....

SECTION 2   Questions 11–20 ⊙ 32

Questions 11–12

*Choose the correct letter, **A**, **B** or **C**.*

11 Who is buried in the tomb of the Taj Mahal?

   A the emperor Shahjahan
   B the wife of Shahjahan
   C the emperor and his wife

12 Where did the white marble come from?

   A India
   B China
   C Persia

Questions 13–16

Label the plan below.

*Write **NO MORE THAN THREE WORDS** for each answer.*

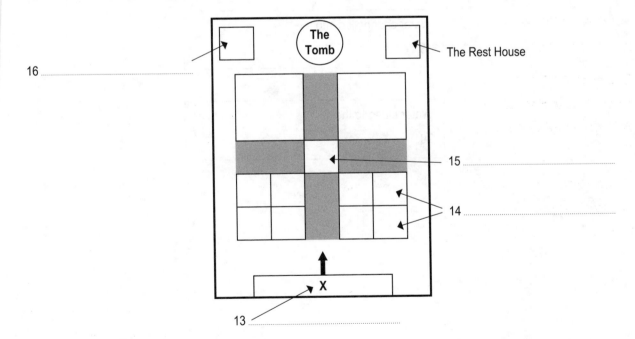

Question 17

*Choose the correct letter, **A**, **B** or **C**.*

17 What is the purpose of the Rest House?

    A a place for the poor to stay
    B a meeting place for pilgrims
    C an architectural feature

Questions 18–20

Complete the flow chart below.

*Write **NO MORE THAN TWO WORDS** for each answer.*

How running water is provided

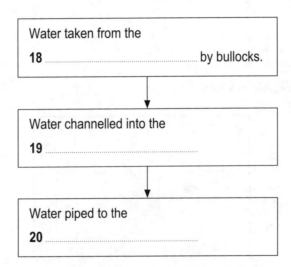

Water taken from the

18 .... by bullocks.

↓

Water channelled into the

19 ....

↓

Water piped to the

20 ....

SECTION 3   Questions 21–30 ⊘ 33

Questions 21–24

*Choose the correct letter, **A**, **B** or **C**.*

21 What background information does Daisy give about rice?

    A Wild rice is grown throughout Asia.
    B Some types of rice need less water than others.
    C All rice varieties have a lovely aroma.

22 Erik says that a priority for rice farmers is to be able to

    A grow rice without fertilizers.
    B predict the weather patterns.
    C manage water resources.

23 Where is the International Rice Research Institute?

    A The Philippines
    B China
    C Japan

24 Scientists in Bangladesh want to find a

    A more effective type of fertilizer.
    B strain of rice resistant to flooding.
    C way to reduce the effects of global warming.

Questions 25–30

Which country do the following statements apply to?

*Choose the correct letter, **A**, **B** or **C**.*

A	Japan
B	China
C	Thailand

25 They grow the most rice in the world.

26 They export the most rice in the world.

27 They aim to increase the nutritional value of rice.

28 Less rice is eaten than in the past.

29 An annual rice festival takes place.

30 A new type of rice is now popular locally.

SECTION 4 Questions 31–40 ⊙ 34

Questions 31–33

Complete the sentences below.

*Write **NO MORE THAN ONE WORD** for each answer.*

RADIO WRITING

31 You may have to ignore some of the ordinary .... of writing.

32 Written words do not indicate things like emphasis, the .... of reading or where to pause.

33 A script needs to sound like a ....

Questions 34–40

Complete the notes below.

*Write **NO MORE THAN THREE WORDS** for each answer.*

Know who you are talking to

Imagine a typical listener:

e.g. imagine telling your **34** .... about a film.

Create an informal tone:

e.g. use words like **35** .... and ....

Work out what you are going to say

Remember: listeners cannot ask questions

you cannot **36** .... ideas

Make your script logical:

■ **37** .... the information.

■ Use concrete images e.g. compare the size of a field to a
38 ....

■ Use the **39** .... to get attention.

Check the script by **40** ....

Practice test: Academic Reading

READING PASSAGE 1

*You should spend 20 minutes on **Questions 1–13**, which are based on Reading Passage 1.*

Climate change heralds thirsty times ahead for most

A new modelling study suggests that increasing temperatures will dramatically affect the world's great rivers

Veteran climate modeller Syukuro Manabe, and colleagues at Princeton University, modelled what effect a quadrupling of atmospheric carbon dioxide above pre-industrial levels would have on the global hydrological (water) cycle over the next 300 years. That looks further ahead than most climate models, but the scenario is inevitable unless governments take drastic action to limit greenhouse gas emissions. Rising CO_2 levels will trigger higher temperatures not only at the Earth's surface, but also in the troposphere, the team says. By factoring this into the models together with changes to levels of water vapour, cloud cover, solar radiation and ozone, the team predicted the effect that climate changes could have on evaporation and precipitation (rain). Both would increase, the researchers found, causing the discharge of fresh water from rivers around the world to rise by almost 15 per cent.

However, while water is going to be more plentiful in regions that already have plenty, the net effect will be to take the world's water further from where the people are. 'Water stresses will increase significantly in regions that are already relatively dry,' Manabe reports in the journal *Climate Change*. He goes on to predict that evaporation will reduce the moisture content of soils in many semi-arid parts of the world, including north-east China, the grasslands of Africa, the Mediterranean and the southern and western coasts of Australia. Soil moisture will fall by up to 40 per cent in southern US states, representing the greatest reduction.

The effects on the world's rivers will be just as dramatic. The biggest increases will be in the far north of Canada and Russia. For instance, the flow of the river Ob in Siberia is projected to increase by 42 per cent by the end of the 23rd century. This prediction could encourage Russia's plans to divert Siberian rivers to irrigate the deserts around the Aral Sea. Similar changes could increase pressure from the US for Canada to allow transfers from its giant Pacific rivers to water the American West. Manabe predicts a 47 per cent increase in the flow of the Yukon river.

By contrast, there will be lower flows in many mid-latitude rivers, which run through heavily populated regions. Those that will start to decline include the Mississippi, Mekong and especially the Nile, one of the world's most heavily used and politically contested rivers, where his model predicts an 18 per cent fall in flow.

The changes will present a 'profound challenge' to the world's water managers, Manabe says. They are also likely to fuel calls for a new generation of super-dams and canals to move water round the planet, like China's current scheme to transfer water between north and south.

Some of the findings are controversial. The UK Meteorological Office's climate model predicts that flows in the Amazon could fall this century, while Manabe's team predicts greater rainfall could increase its flow by 23 per cent. And while Manabe foresees a 49 per cent increase in the flow of the Ganges and Brahmaputra rivers that drain the Himalayas, an international study reported that the Ganges would lose flow as the glaciers that feed it melt away.

Global warming has already increased glacier melting by up to 30 per cent. 'After 40 years, most of the glaciers will be wiped out and then we will have severe water problems,' says Syed Iqbal Hasnain of Calicut University, Kerala, reporting the results of a three-year study by British, Indian and Nepalese researchers. The study finds the biggest impact in Pakistan, where the River Indus irrigates half the country's crops. Flows here could double before crashing to less than half current levels by the end of the century. But the declining flows predicted for the Ganges will also throw into disarray a vast Indian government scheme to avoid drought by diverting water from the country's glacier-fed northern rivers to the arid south.

Meanwhile, a team of researchers in France say that climate change is already affecting the world's rivers. David Labat and colleagues at the government's CNRS research agency in Toulouse in France reconstructed the monthly discharges of more than 200 of the world's largest rivers since 1875. They took discharge data held by the Global Runoff Data Centre in Germany and the UNESCO River Discharge Database and used a statistical technique to fill in gaps left by missing data, or changes to run-off caused by dams and irrigation projects.

Their findings reveal that changing temperatures cause river flows to rise and fall after a delay of approximately 15 years, and the team predicts that global flows will increase by about 4 per cent for every 1° C rise in global temperature. However, climate change over the past few decades has already caused discharge from rivers in North and South America and Asia to increase. Run-off in Europe has remained stable, but the flow of water from Africa's rivers has fallen.

Questions 1–7

Complete the notes.

*Choose **NO MORE THAN THREE WORDS AND/OR A NUMBER** from the passage for each answer.*

Write your answers in boxes 1–7 on your answer sheet.

Syukuro Manabe's climate model
based on: fourfold increase of ....**1**....
period covered: looks ....**2**.... ahead
processes monitored: effects of climate change on ....**3**.... as well as ....**4**....

Syed Iqbal Hasnain's predictions
based on: the loss of ....**5**....
period covered: looks ....**6**.... ahead

David Labat's predictions
based on: data going back to ....**7**....
features studied: 200 of the world's largest rivers

Questions 8–12

Complete the table below.

*Choose **NO MORE THAN THREE WORDS AND/OR A NUMBER** from the passage for each answer.*

Write your answers in boxes 8–12 on your answer sheet.

Predictions about increasing temperatures

	Rivers	Soil
Syukuro Manabe	Overall increase in flow of approximately ....**8**.... Decreases in flow at mid latitudes, in particular for the ....**10**....	Most significant decline in water content will be in ....**9**....
Syed Iqbal Hasnain	Greatest flow increase in ....**11**...., e.g. River Indus Flows will rise and then fall.	
David Labat	Flow rates change about ....**12**.... after the change in temperature occurs.	

Question 13

*Choose **TWO** letters, **A–E**.*

Write your answers in box 13 on your answer sheet.

*Which **TWO** of the following countries are developing systems to solve their own water problems?*

A   China
B   Africa
C   Canada
D   India
E   France

READING PASSAGE 2

*You should spend 20 minutes on **Questions 14–26**, which are based on Reading Passage 2.*

Principles of Persuasion

Successful advertising has to keep up with the times

A By the early twentieth century, key consumer markets for products such as confectionery, soap and tobacco had already become saturated. Though advertisers had developed strategies such as expanding consumer spending through increasing credit, they also turned to advertising messages to help increase sales. As early as 1908, when *The Psychology of Advertising* by Professor Walter Dill Scott was published, advertisers began to formulate theories of human behaviour and motivation which could unlock the consumer's mind through persuasive treatments (Leiss et al. 1990). New approaches to persuasiveness were grouped and systematised in the 1920s into 'reason-why' and 'atmosphere' advertising techniques.

B 'Reason-why' was designed to stimulate demand by constructing a reason for purchase, such as helping to save time, being modern, or being socially acceptable. Reason-why ads were used to differentiate the product from others on the market, as in an example from the 1960s: 'Make sure it's Cadbury's. Because no other chocolate can possibly give you the proper, creamy, Cadbury taste.' The premise was that consumers were essentially rational and made consuming decisions based upon reason. In an expanding market, there is no reason to try to make appeals other than 'reason-why', because consumers continue to buy, but once competition rises and the market flattens, advertisers need to find new appeals. 'Atmosphere' advertising, on the other hand, was meant to evoke non-rational responses such as sexual desire and patriotism from consumers and was useful when the market became saturated and advertisers needed a competitive advantage.

C These approaches tried to get to the essence of what advertising is all about and consequently solve all of the problems of advertising. In reality, advertisers used a combination of the two. New products, for example, at the turn of the century had to be explained, and the reason for using them developed, in the advertising. However, new inventions could not rely just on 'reason-why' ads, they also used suggestion and atmosphere. One technique was to associate the new brand with traditional and cosy settings such as nature and the family.

D A later version of the 'reason-why' advertisement of the 1920s was the Unique Selling Proposition (USP) developed by US agency boss Rosser Reeves in the 1950s. This too was based on 'rational' consumer decisions, but more explicitly tried to find an essence to advertising. Rosser Reeves specified that 'Each advertisement must make a proposition to the consumer. Each advertisement must say to each reader, "Buy this product, and you will get this specific benefit … one that the competition either cannot or does not offer." It must be unique – either a uniqueness of the brand or a claim not otherwise made in that particular field of advertising. The proposition must be so strong that it can move the mass millions, i.e. pull over the new customers to your product' (Reeves 1961).

E A USP could be achieved through the packaging, such as a unique bottle shape or a boiled sweet 'double-wrapped to keep in the freshness'. These differences in the product (the look, shape, size, colour and market position; the biggest/best/leading) are less to do with the advertising and more to do with the manufacturer. The manufacturer may decide to design the product in a certain way to provide the USP, such as an unusual pack design. Whether the consumers were interested enough in the USPs to make them want to buy the product was of little relevance. This imperative for differentiation came from the companies and the competitive market, not from any predilection towards the consumer. The greatest strength of the approach was that it re-emphasised the basic communications principle that to be effective advertising must emphasise difference; it did not matter for what rational or irrational reason the product was differentiated, just that it was differentiated.

F Reason-why and USP are still used today in different settings, especially for new products. However, the speed with which goods lose their difference means that the straightforward explanation of the goods' use, and the appeal of product difference, is lost and other ways are needed to differentiate the product, such as the emotional sell and the advertising 'brand image'.

G David Ogilvy was one of the biggest exponents of the power of the brand to influence consumer-buying decisions, though the term 'brand image' had been used for decades before. Building a brand is as much about establishing familiarity as it is about establishing difference. Even if you are not a Coke addict, you may turn to Coke in a store because you are so familiar with its design and its name and packaging. Any new brands that come on the market have the weight of this to fight against. The new brand has to differentiate through a separate product feature or benefit, or, more usually (if there is no difference), to develop a separate personality so that the brand is remembered as quite distinct.

Questions 14–18

Reading Passage 2 has seven paragraphs, **A–G**.

Which paragraph contains the following information?

*Write the correct letter **A–G** in boxes 14–18 on your answer sheet.*

14 a reference to customers owing money for their purchases

15 an expert's explanation of a particular advertising method

16 an example of how advertising makes a link between the product and familiar situations

17 why current advertising can't rely only on traditional techniques

18 when investigations began into how advertising could appeal to consumer logic

Questions 19–22

Classify the following features as being true of

A 'reason why' advertising
B 'USP' advertising
C 'atmosphere' advertising

*Write the correct letter **A–C** in boxes 19–22 on your answer sheet.*

19 It was created by the manager of an advertising company.

20 Its main approach was to suggest a motive for purchasing the product.

21 It was a useful technique if the customer base was no longer growing.

22 It moved the focus from advertising to what the product looked like.

Questions 23–26

Complete the summary below.

*Choose **NO MORE THAN TWO WORDS** from the passage for each answer.*

Write your answers in boxes 23–26 on your answer sheet.

Brand Advertising

The need for brand advertising was created because of the ....**23**.... with which products today begin to look alike. David Ogilvy is considered a pioneer in this area, although people were using the expression ....**24**.... many years earlier.

In addition to focusing on difference, branding highlights customers' ....**25**.... with a product. A good example of this is ....**26**...., which is instantly recognisable in the shops. Manufacturers of new products have to find a way of matching this.

READING PASSAGE 3

*You should spend 20 minutes on **Questions 27–40**, which are based on Reading Passage 3.*

Roses are blue, violets are red

If you don't like GM food, try flowers instead

Beautiful flowers, like any other beautiful object, can separate the most sensible of people from their money. On special occasions, people invest in a display of beautiful stems and petals to signal their own feelings or intentions. The result is a cut-flower industry in which roses alone are worth $10 billion a year. But that is nothing, compared with what happened in the past. In 17th-century Holland, tulips (the fashionable flower of the day) grew so expensive that people exchanged their bulbs for houses. One bulb of the most sought-after variety, the flaming red-striped Semper Augustus, sold for twice the yearly income of a rich merchant.

For modern flower growers, the equivalent of the Semper Augustus is the blue rose, which horticulturalists have longed for since the 19th century. Any blue rose sent on Valentine's Day this year will have been dyed. But if Yoshi Tanaka, a researcher at Suntory, a Japanese drinks company, has his way, that will soon change. Dr Tanaka is currently overseeing the first field trials of a blue rose developed by Suntory's subsidiary, Florigene. If the trials are successful, a dozen blue roses – even if they do look slightly mauve – could, by 2010, be available in florists worldwide.

What Dutch growers of old and Dr Tanaka's employers both grasped is that rarity, and hence economic value, can be created by genetic manipulation.

The stripes of the Semper Augustus were caused by the genes of a virus. Not knowing that an infection was involved, the Dutch growers were puzzled as to why the Semper Augustus would not breed true. The genetics of blue roses too have turned out to be more complicated than expected. The relevant genes cannot easily be pasted into rose DNA because the metabolic pathway for creating blue pigment in a rose consists of more chemical steps than it does in other types of flower. (Florigene has sold bluish genetically modified carnations since 1998.)

Success, then, has been a matter of pinning down the genes that allow those extra steps to happen, and then transplanting them to their new host.

Mere colour, however, is for unsophisticated buyers. A truly harmonious gift should smell beautiful as well. Sadly, commercial varieties of cut roses lack fragrance. This is because there is a trade-off between the energy that plants spend on making the complex, volatile chemicals that attract people and insects alike, and that available for making and maintaining pretty coloured petals. So, by artificially selecting big, long-lasting flowers, breeders have all but erased another desirable characteristic.

Smell is tougher to implant than colour because it not only matters whether a plant can make sweet-smelling chemicals, it also matters what it does with them. This was made plain by the first experiment designed to fix the problem. In 2001, Joost Lucker, then a researcher at Plant Research International in Wageningen, in the Netherlands, added genes for a new scent into small, colourful flowers called petunias. Chemical analysis showed that the new scent was, indeed, being made, but unfortunately the flowers did not smell any different. As happens in Florigene's blue carnations and roses, Dr Lucker's petunias dumped the foreign chemical they were being forced to create into cellular waste buckets known as vacuoles. Whereas pigments are able to alter a petal's colour even when they are inside a vacuole, because the cell contents surrounding the vacuole are transparent, smelly molecules must find a route to the sniffer's nose by getting out of the cell and evaporating.

Like Dr Lucker, Natalia Dudareva, of Purdue University, in Indiana, eschews experiments with roses, since these plants have scents composed of 300 to 400 different molecules. She prefers to understand basic odour science using petunias and other similar plants, which have about ten smelly chemicals apiece. She has made an encouraging discovery. By studying the many different pathways through which flowers make their fragrances, she has found consistent patterns in the way these pathways are regulated.

Such co-ordinated patterns suggest that a type of protein called a transcription factor is involved. Transcription factors switch genes on and off in groups. If Dr Dudareva is right, cut roses have lost their fragrances not because the genes that encode their hundreds of scent molecules have each lost their function, but because the plants no longer make a few transcription factors needed to turn the whole system on.

This suggests that the task of replacing lost fragrance is more manageable than it seemed at first. But even when the transcription factors in question have been identified, the problem of the energetic trade-off with pigment production and longevity will remain. So Dr Dudareva is also measuring how quickly the enzymes in scent-production pathways work, in order to identify bottlenecks and thus places where her metabolic-engineering efforts would best be concentrated.

Dr Dudareva's methods may also help to improve the job that flower-scents originally evolved to do – attracting insects that will carry pollen from flower to flower. By modifying the smell of crops such as vanilla, which have specific pollinator species, different insects might be attracted. That could expand the range in which such crops could be grown and thus make some poor farmers richer.

Questions 27–32

Do the following statements agree with the claims of the writer in Reading Passage 3?

In boxes 27–32 on your answer sheet write

YES   *if the statement agrees with the claims of the writer*
NO   *if the statement contradicts the claims of the writer*
NOT GIVEN   *if it is impossible to say what the writer thinks about this*

27 Historically, people have been willing to pay excessive amounts for flowers.

28 Farmers who grow flowers are generally richer than other farmers.

29 Blue roses were available for purchase in the 19th century.

30 Dutch plant growers deliberately used a virus to produce the striped Semper Augustus.

31 Blue carnations are more popular than carnations of other colours.

32 Plant breeders are to blame for the loss of smell in today's roses.

Questions 33–36

*Choose the correct letter, **A**, **B**, **C** or **D**.*

Write the correct letter in boxes 33–36 on your answer sheet.

33 Dr Tanaka hopes that his field trials will

    A result in a more expensive flower than the Semper Augustus.
    B produce blue roses that can be sold commercially.
    C show that flowers can be dyed unusual colours.
    D verify the link between flowers and romance.

34 Dr Lucker's experiment with petunias showed that

    A plant fragrances depend on the colour of the petals.
    B the more colourful plants are, the less they smell.
    C plants are able to reject the chemicals that produce smell.
    D colour and smell are equally difficult to introduce into plants.

35 Dr Dudareva prefers to study petunias, rather than roses, because petunias

    A are easier to grow.
    B have a wider range of scents.
    C are found in a wider range of places.
    D have less complex molecular scent structures.

36 In what way could Dr Dudareva's work benefit agriculture?

    A More farmers would be able to grow flowers.
    B A wider range of insects would pollinate certain plants.
    C More unusual flowers could be created.
    D A wider variety of plant species would be grown.

Questions 37–40

Answer the questions below.

*Choose **NO MORE THAN THREE WORDS AND/OR A NUMBER** from the passage for each answer.*

Write your answers in boxes 37–40 on your answer sheet.

37 What items were traded for flower bulbs in 17th-century Holland?

38 What aspect of a rose's internal biology slows down attempts to change its DNA?

39 What is the name of the waste area in which Dr Lucker's petunias were placing foreign chemicals?

40 What is the name of the protein that plants must make in order to release scent molecules?

Practice test: Academic Writing

TASK 1

You should spend about 20 minutes on this task.

The charts below show information about India's trade.

Summarise the information by selecting and reporting the main features, and make comparisons where relevant.

Write at least 150 words.

Exports (£ billion)

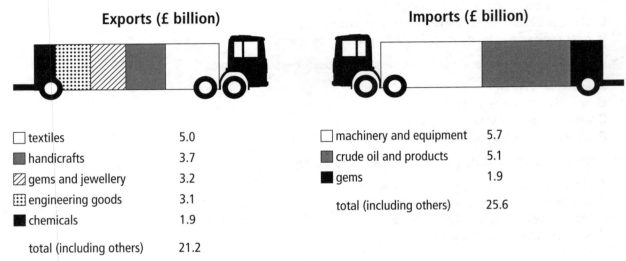

☐ textiles	5.0
◩ handicrafts	3.7
▨ gems and jewellery	3.2
⊞ engineering goods	3.1
■ chemicals	1.9
total (including others)	21.2

Imports (£ billion)

☐ machinery and equipment	5.7
◩ crude oil and products	5.1
■ gems	1.9
total (including others)	25.6

Main trading partners

Exports

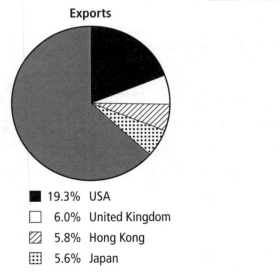

■	19.3%	USA
☐	6.0%	United Kingdom
▨	5.8%	Hong Kong
⊞	5.6%	Japan

Imports

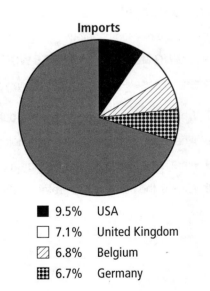

■	9.5%	USA
☐	7.1%	United Kingdom
▨	6.8%	Belgium
⊞	6.7%	Germany

TASK 2

You should spend about 40 minutes on this task.

Write about the following topic.

> *Some people think that it is very important to get a university education.*
> *Others feel we should encourage more young people to take up a trade such as plumbing, painting or building to ensure a good balance of skills in our society.*
>
> *Discuss both these views and give your opinion.*

Give reasons for your answer and include any relevant examples from your own knowledge and experience.

Write at least 250 words.

Practice test: Speaking

Part 1

Ask and answer these questions.

Where do you live?
How long have you lived there?
Would you like to change your home? Why? / Why not?

How often do you watch TV?
When do you usually watch TV?
What's your favourite TV programme?
Did you enjoy watching TV as a child? Why? / Why not?

Are you a tidy person? Why? / Why not?
Were you taught to be tidy as a child? Why? / Why not?
How important is it to be tidy?

Part 2

Record your talk.

> **Describe an item of clothing that you bought for a special occasion.**
>
> **You should say:**
>
> - **why you needed the item of clothing**
> - **what it looked like**
> - **where you bought it**
>
> **and explain why you chose this item of clothing.**

Part 3

Ask and answer these questions.

Clothing and work
Why do some organisations or companies insist that their employees wear a uniform?
Do people change when they put on a uniform?
Will uniforms become more or less popular in the future?

Clothes and choice
Does our choice of clothing reflect our personality?
Are expensive clothes always better quality clothes?
Are people as fashion conscious now as they were in the past?

Practice test: General Training Reading

SECTION 1 Questions 1–14

You should spend about 20 minutes on Section 1.

A LOOK AT THE FESTIVALS THIS SUMMER

A *The Firegathering*

18–20 May

The Firegathering festival returns to an unidentified location somewhere in the Sussex countryside this May. The ticket price is a very agreeable £40; an amount that the organisers promise covers only the costs incurred from staging the event. As well as the cabaret and circus performers, you can expect live performances from local stars. If this looks like it might be right for you, you'd be well advised to book your ticket soon; the event has sold out every year since its beginning four years ago.

B *Sheep Music*

20–22 July

Sheep Music started life as a garden party and has blossomed into a full-scale community event. Even though the advertising has always been limited to word of mouth, the monster turnout in 2005 left organisers worried that the large crowds could ruin the festival's family feel. Luckily July sees the return of this brilliant party. The climax comes in the shape of Saturday night's full-scale parade and fancy dress ball that you just wouldn't expect to happen in the otherwise sleepy Welsh borders.

C *The Big Chill*

3–5 August

Ten years on and The Big Chill could very well be on the verge of becoming a big pop festival like Glastonbury. That said, the many thousands in attendance are still able to relax in the beautiful Eastnor deer park and listen to plenty of music that would otherwise pass them by. Families have always been given a warm welcome and it's fair to say that The Big Chill is probably the most child-friendly of all the medium-sized festivals. If you've never been, you should definitely go.

D *Summer Sundae*

10–12 August

Although only a year old this summer, Summer Sundae has quickly captured the imaginations of Leicester's music lovers. Last year's event was a roaring success, noted by more than a few mentions at the UK Festival Awards. Set in the imposing grounds of De Montfort Hall, the festival has a dedicated kids arena right in the middle of the site. Although the performers are still to be confirmed, the cabins are sure to be there. These small structures are made from wood and feature carpets, storage space and ventilation, and can fit a family for the night.

Questions 1–7

*Look at the festival advertisements **A–D** on page 101.*

For which festival are the following statements true?

*Write the correct letter **A–D** in boxes 1–7 on your answer sheet.*

1 There is no formal marketing of the festival.

2 The acts for the festival have not yet been finalised.

3 The audience was bigger than expected one year.

4 No one knows where the festival will take place.

5 Some accommodation is provided at the festival.

6 No profits will be made from the festival.

7 The festival can be compared with another major music event.

Questions 8–14

Read the library website page on page 103 and answer the questions below.

*Choose **NO MORE THAN THREE WORDS AND/OR A NUMBER** from the Reading passage for each answer.*

8 What place is close to the library?

9 What is the latest time that books can be taken back to the library?

10 What number should the partially deaf ring for information?

11 On which level do the tours commence?

12 What can you show the library as evidence of where you live?

13 What is required if you lose your membership card?

14 How many items are you allowed to order from another branch?

Customs House Library

Located over three floors in the historic Customs House building near the old harbour, the library has books, CDs, videos, DVDs, magazines, newspapers, music scores, audio books, community language books and much more.

Opening hours
Monday to Friday: 10am–7pm
Saturday and Sunday: 11am–4pm
Public holidays: Closed

After hours
Return books every day until 11.30pm on the ground floor.

Contact us
Tel: 9209 8554
Email: library@city.gov.net
Fax: 9202 8561
TTY: 9202 8565 (for hearing impaired)

Free library tours
Public tours: Tuesdays at 1pm – no booking required
Group tours: Thursdays at 10am
Meet on the first floor (lounge area).
Tours take approximately 30 minutes.
No tours on public holidays and from 15 December to 15 January.

Joining
To become a member of the City Library Network, please bring to a branch the following documents:
• proof of your name
• proof of your permanent residential address (e.g. bank statement)
City residents and ratepayers FREE
Click here for non-residents' membership fees and charges.

NOTE Library membership will NOT be granted without proof of your permanent residential address. No membership services are available at the Town Hall branch. Lost or stolen cards incur a replacement fee. *Click here for details.*

Borrowing
Members can borrow up to 10 items for three weeks. This includes
• books, magazines, CDs and talking books – 10 at a time
• videos, DVDs and CDs – 5 at a time
• language kits – 2 at a time
• inter-library loans – 5 at a time
• toys – 2 items plus 1 puzzle at a time

SECTION 2 Questions 15–27

You should spend about 20 minutes on Section 2.

*Read the information from a college website below and answer **Questions 15–21**.*

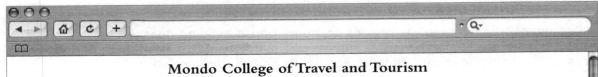

Mondo College of Travel and Tourism

If you plan to work in the travel industry, you will need to have the right skills.

Mondo College offers an on-line certificate course recognised by the travel industry, which will train and qualify you to book airline seats, hotel rooms and rental cars using recognised Computer Reservations Systems (CRS).

You will learn about the domestic and international tourism market, destination information, and how to handle yourself in a range of situations related to the industry. You will also become familiar with a number of travel software packages, making you highly employable in different companies.

Upon successful completion of this course you will receive a nationally recognised Certificate in Travel and Tourism and your new career will take off from there.

In the course you will learn how to:
- operate a computerised reservations system
- sell tourism products and services (see course outline below)
- prepare quotations and process financial transactions
- provide destination information and advice.

> **Sell tourism products and services**
> - Establish rapport with the customer to promote goodwill and trust
> - Tailor options to the cultural needs of customers
> - Provide all options within the agreed timeframe

Workplace training and assessment

Workplace training gives students the opportunity to develop practical job skills such as interacting with people in a professional environment and developing communication skills, as well as an insight into particular job roles and responsibilities. Overall, students have found workplace training improved their chances of getting a job and succeeding at it.

As a compulsory part of this course, students are required to seek a work placement on which they can be assessed. The assessment will involve being observed in a number of roles and all students are required to produce paperwork verifying what they have achieved, signed by a qualified manager or supervisor.

The College provides insurance cover for students who undertake work experience as part of their course. The policy covers personal accidents in the workplace, and will help put employers' minds at ease for the duration of the work placement.

Questions 15–21

Complete the sentences below which are based on the Course information on page 104.

*Choose **NO MORE THAN TWO WORDS** from the passage for each answer.*

Write your answers in boxes 15–21 on your answer sheet.

15 The course qualifies you to make .... for clients using standard computer systems.

16 The course equips you to advise clients on .... as well as overseas travel arrangements.

17 Mondo College teaches you how to .... outlining what a trip will cost.

18 You will learn how to meet the .... of clients depending on their backgrounds.

19 Work placements are a .... of the Travel and Tourism course.

20 Your workplace training must be overseen by a competent ....

21 While you are on placement, you are insured against any ....

Questions 22–27

Read the leaflet below.

Which paragraph contains the following information?

Write your answers in boxes 22–27 on your answer sheet.

22 advice to the trader on how to give information to the public

23 a reference to a problem being hidden from the customer

24 examples of consumer negligence

25 the relevance of cost / quality to performance

26 a situation where legal help may be needed

27 mention of goods bought as presents

Advice for traders on refunding money

When are consumers entitled to a refund?

A Consumers may ask for a refund if the goods they bought are so defective that they should not have been sold, e.g. they don't work, they break down or they develop a serious fault. If an article becomes defective after sale, one of the considerations would be the price paid to the store for the goods (e.g. a $20 watch would not be expected to last as long as a $300 watch).

B Where a dispute arises between a consumer and a trader, the Department of Fair Trading[1] can negotiate with the parties to achieve an acceptable solution. However, the Department cannot instruct the parties what to do. Only a court or tribunal is allowed to make a decision in such circumstances. And remember: consumers cannot ask for a cash refund if they did not pay cash.

When are consumers not entitled to a refund?

C Consumers are not entitled to a refund if they change their mind about a product. This includes when a consumer has found a cheaper product elsewhere, has bought a gift that is unsuitable, or they no longer require the goods.

D They are also not entitled to a refund if they knew about a fault when the goods were bought, for example as seconds. However, if a second has a fault that the consumer was not aware of, or could not have discovered upon a reasonable inspection when the item was bought, their rights are not affected.

E No refund can be made if the consumer is unable to prove when or where the item was purchased. However, traders should not refuse a refund solely because there is no receipt, if they are satisfied that the goods were purchased from their store. Nevertheless, there can be no refund if the consumer is responsible for damaging the goods by not following the instructions, or misusing the product.

F Many stores and traders offer refunds over and above their legal requirements as a goodwill measure to their customers. In this case, traders should display a notice near the cash desk advising their customers of their refund policy.

[1] Government department which looks after the legal rights of consumers and traders

SECTION 3 Questions 28–40

You should spend about 20 minutes on Section 3.

*Read the passage below and answer **Questions 28–40**.*

Open all hours

With the click of a mouse, libraries and museums are reaching a new audience, writes Steve Meacham.

A Museums and libraries used to be thought of as boring and of little relevance to our mobile-phone generation. And yet, over the past decade, something bizarre has happened to the once rarefied world of museums and libraries. Suddenly they've become 'fashionable'. Some call it 'a renaissance', others 'a revolution'. Either way, many of our most august institutions have reinvented themselves. The walls that once protected their vast collections of artefacts and books from the ravages of the outside world have become porous. Now, people are peering beyond the bricks and mortar, seeing libraries and museums for what they always wanted to be – citadels of ideas, stores of human knowledge.

B Even though many sceptics have questioned whether such 'elite' bodies as libraries would become redundant because of the Web – who needs a librarian when you can find out just about anything you need to know on *Google*? – the statistics show the opposite: libraries and museums are thriving like never before. They're marketing themselves to an even wider population, opening their doors 24 hours a day, displaying 'treasures' that until now have had to be locked away under conservation protocols.

C Take the National Library of Australia (NLA) in Canberra. Relatively few Australians ever venture inside. Yet, according to the director general in charge of public programs, 'The library collection of documentary heritage is the largest in the nation. We've got nine million items. Every year the library accepts the equivalent of five semi-trailer loads of new information.'

D 'There's a lot of rubbish on the Internet,' says the chief librarian at the State Library of New South Wales. Search engines like *Google* may be invaluable research tools, she says, but they don't differentiate between truth and fiction. Libraries can advise people which websites have credibility and which don't. Librarians, thanks to the Internet, have become web pilots – highly skilled researchers who are expert in the Internet's electronic tools.

E It is less than a decade since the Australian Museum launched its website. Back in 1995 it was little more than a crude bulletin board, giving details of opening times and admission charges. Now it is one of the most 'information-rich' sites in the country. There are interactive forums, such as those on sea slugs and fish, which are recognised as international leaders.

F As the oldest natural-history institution in the country, the Australian Museum has an estimated 13 million specimens, dating back hundreds of years. Only a tiny fraction can ever be displayed. Preservation, conservation and documentation are vital. Yet digital images of the specimens can be displayed on the museum's website without risk to the specimens themselves. A good example of this is the feathered cape that belonged to the famous navigator and explorer Captain James Cook, that was given to him by the people of Hawaii. Far too delicate to be displayed except for short periods under subdued lighting, it can be viewed permanently on the museum's website. The same goes for threatened species. Thanks to the Web, says the curator, 'We can not only show animals which are rare or endangered, but animals which are extinct.' By their very nature, many documents stored in libraries are too fragile to be displayed. A classic case is William Wills' journal of the ill-fated Burke and Wills expedition, discovered after the explorers' deaths. Scrawled in pencil, it is a priceless piece of Australian history. On the Web every page can be read, a poignant account of a monumental folly.

G A transformation has taken place at another of Sydney's museums, the Powerhouse Museum, where the Soundbite.org project won a prize for innovation in 2003. This was an online digital music studio, which allowed musicians to play with other musicians around the world. It was used by music teachers throughout Australia, New Zealand and Singapore and became an invaluable teaching tool.

H Our libraries are also combining to make it easier to borrow books and it is predicted that soon Australians will be able to go online and order any book in any Australian library and have it delivered to their local library within seven days. Eventually they will be able to have digitalised versions of books sent to them by email. The result, says one of the librarians at the National Library of Australia, is that younger people are being enticed back to libraries. 'People realise libraries are alive. Librarians aren't just looking after dead things.'

Questions 28–35

Reading Passage 3 has eight paragraphs, **A–H**.

Choose the correct heading for each paragraph from the list of headings below.

Write the correct number, i–ix, in boxes 28–35 on your answer sheet.

List of Headings
i A place that rarely receives visitors
ii How one museum received an award for linking people across the globe
iii Looking at real future possibilities
iv Predictions about museums and libraries are proved wrong
v The museum that never closes
vi Items that would not be seen without the Internet
vii The changing face of museums and libraries
viii How one museum has undergone huge technological change in the last ten years
ix Providing a reliable guide to Internet sources

28 Paragraph **A**	32 Paragraph **E**
29 Paragraph **B**	33 Paragraph **F**
30 Paragraph **C**	34 Paragraph **G**
31 Paragraph **D**	35 Paragraph **H**

Questions 36–40

Complete the sentences below.

*Choose **NO MORE THAN TWO WORDS** from the passage for each answer.*

Write your answers in boxes 36–40 on your answer sheet.

36 Unlike search engines such as *Google*, librarians know the difference between fact and .... , and people value this.

37 Museum websites can show .... of fragile, ancient specimens and provide discussion forums on various species.

38 Precious garments such as a .... once worn by Captain Cook can be displayed on a museum website.

39 Libraries contain valuable .... that need to be preserved, such as old travel journals.

40 The future collaboration between libraries and the Internet means it will take only .... to transfer books from one library to another.

Practice test: General Training Writing

TASK 1

You should spend about 20 minutes on this task.

> *You are a regular customer at a supermarket in your town/city. You have recently noticed a problem with some of the products that you usually buy and you have decided to complain about this.*
>
> *Write a letter to the manager. In your letter*
>
> - *explain who you are*
> - *describe your complaint*
> - *say what you think should be done about it*

Write at least 150 words.

You do **NOT** need to write any addresses.

Begin your letter as follows:

Dear Sir or Madam,

TASK 2

You should spend about 40 minutes on this task.

Write about the following topic:

> *Many young people today have their own mobile phone and believe it is essential to their lives.*
>
> *Other people dislike mobile phones and think that they are both a nuisance and an unnecessary luxury item.*
>
> *To what extent do you agree or disagree with these two points of view?*

Give reasons for your answer and include any relevant examples from your own knowledge or experience.

Write at least 250 words.

Recording script

The parts of the script that contain the answers are underlined.

Listening 1

Track 02
Conversation 1

STUDENT Excuse me. <u>I'm looking for</u> the Medical School. Do you know if I'm going in the <u>right direction</u>?

WOMAN Sure, um … <u>Go along</u> this road, here, past the library and past the Great Hall. The Faculty of Medicine is <u>on your left</u>. It's about three minutes' walk from here.

STUDENT Thanks very much.

Conversation 2

MAN 1 I've got this really cool new <u>computer game</u> – it's called *Soccer Superstars*.

MAN 2 How does it work? Can I have a look at it <u>on screen</u>?

MAN 1 Sure. Well, first you choose your own club – you know, Inter Milan, Manchester United … You <u>click here</u> to do that.

MAN 2 Right!

MAN 1 And then you actually manage the team as if you were the club manager. It's all about tactics.

MAN 2 Cool!

Conversation 3

NEWSREADER An express from Newcastle has been derailed outside the station, causing a number of injuries. The Presidential elections have caused a riot in Florida. And gale force storms continue to batter Queensland's north coast causing millions of dollars' worth of damage. This is the <u>six o'clock news</u> – and I'm Sally Broadmoore. <u>Good evening</u>!

Conversation 4

STUDENT Oh, hi! I'd really like to be able to <u>play for</u> one of the university <u>football teams</u>. How do you … like … <u>become a member</u> of the club?

COACH You just have to demonstrate that you're a <u>good player</u>.

STUDENT Right!

COACH We're having trials down here on the oval next Tuesday at six o'clock. So if you come along, we'll <u>see how good you are</u> then.

STUDENT OK – I'll do that.

Conversation 5

STUDENT <u>I'd like to apply for</u> a <u>parking permit</u> for the campus. Have I come to the right place?

ADMINISTRATOR Yes, you have … er … but you have to be a postgraduate student.

STUDENT I'm sorry. I don't quite understand.

ADMINISTRATOR I'm afraid you can only get a parking permit if you're enrolled for a postgraduate degree: a Master's or a PhD program.

STUDENT Oh! That seems rather unfair.

Conversation 6

COMMENTATOR I'm standing down here on the famous Chelsea <u>football ground</u>, and the atmosphere this afternoon is absolutely electric. There isn't a single <u>ticket</u> to be had and the crowds are pouring into the stands. It's going to be an extremely exciting <u>match</u>.

Track 03

WOMAN Good morning. Is this the right place to report a theft?

POLICE OFFICER Yes, it is.

WOMAN Right. I've had my bag stolen. It happened last night when I was …

POLICE OFFICER Slow down a minute. Let's get some details from you first. Can I have your name?

WOMAN Yes. It's … <u>Anna Andersson. That's A double N A, Andersson – A N D E R double S O N.</u>

POLICE OFFICER And what's your address?

WOMAN Do you want my home address or my address here in New Zealand?

POLICE OFFICER Let's start with a local address here.

WOMAN I'm staying in a hostel. It's called <u>Sunrise House</u>.

POLICE OFFICER Sunrise Hostel.

WOMAN No – House, not Hostel.

POLICE OFFICER Oh, OK! Is that the one in Beach Road?

WOMAN Yes, that's right.

POLICE OFFICER Right … Now can you describe the bag that was stolen?

WOMAN Yes … it was <u>a leather bag</u>, <u>a black leather one</u> … but I'm more worried about the contents because it has my passport and my watch in it.

POLICE OFFICER I see. Do you know the passport number?

WOMAN Yes, I think it's <u>4528 … 7709.</u>

POLICE OFFICER 4528 …

WOMAN 7709.

POLICE OFFICER … 7099.

WOMAN No, 7709.

POLICE OFFICER	Oh, and can you tell me what kind of watch it was?
WOMAN	I can't remember the make, but it was quite small, with a silver band.
POLICE OFFICER	OK – no make but … it's a <u>small, silver watch</u>. We'll get this description sent round to all the stations in the area. Meanwhile, I suggest you get in touch with the embassy …

Track 04

PRESENTER	The famous scientist Charles Darwin was a brilliant man, and his <u>wife</u>, Emma, was also intelligent. She liked literature and spoke French, German and Italian well. She was a graceful dancer and an excellent <u>piano</u> player.
	Emma Darwin was born Emma Wedgwood – one of eight children from the well-to-do Wedgwood family, well known to this day for their fine <u>plates and china</u>.
	Emma coped well in society, whereas Charles did not. He wasn't in the least bit interested in music, nor did he have time to read anything but science. Nevertheless, it's said that Emma made a successful and happy career out of the marriage and gave birth to <u>ten children</u> between the years 1839 and 1856. Her life has been documented in a recently published <u>biography</u> called *Behind every great man*.

Listening 2

Track 05

SECRETARY	School of Architecture. Professor Burt's office.
STUDENT	Oh! Good morning. I was wondering if you could give me some information about the forthcoming Architecture 21 conference – dates, enrolment procedures, costs … that sort of thing.
SECRETARY	Well … the conference runs from the <u>18th to the 20th of October</u>.
STUDENT	18th to the 20th of October … Oh good. I'll still be here then and um … where exactly is it being held? Is it at the university as in previous years?
SECRETARY	No, it's actually being held at the <u>Pacific Hotel</u> – we've rather outgrown the university conference facilities, so we've opted for this new venue.
STUDENT	Right – Paradise Hotel.
SECRETARY	<u>No, the Pacific – that's P A C I F I C.</u>

STUDENT	Oh right. And presumably we can get accommodation at the hotel?
SECRETARY	Yes, but you'll need to contact them direct to arrange that. I'll give you the number for hotel reservations. Have you got a pen ready?
STUDENT	Yes, go ahead.
SECRETARY	It's area code <u>zero seven</u> and then <u>nine triple three, double two double six</u>.
STUDENT	And what's the registration fee?
SECRETARY	Individual fees are $300 for the three days, or $120 a day if you only want to attend for one day.
STUDENT	Are there any student concessions?
SECRETARY	There's a 50% concession for students, so that's $150 for the three days, or <u>$60 a day</u>.
STUDENT	And am I too late to offer to give a talk?
SECRETARY	Oh, I'm pretty sure you've missed the deadline for that.
STUDENT	Oh, really? But I've only just arrived here in Australia – is there any way I could have a paper accepted?
SECRETARY	Well, you'd need to <u>talk to Professor Burt</u>, the conference organiser. I can put you through, if you like.
STUDENT	That'd be great. Oh and can I just check the spelling of his name. Is that B U R T?
SECRETARY	Yes, that's correct.
PROF. BURT	Professor Burt speaking.
STUDENT	Oh, hello. My name's John Helstone. I'm an architecture student at London University. I'm here in Australia for three months, looking at energy-saving house designs.
PROF. BURT	Right.
STUDENT	I'm interested in giving a talk on my research at the conference but I believe I may have missed the deadline.
PROF. BURT	Well, strictly speaking you have. <u>The closing date was last Friday</u>.
STUDENT	Oh, no!
PROF. BURT	But we may be able to include your paper if it fits into our program … but you'll have to be quick.
STUDENT	OK. What do I need to do?
PROF. BURT	Send me a summary of your talk. And make sure you include an <u>interesting title</u> for the talk. Something to attract people's attention.
STUDENT	OK. Interesting title. Right. I'm looking at ways of designing buildings for tropical climates that don't rely on the need to include air-conditioning, so I'm sure I can come up with something.
PROF. BURT	Yes, quite. But remember: the outline should be <u>no more than 300 words</u>.

STUDENT	Right. I'll try to keep it down to 300 words, but would 400 be OK?
PROF. BURT	No, not really, because we have to print it in the proceedings and we just don't have the space.
STUDENT	Sure, I understand.
PROF. BURT	And also, can you send me a short CV – the usual stuff – name, age, qualifications, that sort of thing.
STUDENT	Right. OK, short CV.
PROF. BURT	Actually, you can email it to me. That'd be quicker.
STUDENT	Sure. What's your email address?
PROF. BURT	Well the best thing would be to send it to the conference administrative officer at info … that's I N F O at uniconf dot edu dot au.
STUDENT	Right. I'll do that straight away.

Track 06

CLERK	Good morning, Blue Harbour Cruises. How can I help you?
CUSTOMER	Can you tell me something about the different harbour cruises you run?
CLERK	Well … we run three cruises every day, each offering something slightly different.
CUSTOMER	Let me just get a pencil.
CLERK	Firstly, there's the Highlight Cruise, … then we do the Noon Cruise and we also have our Sunset Cruise.
CUSTOMER	Could you tell me a little bit about them? When they leave, what they cost, that sort of thing?
CLERK	Well, the Highlight Cruise is $16 per person and that leaves at 9.30 every morning and takes two hours to go round the harbour.
CUSTOMER	Right … 9.30 … and do you get coffee or refreshments?
CLERK	No, but there's a kiosk on board where you can buy drinks and snacks. And we do provide everyone with a free postcard.
CUSTOMER	Right. And the Noon Cruise? Can you give me some details on that one?
CLERK	Well … the Noon Cruise is a little more expensive – it's $42 per person, and that departs at 12 o'clock, of course. It's actually very good value because it takes about three hours, as it goes round the harbour twice and, of course, for that price you also get lunch.
CUSTOMER	I see … and what about the last one?
CLERK	Well that's $25 a head. And it takes two hours.
CUSTOMER	And when does that depart?
CLERK	We only run that one in the summer months, and it leaves punctually at a quarter past six.
CUSTOMER	And presumably you get a chance to see the sunset.

CLERK	Yes, indeed, which is why it only runs in the summer.
CUSTOMER	And is there anything included?
CLERK	Oh, yes. All passengers receive drinks and snacks, served throughout the cruise. [pause]
CUSTOMER	Can I book for tomorrow?
CLERK	No need to book. Just be down at the quay at six o'clock. All our cruises depart from jetty no. 2.
CUSTOMER	Can you tell me where that is exactly?
CLERK	Yes, no. 2 jetty is opposite the taxi rank. It's clearly signposted.
CUSTOMER	Right … and can you tell me – is there a commentary?
CLERK	Yes, there is. On all the cruises.
CUSTOMER	Do they do the commentary in any other languages?
CLERK	No, it's just in English, I'm afraid.
CUSTOMER	Oh … so I'll have to translate for my friend, I suppose, as she's from Japan.
CLERK	Well, there is a brochure with some information about the places of interest, and that's printed in several languages, including Japanese.
CUSTOMER	Oh, fine.
CLERK	Oh, and one other thing. It gets extremely hot on the upper deck even at that time of day, so it's a good idea to bring a hat. Otherwise you could get quite sunburned.
CUSTOMER	Right. I'll remember that. Thanks very much.

Listening 3

Track 07

1 It's a typical house window really. It's got an outer square frame and then there are two rectangular windows inside the frame. The window on the left has a handle halfway up in the middle and the right-hand side has a small window at the top, with a handle.

2 It's quite a simple design. It looks like one tube but in fact there are two cylindrical tubes – an outer one and an inner one. They're both decorated with stripes. The inner one is longer and thinner than the outer one, so that when you stand it on its end, it looks like a telescope.

3 I'm going to get some new glasses and I really like these. The frame's made of metal and it's quite thin. You can see a darker edge at the top of the lenses but the sides and the bottom have no frame at all. They're good, I think, because I have quite small facial features. Also the lenses are oval, which suits the shape of my face.

Track 08

1

WOMAN How was your first day at university?

MAN Well … it was OK, I suppose …

WOMAN Did you have any actual lectures?

MAN Yes, I went to the introductory psychology lecture in the morning, followed by a psych tutorial, and after lunch I had a sociology lecture at … um … two o'clock, and then I had a history tutorial from five to six this evening.

WOMAN That does make a rather long day!

MAN It certainly does.

2

WOMAN Excuse me. Would you be able to tell me where the Emily Parker Auditorium is? I'm looking for the course information sessions.

MAN Well, you can follow me, because I'm going to the same place. What do you want to study?

WOMAN Well, I'm hoping to be accepted into the medical school, if I get high enough grades in my school exams, but if I don't make it into medicine, I'll probably do medical science. What about you?

MAN Oh, I'm interested in veterinary science. But I'm not sure, at this stage.

Track 09

MARIA So, what's happening on the field trip?

STEVE Um … well, we're going to visit a water treatment plant to see how they process the city's drinking water.

MARIA Oh, that should be interesting. Do you know if it's possible to take photographs of the plant, or are cameras not allowed?

STEVE Not sure. I think we're supposed to include pictures and the lecturer recommended that we bring a pen and notebook because you may want to do some drawings of the dam.

MARIA OK. I'll do that. Should we bring anything to eat?

STEVE No need – all the food's laid on by the people organising the trip. You'll need some good walking gear and spare clothes though.

MARIA Such as?

STEVE Well … I'd recommend that you bring a waterproof jacket of some sort because according to the weather forecast on the radio this morning, it's going to rain.

MARIA Hm. Right. I'll see what I can find.

STEVE And by the way, do you have a cell phone?

MARIA A mobile? Yes, sure.

STEVE Well, make sure you bring that along so we can keep in touch.

MARIA Provided they work up there, of course!

STEVE That's a point!

MARIA See you on Monday then.

Listening 4

Track 10

SPEAKER 1 Oh, you want the south side of the campus, and where we are now at the dance studio is the north end. The best thing is to take the footpath from here to the road. The labs will be right in front of you when you get there. Then go to the crossroads and turn left and go down to the lecture theatre. Then at the junction at the end of that road, you'll see a footpath leading to the block.

SPEAKER 2 We're right next to the admin block, so … you see the footpath that goes round the side of the lake? Well, go north along that path and then … you see where it divides? Well, you need to take the left fork. You'll see the supermarket on your left. The footpath will join the road and then if you turn right, the block will be just along there on your left.

SPEAKER 3 I'm afraid you've come to the wrong place. These are the Graphic Design workshops. Um … what I suggest is that you take the footpath at the back of the workshops, which leads down to the road that you want. Turn right when you get there and follow that road … go straight across both junctions and just keep going. You'll see the block on your left.

Track 11

LECTURER Harnessing the Sun's energy – that is, using the sun to generate power – can be difficult, but these days increasing use *is* being made of the energy from the sun, particularly to heat homes and provide hot water. Have a look at this diagram, which represents solar panels fixed to the roof of a house. It is typical of any system which uses a solar panel to provide hot water.

So how does it work? Well … energy from the Sun travels to the Earth in the form of radiation. This can be *visible* radiation – which is another way of saying 'light'. We also receive *invisible* radiation, which is known as infra red. A lot of this radiation passes through the glass at the front of the solar panel – here on the roof – and hits the surface at the back. This surface is black, because black is good at absorbing radiation, and so the black surface becomes hot. Energy in the form of heat is conducted along the back of the solar panel to these copper pipes. Now … these pipes are filled with a liquid which in turn becomes hot. This can be either oil or water, though oil is usually used. The oil expands and rises up the pipe into the energy exchanger, which is located – up here – in the water tank. Sometimes we have to use a pump as well, to help the liquid along. It's a remarkably efficient system, when you think about it.

Listening 5

Track 12

MINI-TALK 1   We believe there was a game, similar to football, played in Japan as well as in China as far back as 1000 BC. But very little is known about this. The Romans apparently played a similar game, but they had 27 men to a team. The modern game has its origins in England and these days the game is played by women as well as men.

MINI-TALK 2   I think the best known ever would have to be the Brazilian – Pelé. In his time, he was the highest paid and possibly the most famous athlete in the world. He led his national team to win no fewer than three World Cups in 1958, in 1962 and then again in 1970. In November 1969 he scored his 1000th goal. Pelé also won an International Peace Award in 1978 and became a Brazilian national hero.

MINI-TALK 3   The earliest known rules for what we call 'modern' soccer are believed to have been created in 1815 at a famous boys' school in England called Eton College, where the game used to be played. Before this date, there weren't really any rules as such! The rules are now very complex and are constantly under review. From time to time FIFA, the international body governing the game, makes changes to the rules. Referees come under enormous pressure both from the crowds and the players, but it's against the rules to argue with the ref!

MINI-TALK 4   The first World Cup was organised in 1930 by FIFA, the international body governing the game, and this competition was won by Uruguay. The World Cup happens every four years and the competition consists of a number of tournaments being played around the world, leading to an elimination event with 16 teams from 16 different countries. The last World Cup attracted TV audiences of approximately 35 billion people for almost 27 days.

Track 13
Conversation 1

STUDENT 1   Sandra! Are you going to play any sport this season … you know … for one of the university teams?

SANDRA   No, I don't think so. I played basketball last year for the uni. It was fun but it really cut into my time. I've got so many lectures this year that I thought I'd focus on my studies a bit more.

STUDENT 1   Hm, yes, I can understand that. But I'm on a partial sports scholarship, so I'm more or less obliged to sign up for the rowing, and that will involve training three mornings a week plus giving up Saturdays for the competitions.

SANDRA   Well, count me out, but good luck with it, all the same.

Conversation 2

STUDENT   I'm after a book by Patrick White. It doesn't seem to be anywhere on the library shelves.

LIBRARIAN   Which 'Patrick White' are you after?

STUDENT   I think it's called *The Tree of Life*.

LIBRARIAN   Do you mean *The Tree of Man*?

STUDENT   Yes, that's it. Sorry! It's on the reading list for the First Year Australian literature…

LIBRARIAN   Yes, well it's out on loan, I'm afraid. Would you like to reserve it for next week?

STUDENT   No, thanks. I'll have to buy a copy.

Conversation 3

STUDENT   Can I come in?

TUTOR   Sure – come in. Oh hi, Mariella. How's it going?

STUDENT   Oh, OK! But I've run into a bit of a problem with my Economics essay topic.

TUTOR   Right! What's the problem?

STUDENT   Well, initially I wanted to do something on the slump in the IT industry, but I just haven't been able to get enough data, and so I was wondering if you'd be prepared to give me an extension until Wednesday week to get it finished.

TUTOR   Well … as long as you promise …

Conversation 4

GREG   Hi, Frank! It's Greg here.

FRANK   How are you doing?

GREG   Good, mate. Doing anything this evening?

FRANK   Yeah! I've got to finish my Economics dissertation. Why?

GREG   Oh! It's just that there's a free barbecue on at the sports centre – thought you might fancy coming along?

FRANK   Look – I'd love to, but if I don't finish this assignment for Dr Pollard tonight, I may as well give up Economics. In fact, I may as well give up university! I only just scraped a pass in the first semester!

GREG   Oh well. Don't let me keep you from your books.

Track 14

BOOKSELLER	Good morning. Can I help you?
STUDENT	Good morning. Yes, I have a list of books that I'm looking for.
BOOKSELLER	OK – tell me what they are and I'll see if we have them in stock.
STUDENT	Right … well … first of all, do you have a copy of George Orwell's _Animal Farm_? <u>It's a set text</u> for an exam I'm preparing for.
BOOKSELLER	We do normally keep that one in stock. Let me just look it up on the computer. Yes, according to this we have three copies in stock. It's over there – in the Modern Classics section.
STUDENT	Yes, of course. That's where I found _Brighton Rock_ last month. Thanks. And also, I'm an English student and I have a few problems with English verbs and articles, so I'm looking for a book that <u>I can refer to in my own time</u>.
BOOKSELLER	A very popular title we have is _Grammar in Use_ and we have plenty of copies in the Languages section. Or there's _Better Writing_ but it's a bit more expensive.
STUDENT	<u>I'll go with your first suggestion</u>, I think. Thanks. Um, now … there's another course book that I need – _Pride and Prejudice_ – no, wait a minute, I think I can get a second-hand copy of that.
BOOKSELLER	That book's out of stock at the moment, anyway.
STUDENT	OK, and then there's my book club – that's just <u>for my own amusement</u> of course. I think the next book we're discussing is <u>a biography of Nelson Mandela</u>.
BOOKSELLER	Oh, I've just read that myself. It's great. It's over there with the non-fiction books … third shelf, I think.
STUDENT	Thanks.

Listening 6

Track 15
Conversation 1

MAN	What did you think of the _Lord of the Rings_ movie?
WOMAN	I **really** enjoyed it. And I thought the music was great.
MAN	Yes, <u>I thought so too</u>.

Conversation 2

MAN 1	I've been reading about the International Space Station that they're building in space. You know, **I'd love** to spend some time up there.
MAN 2	<u>I can't think of anything worse</u>. And space travel isn't at all good for the body, you know. It draws the calcium out of the bones.
MAN 1	Yes, but I find this stuff **absolutely fascinating**. The Space Station is a truly international venture. I'd go tomorrow!

Conversation 3

MAN	I've just been to the new Tate Modern art gallery in London. I thought it was great.
WOMAN 1	**Did** you? Frankly, <u>I don't think much of it</u>. I prefer the old Tate.
MAN	Oh, **really**? I think it shows an interesting use of space.
WOMAN 2	That's the fashion these days, isn't it? Museums and art galleries all around the world are being housed in old warehouses and power stations. <u>I think it's quite a good idea</u>, really, the concept of recycling buildings!

Conversation 4

SARAH	I'm voting for the opposition party next week. I'm **fed up** with the present government.
MAN 1	I haven't quite decided who to vote for, but you know the old saying, 'Better the devil you know …'
MAN 2	Oh, <u>I'm with Sarah</u>. I think we need a **change**.

Conversation 5

LAURA	Look at this. Sport on the front page of the newspapers again. **Who cares** which team won on Saturday?
MAN 1	Oh, come on, Laura. Just because you're not interested in football …
LAURA	<u>That's not the point</u>. I just think that as a society, we spend **far too much time** talking about sport and **not nearly enough** time worrying about real issues.
MAN 2	<u>I think Laura's got a point</u>. Sport's a **substitute** for things that matter – a way of distracting us.

Conversation 6

WOMAN	What **is** that music you're listening to?
MAN	It's Charlie Parker. Don't you **like** jazz?
WOMAN	No. It gives me a headache. <u>I don't know what you see in it</u>. Can't you play some **decent** music for a change – Mozart or Bach?
MAN	Sorry – I don't have any classical music! It's not my thing. I find it **pretty dull**, to tell you the truth.

Track 16
Beginning A

STUDENT 1	What topic are you researching for your economic history assignment?
STUDENT 2	Well, I've decided to look at the history of postage stamps.
STUDENT 1	That's different.
STUDENT 2	Yes, well … postage stamps played an important role in the development of 19th century commerce. They were quite a novel idea at the time of their introduction.
STUDENT 1	Oh, were they really?

Beginning B

PRESENTER Welcome to this week's edition of *The Sports Show*. Today, we're going to look at the role of the sports coach in elite sport. In the studio we have a group of young athletes and two coaches from two very different sports – football and gymnastics. And let's go first to Charlie McPhee, who's been coaching young footballers for over 25 years. Charlie – welcome to the programme.

CHARLIE My pleasure!

Beginning C

TUTOR OK, everyone! Let's get started. We've got three tutorial papers to get through in the next hour, so … who's going first?

STUDENT 1 We are, Dr Matthews! Cathy and I are doing a joint presentation this week.

TUTOR Oh yes, of course! And can you just remind the rest of the group what area of the media you've chosen to research?

STUDENT 2 Yes, well … we've been looking at the effect of television on young children.

TUTOR Right. Over to you.

Beginning D

TUTOR Good morning, everyone. I'd like to introduce our guest to you – John Watson. We're delighted to have John with us today to share his views on conservation. As Environmental Science students, I know you'll have a lot of questions, so let's kick off by asking him to tell us how he got involved in the environmental movement.

WATSON Thank you, Deborah. It's nice to be here.

Beginning E

PRESENTER Welcome to this week's edition of *Frontiers of Science*. The International Space Station – the ISS – is a floating laboratory, 350 kilometres above the Earth. But what exactly is it and who is behind it? To answer our questions, we are pleased to welcome to the studio Dr Karl Richter, who is a specialist in the field of space research.

RICHTER Delighted to be here.

Track 17

NARRATOR *You will hear two students talking about the topic for an economic history assignment. First you have some time to look at questions 1–5. [pause] Now listen and answer questions 1–5.*

STUDENT 1 What topic are you researching for your economic history assignment?

STUDENT 2 Well, I've decided to look at the history of postage stamps.

STUDENT 1 That's different.

STUDENT 2 Yes, well … postage stamps played an important role in the development of 19th century commerce. They were quite a novel idea at the time of their introduction.

STUDENT 1 Oh, were they really?

STUDENT 2 Yes … because … you know … before they had stamps, the addressee – that's the person receiving the letter, not the sender – used to have to pay for the letter to be delivered, and of course, if he didn't want to pay …

STUDENT 1 … Or maybe if he couldn't pay…

STUDENT 2 Yeah, if he couldn't pay, he could refuse to accept the letter and in effect the post office had to cover the cost. So, they came up with the brilliant idea of having a pre-paid stamp which the sender always paid for.

STUDENT 1 So when was the first stamp produced?

STUDENT 2 Well … the idea for an adhesive postage stamp – one that you could stick onto your letter – was initially devised in Great Britain around 1834. But it took the government until 1839 to accept the idea, and the first stamp was produced in 1840. And that's when they introduced the uniform price.

STUDENT 1 And how much was that?

STUDENT 2 It was one penny for each letter …

STUDENT 1 … No matter where the letter was being sent within Britain?

STUDENT 2 Yes, that's right, because previously each letter was charged, not so much by size or by weight, but according to its destination.

STUDENT 1 Oh, really?

STUDENT 2 The first stamp was called the Penny Black. If you've got one these days they're worth an absolute fortune!

STUDENT 1 They're always bringing out new stamps, though, aren't they, so I figure they must be quite easy and economical to produce.

STUDENT 2 Well, yes, but more to the point it's quite a lengthy business because there are so many stages to go through.

NARRATOR *Before you hear the next part of the conversation you have some time to look at questions 6–10. [pause] Now listen and answer questions 6–10.*

STUDENT 2 First they have to choose the subjects.

STUDENT 1 So what kind of topics are acceptable?

STUDENT 2 Well, the most important thing is that they must be of national interest. Something that represents the country in some way and which is highly recognisable at a glance. So, for instance, characters from books are popular, or you often find examples of national animals and birds.

STUDENT 1 Like the kangaroo on Australian stamps.

STUDENT 2 Yes, exactly. And in the UK you can't have pictures of people who are alive – well, with the notable exception of members of the British royal family, so <u>no *living* people ever appear on Australian or British stamps</u>.

STUDENT 1 That seems a bit stupid.

STUDENT 2 Well, not really. The policy is under review, I believe, but many stamp enthusiasts see good reason for keeping it that way to avoid the possibility of people in power using their influence to get onto the stamps.

STUDENT 1 Oh, I suppose that's a point.

STUDENT 2 One <u>favourite topic in the UK is kings and queens</u>; for instance King Henry VIII, famous for his six wives, appeared on a British stamp together with a stamp featuring each of his wives.

STUDENT 1 Some of the stamps are pretty unusual, aren't they?

STUDENT 2 Yeah. For example, in New Zealand they had a series of stamps the shape of coffee cups.

STUDENT 1 Really! Are you kidding?

STUDENT 2 No – they did! Look … I've got some pictures here. See? … And they all showed people from different eras, sitting in coffee shops, just relaxing. The 90c stamp and the one dollar 20 stamp have people sitting at tables in the café enjoying themselves. And the dollar 50 stamp shows people <u>sitting outside in the sunshine</u>.

STUDENT 1 That's actually really nice.

Listening 7

Track 18

LECTURER Today I'm going to be talking to you about the International Space Station – the ISS, which is a joint venture between <u>20 countries</u>: the five nations of the United States of America, Russia, Japan, Canada, Brazil and the 15 nations of the European Space Agency.

It is the largest and most complex international scientific project in the history of mankind, and as you can imagine, something of this size doesn't come cheap! So how much is it actually going to cost? Well, **despite the fact that** <u>it was estimated to cost 120 billion dollars</u>, it has already gone 8 billion over budget, so now we're looking at 128 billion.

People always want to know the same kind of information about the ISS, so I'll run through the most common questions. **First of all**, they always ask me how we manage with so little water on board the station. Well,

I can assure you that <u>nothing goes to waste</u>. **Because of** the impracticality of transporting large amounts of liquid into space, we have come up with some ingenious solutions. **For instance**, everyone on board, including the laboratory rats, loses water when they exhale or sweat. This humidity goes through a condensation <u>process before being returned to the water supply</u>. **Because**, of course, if we don't <u>re-use the water</u>, the station would need about 20,000 kg of water transported from Earth each year, which just couldn't be done.

Track 19

LECTURER **The next** question relates to what we are going to be doing up there. Well, we'll have teams of astronaut-scientists working in the labs and research will include, **for example**, tissue culture, **though** that won't include plants as such; observations of the Earth from space with a view to <u>improving our maps</u>, and the development of new commercial products. And of course everything we do involves <u>studying life in low gravity</u>, **as** we're in a state of weightlessness. **And then**, **in addition to this**, we'll be keeping a very close watch on the mental state of our astronauts, **because** we are interested in finding out what the long-term <u>effects on the human psyche</u> will be.

Track 20

LECTURER **Another thing** people always ask us is about our daily routine on board the space station.

Well – you need to be real good friends with the others **because** it's a small place! The **first** chore of the day is to ensure all is well with the many systems. **Then** this is followed by breakfast, which is timed to take precisely 45 minutes. Experts have decided that togetherness around the dining table is psychologically important, **so** meals of pre-packed food are eaten together. Mail, which is received overnight, is read around the breakfast table, **followed by** <u>a daily conference. So getting together is inescapable</u>, even in space!

Recreational time's pretty minimal! Some astronauts read, others listen to CDs. One guy I knew just used to stare out the window. **Then** each day, **in order to** offset the ill effects of being cooped up in such a small space, we have two hours set aside for <u>compulsory physical movement</u>. Work rosters occupy six 12-hour days each week. Sundays are for rest and communication, via emails and video conferencing, with family back home on Earth.

Listening 8

Track 21

NARRATOR   Example

LECTURER 1   In previous lectures in this series we have focused on land conservation. Today we are going to look at the need for marine conservation and in particular the effects of commercial fishing on our oceans … because if we are not very careful, a great <u>many fish</u> are likely to end up on the 'endangered species' list.

Track 22

NARRATOR   Listen and answer Question 1.

LECTURER 2   All languages share the same aim, but it seems from linguistic research that there is nothing in any language – for instance in the grammar or sentence structure – that is indispensable, and each language achieves the common aim – that is, <u>to communicate thoughts</u> – in its own way.

NARRATOR   Question 2

LECTURER 3   A ballad is a narrative poem which tells an exciting story. Ballads were first created hundreds of years ago in the days when there were <u>no newspapers</u> and <u>very few books</u>, so people would tell stories instead. Many of the earliest ballads told tales which were frightening and full of superstition.

NARRATOR   Question 3

LECTURER 4   Agriculture is one of the most ancient human activities, so it is remarkable that very little was known until the late 1600s about how plants grow and reproduce. In today's lecture we are going to look at the life of the man, whose name was John Ray, who effectively invented the <u>study of botany</u>.

NARRATOR   Question 4

LECTURER 5   Heat tends to move from places where there's a lot of heat to places where there is less. In today's talk, we're going to look at the three ways in which this occurs. The first of these is conduction. <u>The second way is convection</u>, and the third way is <u>radiation</u>.

Track 23

LECTURER   Good morning, everybody. Now last week we were looking at the positive effects that computers have had on our society. This week I'd like to talk about one of the negatives – computer viruses.

OK. So what is a computer virus? Well, it is a software program that has been created by a human programmer with the single intention of corrupting and destroying useful programs. Put in simple terms, it's a way of causing lots of trouble for ordinary people!

It's known as a virus because, <u>although it's not a biological organism, it functions in a similar way</u> in that it looks for a host, that is, a body – your computer – in which to live and multiply, with the one aim of destroying that host.

Let's go back 50 years. In 1949 the first model of a computer virus program was presented in a paper by John von Neumann. Soon after this was published, a game known as *Core Wars* appeared on the scene. *Core Wars* was initially <u>created for intellectual entertainment</u> by three Americans working on large mainframe computers. By the 1980s, for the very small sum of $2.00 postage, anyone could get details on how to play *Core Wars* and create programs that could escape from the game and destroy other programs.

Computer viruses are picked up in much the same way as their biological counterparts – that is, through contact with others, and this can happen very easily, as literally millions of people are in touch with each other by email every day. Virus programs are often intentionally placed within useful programs such as commercial websites or they are <u>included in software that you might have got from friends or downloaded from somewhere</u> without knowing its real source.

It seems quite hard to believe that anyone would go to all this trouble to intentionally spoil the data of other people, but the rise in the number of computer software infections, and the amount of lost data that we are seeing these days, is proof that these <u>attackers are going to extremes</u> to do just that … going out of their way to create programs that hide inside legitimate software and cause all sorts of errors that their victims will then mistake for hardware failure – believing that the problem lies with their own computer.

There are many types of virus, such as worms and Trojan horses, and each has its own purpose. One function of a Trojan, for instance, is to destroy and delete files on your computer. They attack by generating a lot of email and Internet traffic on your machine until it becomes completely overloaded and you can no longer use your computer. It then does the same to your friends' machines. Bad enough, you may think. But a Trojan also allows the attacker <u>to use the victim's computer to purchase goods with stolen credit cards</u> or access illegal websites.

So, what can we do to combat these people? Well, the first thing is to realise that virus programmers succeed because people are not always careful about where they get their programs from. So, number one – <u>be very careful</u>. And I don't just mean that you should be careful about the source of your software, you also need to take care with emails and avoid any messages which are suspicious-looking. So the second golden rule is <u>'avoid trouble'</u>. For instance, do not open any message that says 'I love you' or 'Win $50'. A third thing we can do involves trying to find out exactly how the viruses work – in other words, we need to <u>understand the viruses</u>. And, of course, <u>there is a good selection of anti-virus software available on the market now to combat the virus plague</u>, so another way of protecting ourselves and our computers is to <u>be well prepared</u>.

If you follow these basic rules, you really shouldn't have any problems.

Speaking 1

Track 24

SPEAKER A   Well … I really like rock music and these days you can download a lot of good songs from the Internet. And that's great!

SPEAKER B   Well, in fact I really only listen to classical music and opera. To be honest with you, I find modern music quite boring. It's just a terrible noise as far as I'm concerned.

SPEAKER C   Actually, my favourite kind of music is film music. I enjoy listening to the sound tracks of movies – especially when I've enjoyed the film and I want to remember it.

SPEAKER D   I suppose you could read the instruction manual, but I think it's better to get your friends to help you.

SPEAKER E   Um … well, using a mobile phone seems to come naturally to young people, but most older people seem to need some kind of actual lesson. So I think the salesperson at the shop should show you the basic features when you buy the phone.

SPEAKER F   Personally, I'm not very good at learning from watching other people. So I think the best way is to sit down with the manual, and read it carefully. At least that's what I'd do.

Speaking 2

Track 25

EXAMINER   Where do you come from?

STUDENT   <u>Well</u>, I grew up in a city called Victoria … <u>which</u> is the capital of the province of British Columbia, in Canada. It's <u>actually</u> not on the mainland <u>but</u> on a large island just to the west of Vancouver, called Vancouver Island … <u>although</u>, just to confuse everyone, Vancouver itself isn't on Vancouver Island!

EXAMINER   What's the best thing about Victoria?

STUDENT   Victoria has a pretty good climate … usually quite warm and certainly much better than the eastern provinces of Canada. I think it's a great place to grow up … <u>you know</u>, not too big, not too small, <u>with</u> some really lovely architecture. <u>And</u> the island itself is just so beautiful, <u>once</u> you get out of the city, that is.

EXAMINER   Is it famous for anything in particular?

STUDENT   <u>These days</u> the island is well known for its eco-tourism … <u>in particular</u> for whale watching. The best time to see the whales is from May to September, <u>so</u> lots of tourists come to the island in summer. I think it's very popular predominantly because it's safe … <u>you know</u> … and clean, and the people are friendly. If you go there, you should visit the gardens, called the Butchart Gardens … <u>even if</u> you're not really into gardens, you just have to go there.

Track 26

EXAMINER   Where do you come from?

STUDENT   I was born in Melbourne, which is the capital of the state of Victoria in Australia. I love Melbourne because it's a beautiful city with lots of examples of 19th century architecture. For example, the wide streets and avenues and grand buildings.

EXAMINER   What's the best thing about Melbourne?

STUDENT   Um … well, perhaps the best thing, for me at least, is Melbourne's sense of style. There's always been a lot of competition between Melbourne and Sydney because we like to think we're … you know … a bit more elegant … smarter clothes, better restaurants, that sort of thing. But it's not really serious.

EXAMINER   Is it famous for anything in particular?

STUDENT   Well, I suppose I'd have to say the trams. They're the major form of public transport in the city and everyone loves them, even though they get in the way of the other traffic! They really give the city a kind of … well … uh … how can I describe it? A kind of European feel, which is what I like about them, I think.

Speaking 3

Track 27

CANDIDATE 1   I'm going to talk about Melbourne Zoo. Melbourne Zoo is probably one of the best zoos I've ever been to … and I'm not that keen on zoos normally … because it's a very open zoo. It's near the centre of the city, next to the Botanical Gardens, and it's really worth a visit.

I actually went there with my family … with my children when they were young … I think it was during the school holidays … and … they were very impressed because … um … for instance, you can see the lions from a bridge – you walk over the top of them and they appear to be quite free, roaming around underneath you. So were the elephants … in fact, they're separated by a kind of moat, that's like a ditch with water in it, and it means that they can't get across it but the impression that you have is that the animals are actually quite free.

The zoo has a great variety of animals and you can see all sorts of creatures from all over the world, though of course, a particular emphasis on Australia … on Australian animals. One interesting thing is that they've kept an old 19th century building, originally built as a monkey cage, as a reminder of what zoos used to be like, in the old days. But these days the monkeys have a much better enclosure and the zoo prides itself on its humanitarian approach. I think it's probably one of the best zoos in the world.

Track 28

CANDIDATE 2   Many years ago when I was in South Africa, I visited a wildlife park called Timbavati, in Natal Province. I went with my two aunts and my sister and we flew into the park in a small plane from Johannesburg, north east, and as we were landing we had to take off again because there was a giraffe on the landing strip. It was so exciting being there. There were no modern buildings; we just had one guide and there were six other people with us and we lived in little mud huts for four days – it was really exciting. We felt as though we were completely on our own, although we had the security of having a guard with a gun. He said he'd never had to use it!

I felt very privileged to be there with all the animals around and only six other people besides us. The guard took us out at dawn and then again at dusk – 'cos that's when you're most likely to see the animals. We also went out at night, once or twice, and that was really amazing – quite frightening though, because you'd see all these little eyes all around you … peering at you. We saw lions, elephants, giraffes, gazelle, everything. It was absolutely marvellous.

Speaking 6

Track 30

SPEAKER A   I don't think we should waste money on trying to build a colony in space because, frankly, I think we have enough problems on Earth which we need to fix first.

SPEAKER B   Personally, I believe museums still have an important role to play in our society. I think it would be a great shame if the government stopped providing the funds to keep them open.

SPEAKER C   That's a hard question! On balance, I think single-sex schools are probably better. They say that girls do much better at single-sex schools, you know, but apparently, boys don't do so well.

SPEAKER D   Well, no, I don't think so, because people should be allowed to make their own choices. So, no … I'm not really in favour of compulsory seat-belts in cars, but obviously we have to have other road rules, such as speed limits.

Practice test

Track 31

NARRATOR   *You will hear a number of different recordings and you will have to answer questions on what you hear.*
There will be time for you to read the instructions and questions, and you will have a chance to check your work.
All the recordings will be played ONCE only.
The test is in four sections.
At the end of the real test you will be given ten minutes to transfer your answers to an answer sheet.

Now turn to Section 1.

NARRATOR   *Section 1. You will hear a conversation between an optometrist and a patient who has come for an eye test.*
First you have some time to look at questions 1 to 6.
[pause]
You will see that there is an example that has been done for you. On this occasion only, the conversation relating to this will be played first.

121

Recording script

OPTOMETRIST Good morning, can I help you?

SIMON LEE Yes. I'm here for an appointment at ten o'clock with the optometrist. I'm a little early. I know its only ten to ten.

OPTOMETRIST Are you Simon Lee?

SIMON LEE Yes, I am.

NARRATOR *The time of the appointment is ten o'clock, so 'ten am' has been written in the space. Now we shall begin. You should answer the questions as you listen because you will not hear the recording a second time.*
Listen carefully and answer questions 1 to 6.

OPTOMETRIST Good morning, can I help you?

SIMON LEE Yes. I'm here for an appointment at ten o'clock with the optometrist. I'm a little early. I know its only ten to ten.

OPTOMETRIST Are you Simon Lee?

SIMON LEE Yes, I am.

OPTOMETRIST I'm Rachel White, the optometrist here today. Come in and take a seat.

SIMON LEE Thanks.

OPTOMETRIST Before we test your eyes, I just need to get a few details from you.
So, Simon, what's your full name?

SIMON LEE Simon Anthony – that's A N T H O N Y. And my family name is Lee: L double E.

OPTOMETRIST And your date of birth, Simon?

SIMON LEE The 1st of June, 1989.

OPTOMETRIST The 21st of June.

SIMON LEE No, the *first* of June.

OPTOMETRIST Whoops … sorry! 1989 – ah, same year my son was born! What's your current address?

SIMON LEE I'm living at a hall of residence.

OPTOMETRIST Which one?

SIMON LEE At University Hall, not far from here, in Adams Terrace.

OPTOMETRIST University Hall … And do you have any medical insurance?

SIMON LEE Yes, I'm fully covered.

OPTOMETRIST And who are you insured with?

SIMON LEE I'm with 'Health for Life'.

OPTOMETRIST Healthy Life.

SIMON LEE No. People always get that wrong. It's 'Health for Life'. They're part of some big insurance company.

OPTOMETRIST Good! Now, Simon. Have you ever had your eyes tested before?

SIMON LEE Yes, once. But not recently. It was when I was still at school.

OPTOMETRIST So roughly when would that have been?

SIMON LEE Probably around September 2007. No, on second thoughts, it must've been the year before – September 2006. And my eyesight was fine then.

OPTOMETRIST But you're having a little difficulty now, are you?

SIMON LEE Well, yes … since I started at university, I've been having difficulty with distance vision. I can't always see things in the distance.

OPTOMETRIST Well, let's have a look. Now I'm just going to cover your left eye. Can you read the top line?

SIMON LEE Yes. R … B … Q … S …

NARRATOR *Before you hear the rest of the conversation you have some time to look at questions 7 to 10.*
[pause]
Now listen and answer questions 7 to 10.

OPTOMESTRIST Well, Simon. Your eyes have obviously got a little worse since your last test and I think you're going to need to wear glasses … er … not all the time and … not so much for reading or close work but definitely for driving.

SIMON LEE Right. Yes. I thought that was probably the case.

OPTOMETRIST So now you need to choose some frames. There's a wide range to choose from, as you can see.

SIMON LEE Can you give me some idea of the difference in cost? I quite liked the idea of some frameless glasses.

OPTOMETRIST Mm. Did you? Well, the prices vary enormously, like everything, but the frameless ones are the most expensive. The cheapest are the ones with the full frame.

SIMON LEE Mm, perhaps I'd better go for those.

OPTOMETRIST Or why not try these ones with the half frame?

SIMON LEE They're not too bad.

OPTOMETRIST Yes. They look quite nice and they're strong – far less likely to break than the frameless ones.

SIMON LEE Oh, that's a good point. OK, I think I'll take those ones.

OPTOMETRIST If you pop back next Monday, I should have them ready for you. And you can pay for them when you pick them up.

SIMON LEE Thanks very much. Can I pay by credit card?

OPTOMETRIST You can, but there will be a slight charge if you do that.

SIMON LEE Right. I'll pay by cash then, if you don't mind.

OPTOMETRIST No problem. Cash, credit card, debit card. All the same to us. See you on Monday.

NARRATOR *That is the end of Section 1. You now have half a minute to check your answers.*
[pause]
Now turn to Section 2.

122

Track 32

NARRATOR *Section 2. You will hear an extract from an audio guide to the Taj Mahal.*
First you have some time to look at questions 11 to 16.
[pause]
Now listen carefully and answer questions 11 to 16.

GUIDE Welcome to our audio tour of the Taj Mahal.

The Taj Mahal is the most popular tourist attraction in India. It is also one of the most spectacular buildings of the world, and is considered as a symbol of love. But how many people realise that it was actually built as a tomb or burial place for the Emperor's wife?

The Taj Mahal was built by the Mughal Emperor Shahjahan to commemorate his beloved wife Mumtaz Mahal when she died, and, although this was not his original intention, for he had planned to build a black marble tomb for himself, they <u>both lie side by side</u> in the tomb today. Emperor Shahjahan's two greatest passions were architecture and jewellery and both are represented here in all their splendour.

The most skilled architects and craftsmen came from across India and countries as far away as Persia and Turkey. Much of the structure was built in white marble that was carried by a thousand elephants all the way from <u>the Indian region of Rajasthan</u> some 300 kilometres away. Crystal and jade came from China, sapphires from Sri Lanka and turquoise from Tibet.

But there's a lot more to the Taj Mahal than just the tomb, so let's have a look at the overall plan before we take a walk through the magnificent gardens. Your tour begins here at the point marked with an X on the plan. This is known as <u>The Main Gateway</u>. Walk through the gate and you come into an elaborate garden. There are two marble canals studded with fountains, which cross in the centre of the garden, dividing it into four equal squares. Each of these four quarters is then sub-divided into flower beds. So there are 16 <u>flower beds</u> altogether. The tomb stands majestically at the north end, not in the centre as you might have expected.

Instead, at the centre of the garden, halfway between the tomb and the gateway, there's <u>a raised pond</u> which provides a reflection of the Taj Mahal. It's a magnificent sight. On either side of the tomb there are buildings made of red sandstone. The one to the west – to the left on our plan – <u>is a mosque</u>. It faces towards Mecca and is used for prayer. On the east side of the Taj is a building known as the Rest House. It's like the twin of the mosque, but because it faces away from Mecca, it was never used for prayer.

NARRATOR *Before you hear the rest of the guide you have some time to look at questions 17 to 20.*
[pause]
Now listen and answer questions 17 to 20.

GUIDE Many people have asked what the Rest House was for. Was it a place for pilgrims to stay? Was it a meeting hall of some kind? Perhaps the most likely answer to this question is that its purpose is purely aesthetic, to act as a visual balance for the mosque and <u>to preserve the symmetry of the design</u> of the whole complex.

Let's have a look at some of the engineering features of the garden. For one thing, they require a constant supply of running water. When it was built, water was <u>drawn from the river</u> manually, using an elaborate rope and bucket system, pulled by a team of bullocks. The water was then brought through a broad water channel and held in a number of <u>supply tanks</u>. These tanks were at varying heights off the ground and were ingeniously designed to store the very large amounts of water required. Using an elaborate system of underground pipes, the water was then distributed from the supply tanks to each of <u>the fountains</u>. To ensure that the water pressure was the same throughout the garden, there was a copper pot under each fountain connected to the water supply. It was undoubtedly a brilliant system.

NARRATOR *That is the end of Section 2. You now have half a minute to check your answers.*
[pause]
Now turn to Section 3.

Recording script

NARRATOR *Section 3. You will hear a tutor and two students discussing the crop rice.*
First you have some time to look at questions 21 to 24.
[pause]
Now listen carefully and answer questions 21 to 24.

TUTOR Good morning, everyone. So … following on from our tutorial on European agriculture last week, Daisy and Erik are going to talk about the most commonly grown crop in Asia, which is, of course, rice. Erik, can you tell us what you've been working on?

ERIK Yes, sure … We've been looking at the role of rice in a number of countries, how it's grown, ways of increasing production. As I'm sure you know, rice is the staple diet throughout Asia and, in fact, 90 per cent of the world's rice is grown and eaten there. Daisy's got some background on that.

DAISY Um … well, rice was originally a wild plant which started out in the tropical regions of Asia, but there are literally hundreds of varieties today and each with different qualities. For instance, one will survive floods, while another will grow in relatively dry conditions. A third has a really lovely smell. But wherever it grows, rice needs a lot of water.

TUTOR What do you mean by 'a lot'?

ERIK Well, it takes about 5,000 litres to get a kilogram of rice. This can be supplied either naturally or by irrigation. And as most rice-growing countries suffer from unpredictable weather, including drought – water management really is the key.

DAISY Research has become so important now that each rice-growing country in Asia has its own research institute, whether we're talking about Japan, China or Bangladesh … and they're all co-ordinated by a group in the Philippines called the International Rice Research Institute.

TUTOR Interesting.

DAISY Bangladesh, for instance, has been successfully using different rice varieties and fertilizers for 30 years. But because it's such a flat, delta country, it's very difficult for the water to drain away after the monsoon season, so they need to find special rice crops that can survive the floods. And with global warming, the situation is more urgent than ever.

NARRATOR *Before you hear the rest of the discussion you have some time to look at questions 25 to 30.*
[pause]
Now listen and answer questions 25 to 30.

ERIK Now I'd like to move on to our comparative study. As you can imagine, China is the world's biggest rice producing country. Collectively the Chinese people probably eat more than three billion bowls of rice every day!

TUTOR Quite a statistic!

ERIK And of course, rice plays an important cultural role too.

DAISY We then compared China to Thailand. You know, even though Thailand only has about 64 million people, it is the world's number one exporter of rice. Not China as you might imagine.

TUTOR Is that so?

ERIK Yes. They send their rice everywhere … in particular to Europe, as well as Africa and the Middle East. Apparently the fact that 'jasmine rice' is growing in popularity is one reason why Thailand's rice export industry is doing so well. People want something a bit different.

DAISY And, of course, Thailand is well suited to rice growing – good climatic conditions, and lots of fresh water.

ERIK Going back to China for a minute, we should mention that at the rice research institute in Hangzhou they are working on ways of improving rice yields, using less water.

TUTOR By yields you mean … the amount they can grow?

ERIK Yes. They're trying to find ways to get more rice from less land, improve the taste, but also have other things in it besides carbohydrates so that it's healthier – better for you.

TUTOR Good idea, considering it's the staple food.

ERIK And then you've got Japan, which is totally self-sufficient when it comes to rice. This is basically because they have a high tariff on imported rice, so everyone buys the home-grown product. And they don't export much.

DAISY Yes, but you know, even though rice is a kind of sacred crop there, consumption is only half what it was in the 1960s. This trend isn't evident in Thailand or China.

TUTOR Interesting that you mentioned how rice is almost sacred in Japan. Because I believe in Thailand it also plays an important cultural role.

DAISY Absolutely! They have the 'royal ploughing ceremony' every year, which the King always attends and he actually scatters a new stock of seed to the farmers, who pour into Bangkok for the event.

TUTOR What about the global interest in organic farming? Is there such a thing as organically grown rice?

ERIK Yes – indeed. And the Japanese are getting quite a taste for it, apparently. There's an experimental farm near the city of Akita in the Japanese rice belt – famous for its Sake, by the way – which has pioneered organic rice production, and now it's sold all across the country. It's a bit like the recent popularity of jasmine rice in Thailand, but that's for the export market, of course.

TUTOR Interesting how attitudes change, isn't it?

NARRATOR *That is the end of Section 3. You now have half a minute to check your answers.*
[pause]
Now turn to Section 4.

Track 34

NARRATOR *Section 4. You will hear part of a lecture about writing for radio.*
First you have some time to look at questions 31 to 40.
[pause]
Now listen carefully and answer questions 31 to 40.

LECTURER We're going to move on today to look at some of the key principles of writing for radio.

Of course the main thing that you have to remember is that a radio script is not written to be read, but to be spoken and heard. Now putting this into practice is more difficult than it seems because writing as we speak involves abandoning many of the normal 'rules' of writing that have been taught to us from an early age. This is because we need to concentrate on how the piece *sounds*. Written words convey information, but they don't convey the *full meaning* of what you want to say … they don't tell you what to emphasise, what speed something should be read at, or where the pauses should come, so these have to be indicated in a script.

Whatever is said on radio – whether it's a link to a magazine programme, a film review, or even a voice piece in the news – needs to sound as if it is coming from the mind of the speaker – almost like part of a conversation – rather than something that is being read.

Before you begin to write, it's a good idea to know who you're talking to, to visualise a typical member of the radio station's audience. If you're writing a film review for a local audience, for example, think about how you would tell your grandmother about the film, or if you're reviewing a pop concert, think about how you would tell your friend about the band.

The words have much more impact if each person feels they are being spoken to directly. So your tone needs to be informal – rather than using impersonal words like 'listeners' or 'the audience', you can make it more informal … include them in what you're saying by referring to 'us' and 'we'.

Once you know who you're talking to, the next thing is to work out what you're going to say. Don't forget that the person listening to you has no opportunity to ask questions, and in the same way, you can't repeat what you've just said. For these reasons it's important that your script is logical and progresses smoothly.

Too many facts too close together will cause confusion, so space them out evenly. The best scripts allow listeners to visualise what you're describing. For example, instead of giving the physical dimensions of a field, describe it as being the size of, say, a football pitch; if you're talking about a tall building, relate it to – perhaps – a ten-storey block of flats.

Now, all scripts need something that will grab the attention of the listener. You need something that will make them say, 'Hey, I want to stop and listen to this.' So the first sentence has to do this for you … it needs to be intriguing, interesting – and then it needs to be backed up by a second sentence that explains what you're talking about. The last sentence should also give your listeners food for thought and can be in the form of a question, or a statement that sums up the item.

After you've finished your script you need to polish it up and the most effective method of doing this is by reading it aloud. This also helps you to avoid tongue twisters or words that you might find awkward to pronounce.

NARRATOR *That is the end of Section 4. You now have half a minute to check your answers.*
[pause]
That is the end of the Listening test.
At the end of the real test you will have ten minutes to transfer your answers to the Listening answer sheet.

Answer key

Listening 1

2

Extract	Picture	Situation	Number of speakers	Key words	Do the speakers know each other?
1	b	Asking for directions on campus	2	I'm looking for, right direction, go along, on your left	No
2	f	Friends chatting at home	2	computer game, on screen, click here	Yes
3	a	TV news	1	six o'clock news, good evening	–
4	h	Finding out about joining a team	2	play for, football teams, become a member, good player, see how good you are	No
5	g	Trying to get a parking permit	2	I'd like to apply for, parking permit	No
6	c	Introduction to TV sports commentary	1	football ground, ticket, match	–

3

A Police report – stolen items
B Life of Emma Darwin

4

A: Type of information

1 name
2 name or number of building
3 adjective – fabric, style, colour
4 number
5 adjectives – type, colour, material

B: Type of information

6 family relation
7 game/instrument/sport
8 subject/item
9 number and children
10 media item: book/film/play/TV programme

5

1 Anna Andersson
2 Sunrise House (not Hostel)
3 black leather / leather black
4 4528 7709
5 small, silver

6

6 wife
7 piano
8 plates (and) china
9 ten children / 10 children
10 biography/book

Listening 2

1

a Table A is about food eaten by animals in zoos. Table B is about important dates, people and events in hot-air ballooning.
b They tell you the type of information you need to listen for.
c across
d a type of food
e a type of gas
f Because there is no information on the recording about this.

126

2

Full question	Type of information
1 What does the man want to study at university?	a subject
2 Where/When was Louis Pasteur born?	a place / a date
3 How much water do New Yorkers consume each day?	a measurement of fluids
4 What do you need to calculate longitude at sea?	an instrument / a piece of equipment
5 Which game has a more difficult scoring system than soccer?	a game
6 What are spring rolls made of?	a type of food

3

a registering for a conference

b Full questions
  1 When is the conference?
  2 Where is the conference?
  3 What is the phone number for reservations?
  4 What is the day rate for a student?
  5 Who should he contact?
  6 When is the closing date for giving a talk?
  7 What should the summary have?
  8 What is the maximum number of words?
  9 What else should he send?
  10 What is the email address?

c Type of information needed
  1 a date (more than one)
  2 a place
  3 a number
  4 a price ($ or £)
  5 a name
  6 a date or day of the week
  7 an instruction / an item
  8 number (of words)
  9 an item
  10 a name

4
  1 18th to 20th October // 18–20 October // 18–20 Oct
  2 (the) Pacific Hotel
  3 07 9333 2266
  4 $60
  5 Professor Burt // Prof Burt
  6 last Friday
  7 (an) interesting title
  8 300 words
  9 brief CV // short CV // short Curriculum Vitae
  10 info

6
  1 Sunset
  2 (a) (free) postcard
  3 $42
  4 lunch
  5 6.15 // quarter past six
  6 drinks (and) snacks
  7 taxi rank
  8 English
  9 Japanese
  10 hat

Listening 3

1
  1 pointed   4 end / top
  2 cone   5 sides
  3 circular   6 bottom / base

2
  1 C   2 A   3 C

3
  1 frame   4 side
  2 opening   5 circular
  3 cylindrical 6 tubes

4
Number 1 is a question and 2 is an unfinished sentence.
  1 key words: which lecture / afternoon
  2 key words: wants to study
  1 Answer: B   2 Answer: A

5
D, F, G (*in any order*)

6
camera – he's not sure about this
drinking water – they are going to see the water treatment plant that processes this
food – he says there is no need
radio – he refers to listening to the weather forecast

Listening 4

1
  1 beside   5 links
  2 next   6 north-east
  3 opposite   7 southern
  4 closer   8 before

2
Speaker 1 – **A**
Speaker 2 – **C**
Speaker 3 – **B**

3 Forms of alternative energy
1 wind farm – the wind moves rotating blades on large wind turbines
2 hydro-electricity – water in a dam forces turbines round to create electricity
3 solar energy – panels trap heat from the sun, which can be used for heating
4 wave power – energy is captured using a floating buoy
5 bio fuel – a substitute for oil/petrol is made from plants such as sugar cane

Other sources of energy are: geothermal power using the earth's heat, biomass using biodegradable materials and nuclear power made from a controlled nuclear reaction to produce heat.

4

Noun	Verb	Adjective
increase	to increase	increasing
heat	to heat	hot
sun		solar, sunny
provision	to provide	
representation	to represent	representative
type	to typify	typical
use	to use	useful, useless

5
1 solar panel
2 copper pipe(s)
3 oil or water (*must have both*)
4 water tank
5 pump

Listening 5

2 and 3

1	B	Similar game played in Japan and China. Today women also play.
2	A	Pelé – Brazilian – won 3 World Cups – national hero
3	E	Rules date from 1815 – FIFA changes the rules
4	D	First played in 1930. Won by Uruguay. Every 4 years. Audience of 35 billion.

5

Books	Assessment	Types of class
on loan	assignment	tutorial
reading list	dissertation	lecture
out of stock	extension	seminar
biography	essay	
set text	exam	
library	pass	
bibliography	fail	
non-fiction		

6 Rephrasing
1 A preferable to having to study
  B takes up time
  C aggressive/spirited

2 A He is interested in it.
  B It is compulsory reading for the course.
  C He won't be here on Monday.

3 A She wants to write about something different.
  B She needs to get more data for her essay.
  C The deadline for the essay is too soon.

4 A needs to get better marks
  B would like to study something else
  C is meeting Dr Pollard tonight

Answers
1 B 2 B 3 C 4 A

7
1 A 2 C 3 E

Listening 6

1

	Topic	Number of speakers	Do they agree?
1	a movie	2	Yes
2	space station	2	No
3	art (gallery)	3	No
4	politics	3	No
5	sport	3	No
6	music	2	No

2

	Words stressed to emphasise meaning	Words used to agree or disagree
1	really	I thought so too.
2	I'd love absolutely fascinating	I can't think of anything worse.
3	Did you? really?	I don't think much of it. I think it's quite a good idea.
4	fed up change	I'm with Sarah.
5	Who cares …? far too much time not nearly enough substitute	That's not the point. I think Laura's got a point.
6	is like decent pretty dull	I don't know what you see in it.

3

A	conversation at university	2	history of stamps
B	radio programme	2	sport
C	tutorial	3	children and TV
D	lecture	2	environment
E	radio programme	2	space research, science

4

1	A	6	books
2	B	7	kangaroo
3	C	8	living people
4	A	9	kings and queens
5	C	10	C

Listening 7

1

even though – signals an opposite or concession

even if – signals an unlikely possibility

secondly – second point in a sequence

as – provides a reason (followed by a verb)

for instance – provides an example to clarify a situation

finally – indicates the speaker is making one last point

not only – signals an additional related point (often followed by *but*)

regardless of – signals that the point is independent of what follows in the statement

because of – provides a reason (followed by a noun or gerund)

2

A	finally	D	secondly	G	Because of
B	even though	E	Not only		
C	For instance	F	Even if		

5

1	C	2	B	3	C

6

5	Five countries are named initially.
15	*15 nations of the European Space Agency*
20	*a joint venture between 20 countries* = correct answer
$8bn	*over budget*
$120bn	*it was estimated to cost $120 billion* = correct answer
$128bn	total and current cost
using little	*so little water* is mentioned
transporting	*the station would need 20,000 kg of water transported from Earth… couldn't be done*
recycling	*nothing goes to waste / returned to the water supply / re-use the water* = correct answer

7

Words you might hear on the recording are:

A	solar energy	*solar panels, sun*
B	plant cultivation	*growing things*
C	mapping	*maps, directions*
D	weather patterns	*weather words, e.g. wind, rain, cloud*
E	studies in weightlessness	*gravity*
F	psychology	*mental, mind*
G	nutrition	*food words, e.g. health, fat*

Answers: C, E, F (*in any order*)

8

Words you might hear on the recording are:

A	turn on the computers	*start up*
B	cook meals	*make food*
C	attend meetings	*have a conference, talk to each other*
D	listen to CDs	*play music*
E	take some exercise	*physical activities, movement*
F	communicate with family	*write emails, speak on phone*

Answers: C, E (*in any order*)

9

Signpost words are in bold in the Recording script.

Listening 8

1

1 to communicate thought(s)
(purpose – *aim*)

2 newspapers and books
(were absent – *when there were no …*)

3 botany // plants
(a pioneer – *invented the study of*)

4 convection and radiation
(heat is transferred from – *heat tends to move*)

2

1	A	6	Be very careful
2	B	7	Avoid trouble
3	C	8	Understand (the viruses)
4	B	9	Be well prepared
5	C	10	C

Reading 1

1

Topic: jet-lag

Sentence containing main idea: *If his journey has taken him westwards, however, he will probably have an easier time adjusting to his new schedule than if he has travelled east.*

2 B

3 humour / laughter

4 A

5

1 guidebook – a book that provides information for visitors

2 outdated – out-of-date, containing old information which may no longer be true

3 shelf-life – the period during which a product can be sold

4 backpacker – someone who travels with a pack/rucksack on their back

5 non-problematic – straightforward

6 B

7

1 vast majority

2 lies at the heart of

3 adjust

4 Conservationists; species

5 go to enormous lengths

6 perplexing

7 findings

8 serious repercussions

8

1 C	3 E	5 D	7 B
2 A	4 C	6 A	

9

Possible answers

1 a main reason for

2 a large variety of

3 attract

4 at children's head height – so they can see them

5 easy to touch/grab

6 in fact / in reality

7 the most recent trends/fashion

8 tell the difference

Star phrase

3 Many consumers are susceptible to the promises made in advertisements.

Reading 2

1

1 South Carolina   4 Israel

2 John Sadler   5 peppers / tomatoes / grapefruit

3 Leafsen

2

1 yield(s)   6 irrigation system

2 water usage   7 periodically

3 crops   8 consumption

4 sure sign   9 stem

5 conventional   10 (water) savings

3

1 (the/an) electronic sensor   7 Leafsen

2 periodically   8 sensor

3 tomato (plants)   9 thickness

4 60 per cent   10 computer

5 (their) temperature   11 processor

6 (their) stem thickness

4

2 yield   8 recommendations

3 irrigated   9 reliable

4 consume   10 operation

5 unhealthy   11 marketed

6 adjustments   12 fruitful

7 measurements

Star phrase

3 Young animals are dependent on their parents for food and shelter.

Reading 3

1

1 Using a cellphone / mobile phone before you go to bed could affect how you sleep.

2 Chillies may help people to have a better quality of sleep and to need less sleep.

2

Structure: They begin with the main idea, which is then exemplified through research findings. They end by commenting on the limitations of the research.

Content: They both provide research results on issues related to human health / well being.

3

1 main idea

2 further support

3 topic

4 C

5

1 urban pedestrians   5 burning buildings

2 ant traffic   6 shopping crowds

3 traffic congestion   7 two-way traffic

4 traffic laws   8 a forked bridge

6

1 NG	3 F	5 T	7 T
2 F	4 T	6 NG	

7

1 seek   4 funded   7 negotiating

2 unravelled   5 meet   8 investigated

3 announced   6 dashing   9 conceded

Star phrase

3 I'd like to go to the gym more often, but I can't cope with all the different types of equipment.

Reading 4

1

1 v	3 vi	5 i	7 iv
2 x	4 ix	6 ii	8 vii

2

1 like new
2 not unusual
3 double / twofold
4 guardian to / keeps / looks after
5 careless
6 machines for the home
7 standard reference unit
8 insect specialists

3

Word	Part of speech + how it is formed	Meaning
collection	noun – *collect* + *ion*	group of items that have been put together
pressing	adj – *press* + *ing*	under pressure of time – urgent
storage	noun used as adj – *store* + *age*	used to store / keep
sloppy	adj – *slop* + *py*	slop = spill sloppy = messy
increasingly	adv – *increasing* + *ly*	more and more
valuable	adj – *value* + *able*	having worth / value
polluted	verb – *pollute* + *d*	suffering from / dirty from pollution
unimaginable	adj – *un* + *imagine* + *able*	cannot be imagined
catalogue	verb in same form as noun	to list (in a catalogue)
goodwill	compound noun *good* + *will*	friendly feelings, support

4

1 7/seven years
2 2/two per cent / percent
3 research
4 radioactivity / radioactive materials
5 computers
6 age
7 industrial revolution
8 Entomologists

Star phrase

3 The authorities are planning to introduce road charges on the grounds that there are too many cars on the road.

Reading 5

1

1 Paragraph 1: As a product, chocolate has a lot going for it, appealing to all ages, both sexes and all income brackets.
2 Paragraph 2: It also increasingly transcends national boundaries.
3 Paragraph 3: Media expenditure on confectionery exceeds that for any other impulse market.
4 Paragraph 4: Innovation is also essential for ongoing success, despite the chocolate market being dominated by 'consistent performers'.
5 Paragraph 5: Producers believe that special editions offer the consumer a new and exciting variation of a product, while suggesting the same consistent quality they associate with familiar brands.

2 and 3

Type of answer

2 a number – probably markets, places or countries
3 a time or place – probably a country or continent
4 a type of consumer, or an adjective such as 'other'
5 a number – a sum or percentage

	Scan for	Word(s) in passage	Re-wording in summary	Answer
1	UK, 1997	value decade	worth ten-year period	£5.2bn
2	Swiss Nestlé	exported more than	supplies over	100 countries
3		fast growth	rapid sales increases	Asia
4	UK market, British	a mere … whereas	eat more than (comparison)	American
5	European market	accounts for	amounts to	a third

4

1 K	3 M	5 H	7 I
2 D	4 A	6 P	

5
1 chocolate
2 from the total UK confectionery market figures after chocolate sales have been removed
3 the chocolate confectionery market
4 Asia
5 £12bn
6 the fact stated in the previous clause
7 long-established brands
8 boxed chocolates

6

Verb	The person	Related phrases
market	marketing executive, etc.	the (product/country) market
sell	seller/salesperson	good/poor sales/sales growth
grow	grower	fast/slow growth
retail	retailer	retail trade/industry
brand	–	brand image
industrialise	industrialist	the (product) industry
stock	stockist	check stock, stock-taking
launch	–	product launch

Star phrase
3 The improvements that were made in the curriculum account for the excellent exam pass rates.

Reading 6

1
a copy, imitate
b an introduction to the idea + a review of the two research projects + a conclusion

2
a Whether chimpanzees learn from copying their parents or by experimenting on their own.
b They set up experiments.
c That apes copy and that they need to do this to survive.

3
B, D, G (*in any order*)

4
B Lines 15–17: *'the young chimpanzee learned how to open the nut by trial and error, not by imitating his mother'*

D Lines 45–46: *'although the accuracy of their copying tends to be poorer'*

G Last lines: *'learning from elders is crucial to growing up as a competent wild chimpanzee'*

5
A Lines 5–6: *'in scientific circles the question of whether apes do 'ape' has become controversial'*

C Lines 30–31: *'The clearest way to establish how chimpanzees learn is through laboratory experiments.'*

E Lines 52–55: *'the chimpanzees in the zoo exhibited a greater range of activities than … we had seen in the wild'*

F Line 65: *'activities such as ant-dipping'*

6

		A	B	Answer
1	Two different groups of chimpanzees were observed.	✓	✓	C
2	Some of the food items in the experiment were not real.	✓	✗	A
3	The experiment was conducted on humans.	✓	✗	A
4	The chimpanzees were not shown how to do anything.	✗	✓	B
5	Rewards were used for successful behaviour.	✗	✗	D

7

Word	Meaning	Other forms?
controversial	causing disagreement	controversy
implications	future possible effects	(to) imply
collaboration	working together	(to) collaborate
recorded	noted in writing	(a) record
subjects	things or people being studied in an experiment	
monitored	watched carefully	
exhibited	showed	exhibit
interpreted	decided what something means	interpretation
findings	results / discoveries	find

8
1 A 3 A 5 D 7 C
2 B 4 C 6 A

Star phrase
3 People often fail to realise the extent to which bad language can have an influence on children.

Reading 7

1

A1 It doesn't say.

A2 social standing

A3 a NO   **b** YES   **c** NOT GIVEN

B1 The writer is suggesting that publishers should look ahead and help authors whose books might sell long-term.

B2 make stronger / support (financially in this case)

B3 a YES   **b** NO   **c** NOT GIVEN

B4 bestsellers

C1 not confident

C2 *scant* – very little; *generating* – producing

C3 complex

C4 a NO   **b** NOT GIVEN   **c** YES

D1 The writer agrees with them.

D2 *biodiversity* – wide range of species; *triggered by* – caused by

D3 a NOT GIVEN   **b** NO   **c** YES

D4 a mass extinction of species

E1 The writer can see why it happened. (*It was thus understandable …*)

E2 *scrutiny* – careful investigation; *acquit* – find innocent; *wanting* – ineffective

E3 a NO   **b** YES   **c** NOT GIVEN

2
1 NOT GIVEN   4 YES
2 NO   5 NO
3 NOT GIVEN   6 YES

Star phrase
3 Do the effects of global warning mean that there is a case for restricting air travel?

Reading 8

1
a They are both brochures for a museum.
b They are written for visitors to the museum.

2
1 In Antibes / In France
2 Picasso
3 Wednesdays and holidays
4 June – September / June to September
5 The Vampire submarine

6 The harbour
7 (the) Volunteers' desk
8 Use flash (photography)
9 Christmas Day

4
a That physiotherapy can help people who have injured themselves playing sport.
b Customers at a pharmacy / chemist's shop
c Three. The first part is a paragraph of continuous text and the next two parts are lists of points.

5
1 D   2 A

6
1 vital   4 prevented
2 well-being   5 overuse
3 cause   6 enabling

7
1 TRUE   6 NOT GIVEN
2 FALSE   7 Friday
3 NOT GIVEN   8 sun screen
4 FALSE   9 red and yellow // yellow and red
5 TRUE   10 wear a seatbelt

Reading 9

1
1 sociology   5 guest
2 stimulate   6 lectures
3 discussion and debate   7 international
4 prominent   8 speaker

2
1 E   2 D   3 F   4 A

3
i 3   iii 8   v 4   vii 1   ix 9
ii 2   iv 10   vi 6   viii 7   x 5

4
1 iii   3 ii   5 viii
2 vi   4 v   6 i

5
1 (some) practical work
2 June and November / end of semester
3 travel (costs)
4 (the) canteen
5 The Student's Club

6
1 assignment   6 student card
2 guidelines   7 to enrol
3 semester   8 discount
4 co-ordinator   9 exhibition
5 reimbursement

7

1 enrol
2 co-ordinator
3 semester
4 department

5 assignments
6 guidelines
7 student card
8 discount

Reading 10

1

It is about the latest training techniques for elite sportsmen and women.

2

1 professional
2 researchers
3 velocity
4 reckon
5 fatigued
6 staff

7 at the forefront
8 talent
9 athletes
10 international counterparts
11 the field
12 monitoring

3

1 E   3 D   5 F
2 F   4 A   6 H

4

1 G netball coach
2 E skills acquisition specialist at the AIS
3 A athlete / champion hurdler
4 D Head of Physiology at the AIS
5 B Australian rugby coach

5

1 D   3 B   5 C
2 A   4 D   6 A

6

1 A   3 O   5 N
2 K   4 H   6 F

Writing 1

1

1 amount/quantity of
2 number of; amount of
3 levels
4 figures

5 level of
6 quantities/amounts of
7 amount of
8 numbers of

2

1 small
2 large amount/quantity
3 huge number
4 high

5 small number
6 large amount/quantity
7 low
8 a greater amount of / more

3

Possible answers

A Chart A shows the amount of fish caught in the three major oceans between 1975 and 2000.
B Chart B provides actual and projected population figures for China and India between 2000 and 2050.

1 amount/quantity of; greater than
2 smallest amount/quantity of
3 A larger amount/quantity of / More
4 higher
5 a greater number of / more

Writing 2

1

1 rising
2 rise
3 have risen … to/by
4 fell … to … rose

5 will rise … will fall / are predicted to rise … are predicted to fall

2

1 decrease in the / downward trend in the
2 increase in / upward trend in the amount of
3 decrease in the / downward trend in the
4 there was a downward trend in crime levels
5 increase / upward trend

3

Suggested answers

3 rises sharply to
4 drops dramatically
5 lowest point

6 steady rise to
7 steep fall
8 returns to

4

Possible answer

The graph shows the amount of electricity people use when they are watching a World Cup football match. Overall, the demand fluctuates, with clear peaks and troughs at certain times during the match.

5

Possible answer

The table compares the number of male and female school-leavers entering university over a forty-year period. The percentage of Japanese students attending university rose steadily from 1960. At that time, a very small percentage of women went on to university and only 15 per cent of men received a university education, whereas nowadays, these figures are significantly higher.

6

Possible answer

Between 1960 and 2000, the increase in the percentage of women going to university in Japan was fairly steady, although from 1990 to 2000 figures rose more sharply. By 2000, it was estimated that 25 per cent of Japanese girls leaving school were entering university education, but this was still a smaller percentage than the figure for boys.

Generally, the male pattern showed more variation. Figures rose to a high of 40 per cent between 1960 and 1980, which represented the longest period of increase. It was followed, however, by a slight fall in numbers between 1980 and 1990, but then in 2000 the figures returned to just above the 1980 level.

Overall, the table shows an increase in the percentage of students of both sexes going to university. However, the rate of increase for girls is far greater than for boys, with over eight times the percentage of girls going to university in 2000 than in 1960.

Writing 3

1

1	over	3	from	5	by	7	at
2	in	4	to	6	to		

2

1 It is forecast that the popularity of science subjects at university will fall sharply over the next ten years.
2 It is estimated that pollution levels in the 1900s were higher than they are today.
3 It is forecast that global population figures will reach 10 billion by 2050.
4 It is predicted that more children than adults will be obese by 2030.
5 It is predicted that the number of hours people spend watching TV will fall, while the amount of time they spend using technology will rise.
6 It is estimated that the average British person consumes / will consume 74,802 cups of tea in their lifetime.

3

1 The popularity of science subjects at university is forecast to fall sharply over the next ten years.
2 Pollution levels in the 1900s are estimated to have been higher than they are today.
3 Global population figures are forecast to reach 10 billion by 2050.
4 More children than adults are predicted to be obese by 2030.
5 The number of hours people spend watching TV is predicted to fall, while the amount of time they spend using technology is predicted to rise.
6 The average British person is estimated to consume 74,802 cups of tea in their lifetime.

4

1 Between 2005 and 2006 the amount of rainfall decreased, hitting a low of 2mm per month in the summer of 2006.
2 Standards in hospitals rose in the 1960s, showing a 20% improvement over the previous decade.
3 The average number of hours children spend on computers is predicted to increase over the next five years, reaching a peak of ten hours per day.
4 Sales figures for 2007 fluctuated, being high at the beginning of the year and low at the end.

Writing 4

1

1	features	4	figure
2	popularity	5	industry
3	resources		

2

1	faster	6	both
2	smallest/narrowest	7	15.6
3	while/whereas	8	compared to
4	However, Whereas	9	most
5	smaller/lower		

3

2	are fermented	8	taken
3	(are) removed	9	buying
4	are left	10	(are) loaded
5	turn	11	be made
6	are spread out	12	eaten
7	pour		

Writing 5

1

Sample answer – other answers are possible.
Problems: working conditions / too much sitting down / too many staff in one room
Suggestions: provide better seats / better headphones / reduce number of people

4

The first sentence has been copied from the rubric and there are poor links between sentences. The material is not well organised.

5

Sample answer
Last Friday was my mother's birthday and so I decided to take her to the theatre to see a concert. A South African group were playing, called 'The Swing Band', and they put on a wonderful performance.

6

- Ticket from neighbour
- 'Jangle Jive' an African percussion band
- Wasn't busy, so went along
- Colourful clothes, scenery
- Music – Jungle Rhythms – best, animal sounds
- Lasted 15 minutes
- Playing near her/him
- Recommend he/she goes
- Will enjoy drums

7

Paragraph 1: I must tell you / I didn't know / but / with
Paragraph 2: As / and / As for / the most memorable / which / and
Paragraph 3: I'm pretty sure / I really recommend / You may think / but / Even

Writing 6

1

1 D *I would like to enquire about*
2 E *I would like to book*
3 A *It is disappointing that*
4 B *I'm attaching the details as I know you'd love it there.*
5 C *I'm so sorry*

2

Possible answers

1 Please could you avoid always putting your rubbish out on the wrong day, as this means that the rubbish sits on the pavement all week.
2 I'm really sorry that I missed the meeting this morning. The traffic in the city was terrible and I got to work over half an hour late.
3 I'm extremely grateful to you for lending me your car while mine was at the garage being repaired. I know you won't accept any money, so I have filled the tank for you.
4 I am trying to organise a surprise birthday party for Dad on 24 June and I was wondering if you would both be able to come.
5 Last week I left a jacket and pair of trousers with you for dry cleaning. However, I am very disappointed with the service because the trousers now have a large hole in them, and the suit is ruined.
6 Don't forget that we have a meeting with the landlord on Friday at 6 p.m. to discuss the renewal of the lease. I would really appreciate it if everyone could be here, as this is quite important.

3

1 could
2 will go
3 would appreciate
4 arrived
5 will not be
6 would be; could

4

1 … I suggest (that) you employ more staff.
2 … I suggest (that) you look on this website. / I suggest looking on this website.
3 … (may) I suggest (that) you take another week to complete it.
4 … I suggest (that) the salespeople check all the boxes.
5 … Can you suggest a convenient time?

Writing 7

1

A only has one topic or part to discuss: the role of personal relationships in achieving a happy life. Other issues could also be covered, such as health and money, and this would improve your answer because you would need to compare and contrast the things that make people happy.

B has more than one part: male/female approaches to study must both be discussed. If only one area is covered, you will lose marks.

2

Main idea	Supporting points
Men and women organise study differently	1 Women work in groups / discuss 2 Men work alone / less support

3

Main idea	Supporting points
Differences depend on type of person rather than on if they are a man or a woman	1 Both men and women leave things till the last minute 2 Both men and women use things to help them plan their time

5

1 Although
2 also
3 rather than
4 Similarly
5 This is because
6 such as

6

a Friends are important in life.
b No.
c It is very repetitive and lacks ideas.

7

Possible answer

Friends play an important role in my life and it would be difficult for me to live without them. Most significantly, they support me in a number of ways: by providing advice when I need it and good company when I want to go out and enjoy myself. Generally speaking, these are the aspects of friendship that are easy to define.

Other aspects of friendship are less easy to explain but an important one is that there is often a bond between friends that keeps them together. Although friends can be annoying sometimes, this bond helps us forgive them for their faults. As a result, the friendship becomes even stronger.

Writing 8

1

a *come up with new ideas / are terribly important / good imitators*
b The writer thinks both skills are important, as stated in the opening paragraph.
c The main ideas are in bold below.
d The supporting points are in italics.

e 1st paragraph – introduction, states writer's position
2nd paragraph – relates to the importance of those who produce consumer goods
3rd paragraph – develops the idea that those who copy well have a role in society
4th paragraph – highlights a more important aspect of discovery that cannot be copied easily

f The writer summarises the points made in the answer and restates her/his position through doing this.

Sample answer

I certainly agree that people who come up with new ideas are terribly important to our society. However, I also think there is a role in society for good imitators.

No one would deny that certain individuals must be thanked for providing us with facilities that we use every day. *Where would we be, for example, without basic items such as the washing machine, the computer and, more recently, digital cameras and mobile phones?* These inventions are now used so regularly that we tend to take them for granted.

In fact, the society we live in today has become increasingly consumer-oriented and, while it may be possible to constantly update and improve consumer goods, *not everyone in my country can afford them.* Furthermore, *not everyone lives in an area that has access to the latest models on the market.* For these reasons, **it is useful if someone can provide good copies of expensive products.**

Having said that, **certain innovations have a more serious impact on our lives than others and cannot easily be replicated.** *Vital medicines like penicillin and vaccines against dangerous diseases also exist because people made continual efforts to develop them. Scientific ideas such as these enable us to live longer and avoid illness.*

Undoubtedly, scientists and engineers work extremely hard to make life better for us. In some areas, their work just adds comfort to our lives, and if people copy their ideas, it allows a wider population to benefit from them. However, in other areas, their contribution is unique, cannot be copied and without it we would be unlikely to survive or move forward.

2
Possible answers
b gives sense of pride in studies
c reflects on quality of teaching
e the home
f individual study areas
h staffing needs
i cost of facilities and equipment

3
a Introduction: The sentence suggests that the writer is going to begin exploring the topic.
b Conclusion: 'Taking all the arguments into account' means that the writer is referring back to opinions and views that have already been stated.
c Conclusion: The writer's use of 'so' indicates that previous arguments are being referred to.
d Introduction: The writer's use of questions suggests that these ideas will be discussed further.

4
Possible answers
a On the whole, it must be the case that a neat, tidy college or university will promote good study habits among students.
b At first glance, the statement seems reasonable, but I wonder whether the condition of the place we learn in has any effect on the way we study.
c I certainly agree that it is good to study in pleasant surroundings; however, it is questionable whether these have any direct impact on the success of our studies.
d The statement may be true, but I think we have to question, first of all, what is meant by 'study well' and whether this refers to the way we study or the overall success of our studies.
e I am taking the term 'environment' to mean the building or campus where students work, rather than the surrounding area, which I feel is less important.

5

Sample answer	
The idea that a marriage should be arranged by the parents of the couple, or by other members of the family, is quite acceptable in some societies, yet completely out of the question for others. So the way you see the pros and cons of each system will depend on your cultural background.	*Introduces both systems and states main difference.*
In western cultures, it is very unusual for marriages to be arranged. Most young people in these societies do not agree that their parents should choose their partner for life. They feel that young people should have a right to choose for themselves, even if they make a bad decision.	*Gives view against arranged marriages, with support.*

However, even when marriages are not arranged, it is often the case that parents want to approve of their children's partners. This is because it is always easier for the couple concerned if the parents support the relationship and welcome the grandchildren. So to a certain extent, parents still play a positive part in the marriage process.	*Concedes that there are comparisons between arranged and non-arranged marriages.*
People who have arranged marriages often argue that the likelihood of the marriage lasting is greater when it is set up in this manner. Parents can be assured that their children are joining a family of similar economic and social background, and this, in the long run, produces a more stable society.	*Argues in favour of arranged marriages and supports the view.*
In the end, the important thing to ensure is that people are never forced into a marriage that will make them unhappy or lead to an unequal relationship, where one partner is exploited by the other. In my view, this principle should apply in all societies and situations.	*Concludes and gives personal position.*

Writing 9

1

1	f	**3**	c	**5**	b
2	a	**4**	d	**6**	e

2

1 I tend to disagree / I strongly disagree with this view.
2 As far as I am concerned …
3 In my view/opinion, children should …
4 Even though there are …
5 In my view …
6 I feel it is good that rich nations …
7 To conclude, / In conclusion, …
8 To sum up, I would support …

3

Suggested answers

1 In my view, it is unethical for parents to choose whether they have a boy or a girl.
2 Despite the fact that a lot of steps have been taken to help old people, we still need to do more.
3 It is doubtful whether antibiotics will continue to be effective in the long term.
4 There is little evidence to support the view that fat is bad for you.

5 Although students get tired, they still stay up late.
6 I am unconvinced that tourism benefits poor nations.
7 It is generally believed that animal testing is justifiable.

4

1 Some people consider money to be the most important aspect of life.
2 Many conservationists consider humans to be responsible for the loss of wildlife.
3 Teachers are not considered to be as important as doctors.
4 My grandparents considered education to be very important.
5 In Europe, bread is considered to be a staple food.
6 Have you considered your future?

5

1	in favour	**5**	Although
2	I mean	**6**	doubt
3	to be	**7**	believe/think
4	rather than	**8**	In fact

Writing 10

1

a *Actually*, *As well* and *On the other hand* are used incorrectly.
  Actually is the wrong register (too informal). A linker isn't needed here.
  As well is syntactically incorrect; here we would say *Also* or *In addition*.
  On the other hand is wrong because it does not introduce a contrasting point.

b By replacing the rhetorical question with a sentence that leads into the reasons that follow.
  By avoiding the repetition of 'people'.
  By developing the supporting point better – here the student really repeats the same point as part of the development, e.g. it would be very expensive to do this + and some people can't afford it.
  By ending the paragraph with a related, rather than new, idea.
  By using a wider range of language.

2

a It relates the idea to research and the task, and it sets a clear focus for the reader by referring to hotels.
b Linkers: *To begin with, Secondly, though, Besides, even if, And lastly*
  Reference words: *one, this, these, there*
c It means 'in addition' and links the idea of the danger of the journey to the moon with the problem of survival in a different atmosphere.
d To highlight the improbability (in her view) of ever being able to do this. It also adds a touch of humour.

3

1	eager	**5**	put off
2	check into	**6**	get there in one piece
3	far-fetched	**7**	alien environment
4	extremely wealthy		

4

Possible answers

1 I tend to think this is a rather one-sided claim.
2 Surely this is a rather uncharitable attitude.
3 I think this is a very positive development.
4 In my view, this is a particularly cruel activity.
5 I feel this is a very unhealthy approach to life.

5

1 generate
2 methods
3 dangerous
4 experience
5 the pro-nuclear scientists
6 contribute to
7 resources
8 practical/sensible/useful (others possible)
9 reliable
10 Basically
11 run out
12 making sure / ensuring

Speaking 1

1

a Key words: **1** kind of music / like
2 best way / learn / new mobile phone

b This is the 'topic vocabulary'. You need to produce a range of accurate vocabulary related to the topic to get a good mark.

2 and 3

	Words/phrases that are stressed	Reason for stress
A	*really like* *these days*	to emphasise how much to compare with the past
B	*really only* *quite boring* *terrible noise*	to introduce her narrow response to illustrate her view
C	*favourite* *especially* *to remember it*	to emphasise one kind of music to round up her explanation
D	*I suppose* *better*	to introduce a concession
E	*naturally* *young/older* *lesson* *when you buy*	to emphasise how easy it is to bring out the contrast between young and old to highlight her idea to illustrate when the lesson should take place
F	*Personally* *best way* *I'd do*	to indicate that this is her own opinion to emphasise how she personally would do it

4 and 5

	Verb	Tense needed for answer	Type of vocabulary needed
1	do you like to spend	present simple, e.g. *I like …ing*	leisure activities, sports, shopping
2	do you enjoy	present simple + gerund *like watching / enjoy doing something*	types of television programmes, e.g. *reality TV, serials, current affairs, films, documentaries* music, DVDs
3	did you play	past tense, e.g. *played, used to play*	names of sports, e.g. *football, basket ball, athletics, badminton*
4	do you want to do	future, e.g. *will, going to, hope to, intend to*	further education and other plans, e.g. *get into university, study, go on holiday, get married*
5	is	present simple	names of meals, e.g. *breakfast* explanation, e.g. *a social event, a relaxing time of the day*
6	is to learn / to use	present simple infinitives	ways of learning, e.g. *on your own, from a tutor, with a friend*
7	do … compare wear / used to wear	present simple and past tenses, e.g. *used to wear, wore*	types of clothes, e.g. *casual clothes, T-shirts, jeans, formal wear, suit*
8	would you … get	conditional, present simple	qualities of emails and letters, e.g. *formal, friendly, quick, efficient, cheap, reliable*
9	do you prefer	present simple	qualities of library, e.g. *quiet, access to books and computers, opening hours* qualities of home, e.g. *more relaxed, comfortable*
10	are you studying	present continuous, present simple, conditional e.g. *I would like to …*	reasons, e.g. *useful, need it for my studies, my future job, international language, to communicate with people from other countries*

Speaking 2

1

1 I	**4** J	**7** C	**10** A
2 F	**5** B	**8** D	
3 E	**6** H	**9** G	

2

A sport – 10 football
B airports – 5 plane
C from a small village – 7 come from
D student, job – 8 studying, working
E Spanish – 3 languages other than English
F cake, card, present – 2 birthdays
G only child – 9 brothers or sisters
H recipes – 6 cook
I staying – 1 live
J weekend break – 4 holiday

3

A and in fact
B except that
C which
D but
E although
F and
G but, so
H especially when
I Actually, because
J although, who

4

1 actually		**6** In fact
2 and		**7** except
3 which		**8** but
4 especially		**9** and
5 but		**10** so

5

	Main information	Additional information	Linking words, fillers
Name of place	Melbourne	Capital of Victoria Beautiful, wide streets, grand buildings	*which because for example*
Good points	Style / fashion conscious	More elegant, smarter clothes, better restaurants than Sydney	*because you know that sort of thing but*
Famous for	Its trams	European feel	*Well, I suppose even though which*

Speaking 3

1

a Yes
b her children / she gives examples of the animals / the old monkey cage
c The present simple is used to describe the state/situation and to express opinion.
d Melbourne Zoo is good because of its design.

2

Key words used: *South Africa, wildlife park, small plane, landing strip, take off, modern buildings, guide, mud huts, security guard with gun, animals, dawn, dusk, peering eyes, names of animals*
Adjectives used to express feelings: *exciting, privileged, amazing, frightening, marvellous*
Main tense used: past simple – telling a story in the past
Speaker's main point: The trip was really different and exciting.

3

Possible answers: authority, optimism, enthuiasm, wealth

4

Possible answers

The dinosaurs were alive way back in **time**.
What is **the time**?
Life is precious.
How long is **the life** of an AAA battery?
Health should come before anything else.
The health of a nation depends on the wealth of that nation.
Love is sweet.
The love of a parent for a child is unlike any other emotion.
Beauty cannot be bought or sold.
I was struck by **the beauty** of the young race horse.

5

1 a	**6** the	**11** the
2 –	**7** the	**12** a/the*
3 the	**8** –	**13** –
4 –	**9** –	**14** a
5 –	**10** –	**15** –

* *a vet* = any vet; *the vet* = the vet who is known to them

6

Possible answers

The reason I don't like *Al Pacino films is that they are usually too violent.*
One of the problems with *university is that there is so much reading to do.*
One of the good things about *swimming is that it exercises all the muscles in your body.*
What I enjoy about *surfing the net is that it provides a lot of useful information.*

Speaking 4

1

1 He used to get a lot of enjoyment from his work.
2 I am pleased with my achievements at college.
3 I believe that success comes from hard work / working hard.
4 I had great respect for the way my colleagues handled the problem.
5 Regular exercise has tremendous benefits for most people.
6 I made a very detailed record of the observations we made on our geography field trip.
7 Improved transport systems should lead to a reduction in the amount of time people spend in their cars.
8 We need to make some improvements to the health system in our country.
9 My grandfather lost the ability to speak properly after his illness.

2

1 strong	4 true	7 wonderful
2 usual	5 bitterly	8 heavy
3 regular	6 common	9 genuine

3

Possible answers

1 … I had enough money.
2 … will definitely take it.
3 … do well enough in my exams.
4 … I got the chance to do so.
5 … will be very disappointed.
6 … will get a scholarship to fund my studies.
7 … I can't get a visa.

4

The tenses will need to be conditional or present. The content of the talk will be drawn from your imagination rather than based on a past experience.

Speaking 5

1

A, C and F

2

a F   b B   c E   d C   e D

3

1 in the wild
2 advantages
3 animal behaviour
4 are in danger of extinction
5 laboratory
6 in their natural environment
7 cage
8 cruel

5

A – topic 1   B – topic 5

Speaking 6

1

1 d whether … or	4 e will look like / date
2 a Why …?	5 b Do you think …?
3 c How …?	

2

1 Apparently the government is planning to remove the tax …
2 Frankly, I think the monarchy …
3 Personally, I am not in favour of sports like fox-hunting …
4 Regrettably, we still have no cure for …
5 Obviously, some people enjoy horror movies because …
6 Theoretically, a free national health service is a wonderful idea, but in practice …
7 …, so hopefully, we will see a change in smoking habits.
8 I seriously believe we should be doing everything possible …

3

A 5	C 9	E 7	G 4	I 6
B 2	D 1	F 8	H 3	J 10

4

A frankly	B Personally
C apparently	D obviously

Possible questions

A How do you feel about the International Space Station?
B Some people feel that museums are out of date and that all government funding should be withdrawn. What is your view on this?
C On the subject of girls' and boys' schools, how do you feel about single-sex schools? Do you think they are a good idea?
D In some countries, it is illegal not to wear a seat-belt when you are in a car. Do you think this is a good law?

Practice test

LISTENING

Section 1

1 Anthony
2 1(st) June
3 University Hall
4 Health for Life
5 September 2006
6 (in the) distance
7 (for) driving
8 (the) full frame / full frame glasses
9 (they are) strong
10 (in/by) cash

Section 2

11 C
12 A
13 (The) Main Gateway
14 (the) (16/sixteen) flower beds
15 (a/the) (raised) pond
16 (a/the) Mosque
17 C
18 river
19 (supply) tanks
20 fountains

Section 3

21 B	23 A	25 B	27 B	29 C
22 C	24 B	26 C	28 A	30 A

Section 4

31 rules
32 speed
33 conversation
34 grandmother
35 us (and) we
36 repeat
37 space (out)
38 football pitch
39 first sentence
40 reading (it) aloud

ACADEMIC READING

Section 1

1 (atmospheric) carbon dioxide
2 300 years
3 evaporation
4 precipitation (rain)
5 glaciers
6 40 years
7 1875
8 15% / 15 per cent
9 southern US states
10 (River) Nile
11 Pakistan
12 15 years
13 A and D

Section 2

14 A	19 B	23 speed
15 D	20 A	24 brand image
16 C	21 C	25 familiarity
17 F	22 B	26 Coke
18 A		

Section 3

27 YES	34 C
28 NOT GIVEN	35 D
29 NO	36 B
30 NO	37 houses
31 NOT GIVEN	38 (its/the) metabolic pathway
32 YES	39 (a/the) vacuole / vacuoles
33 B	40 (a) transcription factor

ACADEMIC WRITING

Task 1 Sample answer

India has a range of imports and exports and a number of trading partners. Overall, India imports £25.6 billion worth of goods, compared to £21.2 billion worth of exports.

The biggest import item is machinery and equipment at £5.7 billion and a similar amount is spent on importing crude oil and related products. India's other main import is gems – £1.9 billion worth – but it also exports £3.2 billion worth of gems and other jewellery. This, however, is the second biggest export. India's biggest export is textiles at £5 billion, followed by handicrafts, at £3.7 billion. Other big exports include engineering products and chemicals.

As far as trading partners are concerned, India's biggest partner for both imports and exports is the USA. 9.5% of imports come from there and 19.3% of exports, which is considerably more, go there. The UK is India's second biggest trading partner and India also exports just over 5% of goods to Hong Kong and Japan, and imports a similar percentage of goods from Belgium and Germany.

172 words

Task 2 Sample answer

For some people, going to university is a goal in itself, regardless of where it takes them. They aim for this, or for a professional career, because they follow their parents, or equally because their parents did not have this opportunity and want it for their children. But is everyone who studies at university doing what is right for him or her? And do we need all these qualified people?

Of course a functioning society needs to have a balance of skilled people. We need doctors and dentists to look after our health, historians and teachers to inform us, and engineers to design roads and computer programs. But we also need plumbers and builders and IT specialists, and many others, to build and maintain everything.

In many developed countries fewer and fewer people are encouraged to take up a trade, because they are told that university is smarter. Usually, if you are successful at university, you can get a well-paid job, though there is no guarantee of this. However, a trade can provide great job satisfaction and good wages because there is such a shortage of skilled people.

Some countries have a policy of training people in technical schools from a young age. In my country, for instance, we have two types of secondary school and you choose quite early which path you want to take, and I think this is good.

In my opinion everyone has his or her role to play in society and we should encourage people to do what suits them best. On top of this, though, we also need to make sure that society respects a technical education as highly as an academic one, so that everyone feels valued.

284 words

GENERAL TRAINING READING

Section 1

1	B	8	(the) (old) harbour
2	D	9	11.30pm
3	B	10	9202 8565
4	A	11	(the) first floor
5	D	12	(a) bank statement
6	A	13	(a) replacement fee
7	C	14	5/five

Section 2

15	reservations	22	F
16	domestic	23	D
17	prepare quotations	24	E
18	cultural needs	25	A
19	compulsory part	26	B
20	manager / supervisor	27	C
21	(personal) accidents		

Section 3

28	vii		
29	iv	36	fiction
30	i	37	digital images
31	ix	38	feathered cape
32	viii	39	documents
33	vi	40	7/seven days
34	ii		
35	iii		

GENERAL TRAINING WRITING

Task 1 Sample answer

I am writing to complain about the quality of your fresh fruit; in particular your soft fruit, such as pears, oranges, peaches and plums.

I have done my food shopping at your supermarket since I moved to this area five years ago. You have a good range of products and your staff are very helpful. However, in the last few weeks I have noticed that the fruit that I buy from your shop goes brown very quickly and has no taste. Several times now, I have had to throw it away because of this.

Personally, I think it is unacceptable for a supermarket that has a good reputation to expect customers to pay for sub-standard produce. I am quite sure that other shoppers have had a similar experience and I think you should correct this situation; otherwise you may find that we go somewhere else to do our shopping.

Yours faithfully,

Katy Siu

151 words

Task 2 Sample answer

When mobile phones were first introduced, they were big, expensive and costly to use, and only a few people could afford them. They were a kind of status symbol. Today, however, mobiles are much smaller and cheaper, and you can easily keep one in your pocket. As a result many people all over the world own a mobile phone.

People of all ages have become so used to the convenience of being able to contact people anywhere, at any time, that they cannot imagine life without their mobiles. My father would not be able to run his business without using his phone day and night for deals and transactions. In fact, some people no longer have ordinary telephones in their homes and I think this trend is likely to continue.

People from an older generation who have not grown up with this technology may say that mobile phones are a nuisance, especially when they ring in public places, such as the cinema. Even mobile-phone owners like myself can find this annoying. However, it is not difficult to switch off your phone, or turn down the ring tone, in order to avoid irritating people.

We cannot turn the clock back. Now that we have this technology, I think we should use it. Having a mobile phone makes people feel safe, because they can get in touch with friends or parents very easily, and can send text messages cheaply. The phones themselves can be expensive but the advantages they bring are surely worth the money.

252 words

Acknowledgements

The authors and publishers would like to thank the teachers and consultants who commented on the material:

Australia: Garry Adams, Katherine K. Cox, Luke Harding, Kathy Kolarik, Susy MacQueen; UK: Ros Hallam, Karen Saxby, Roger Scott.

Development of this publication has made use of the Cambridge International Corpus (CIC). The CIC is a computerised database of contemporary spoken and written English which currently stands at over one billion words. It includes British English, American English and other varieties of English. It also includes the Cambridge Learner Corpus, developed in collaboration with the University of Cambridge ESOL Examinations. Cambridge University Press has built up the CIC to provide evidence about language use that helps to produce better language teaching materials.

The authors and publishers acknowledge the following sources of copyright material and are grateful for the permissions granted. While every effort has been made, it has not always been possible to identify the sources of all the material used, or to trace all copyright holders. If any omissions are brought to our notice, we will be happy to include the appropriate acknowledgements on reprinting.

The Economist for the extract on p. 20 from the article 'Early birds get it', The Economist 28 July 2001, for the extract on p. 20 from the article 'Orang-utans on the brink', The Economist 10 March 2001, for the extract on pp. 29–30 from the article 'Behind the scenes at the museum,' The Economist 23 December 2000, for the extract on p. 40 from the article 'Let the good times roll', The Economist Intelligent Life, Summer 2005, for the extract on p. 41 from the article 'Saving the rainforest' The Economist 12 May 2001, for the extract on p. 41 from 'Fingering fingerprints' The Economist 16 December 2000, for the graph on p. 53 from 'Move Over China' The Economist 31 March 2001, for the table on p. 55 from 'A degree of progress', The Economist 16 February 2000, for the article on pp. 95–96 'Roses are blue, violets are red' The Economist 8 February 2007. Copyright © The Economist Newspaper Limited, London; New Scientist Magazine for the extract on p. 20 from the article 'Comic Relief' New Scientist 27 May 2000, for the article on p. 23 'Fruitful Drinking' New Scientist 12 May 2001, for the extract on p. 26 'Talk about REM' New Scientist 15 October 2005, for the extract on p. 26 'Spice up your Nights' New Scientist 15 October 2005, for the extract 'Herbal Medicine' from 'Swallow it whole' on p. 42 New Scientist 26 May 2001, for the article 'Climate change heralds thirsty times ahead for most' on pp. 89–90 New Scientist 22 May 2004. Copyright © New Scientist; Jeannette Hyde for the extract on p. 20 'Cutting corners on the world' from The Times Weekend, 5 December 1998. Used by kind permission of Jeannette Hyde; Anova Books for the extract on p. 22 'Children and Consumerism' from Consumerism by Alex Woolf, published by Batsford, part of Anova Books Company Limited; Charles Jonscher for the extract on p. 26 from Wired Life published by Bantam Press. (Copyright © Charles Jonscher 1999) Used by permission of PFD on behalf of Dr Charles Jonscher; Richard Macey for the article on p. 27 'Ants show us the way forward'

from Sydney Morning Herald 10 November 2005. Used by kind permission of Richard Macey, Sydney Morning Herald; Sarah Perrin for the extract on pp. 32–33 'Soft centres – hard profits', first published in Accountancy April 1998; Scientific American for the article on pp. 36–37 'Do apes ape?' by Andrew Whiten and Christophe Boesch, Scientific American January 2001. Reprinted with permission. Copyright © January 2001 by Scientific American, Inc. All rights reserved; Nicholas Clee for the extract on p. 40 from Eating Wildebeest. Reproduced by kind permission of Nicholas Clee; Jacquelin Magnay for the article on p. 50 'Creating the champions', Sydney Morning Herald, Good Weekend Supplement, 18 June 2005. Reproduced by kind permission of Jacquelin Magnay; The Guardian for the graph on p. 55 'Demand for electricity during a televised Word Cup football match', The Guardian 18 October 1994. Copyright © Guardian News & Media Ltd 1994; The Sunday Times for the table on p. 58 'Comparison of top performance between men and women in five major running events', Sunday Times 1 June 1996. Copyright © NI Syndication; Taylor & Francis for the extract on pp. 92–93 'Principles of Persuasion' from The Advertising Handbook edited by Sean Brierley. Copyright © 1995, 2002, Sean Brierley. Reproduced by permission of Taylor & Francis Books UK; Brown Reference Group for the charts on p. 98 from Nations of the World, India by Anita Dalal. Copyright © The Brown Reference Group plc; Insight Magazine for the text on p. 101 'Festivals this Summer' from Insight City News, 19 April 2007. Reproduced by permission of Insight Magazine; NSW Office of Fair Trading for the adapted text 'Advice for traders on refunding money' on p. 106 from www.fairtrading.nsw.gov.au/shopping/refundsandrepairs.html. Adapted with permission from the NSW Office of Fair Trading, Australia; Steve Meacham for the article on pp. 107–108 'Open all Hours' Sydney Morning Herald, 17 April 2004. Reproduced by kind permission of Steve Meacham.

The publishers are grateful to the following for permission to include photographs [Key: l = left, r = right, t = top, c = centre, b =bottom]:

Alamy/© Wild Pictures, p. 27, /© Narrative Images LLC, p.42,/© Tim Mossford, p.56; /© Stan Kujawa, p.61; Corbis ©/Najlah Feanny, p. 15; © Gareth Boden Photography p. 121; Getty Images/Sport, p. 12, /© Minden Pictures, p. 36; NASA, p. 16; © Neil Rawlins/Photographers Direct p. 22; © Paul Mulcahy, p. 32; © Science Photo Library, p. 5.

The publishers are grateful to the following for their illustrations:

Stephane Gamain: p. 9, p. 11 (t); Dylan Gibson: p. 4, p. 8 (c, b), p. 16, p. 18, p. 72, p. 77 (t, r), p. 83; Kamae: p. 11 (b), p. 24; Julian Mosedale: p. 19, p. 51, p. 69, p. 77 (t, c); Ian West: p. 57, p. 64, p. 79; Vicky Woodgate: p. 5, p. 7, p. 8 (t), p. 10, p. 59.

Freelance picture research by Alison Prior

The publishers are grateful to the following contributors:
Alyson Maskell: editorial work
Sarah Hall: proofreading
Ian Harker: audio recordings